Glad Rags II

Glad Rags II

Leigh Charlton and Annette Swanberg
Photography by Leigh Charlton

A Directory to Discount Fashions in Los Angeles and Orange Counties

Chronicle Books / San Francisco

Glad Rags II's cover was photographed on Santa Monica beach by Leigh Charlton. Woman's chintz jumpsuit and metallic belt from Importique modeled by Wesley Hudnall. Child's moire satin dress from Jack & Jill modeled by Deva Tamburri.

Back cover photographed by Leigh Charlton. Antique beaded shoes from the Melon Patch. Legs courtesy Annette Swanberg.
Fashion coordination, make-up, and hair styles for *Glad Rags II* photographs by Leigh Charlton with gracious assistance from the models.

Library of Congress Cataloging in Publication Data
Swanberg, Annette.
    Glad Rags II.
    Updated, rev., and expanded ed. of: Glad rags. c1979.
    Includes indexes.
    1. Clothing trade—California—Los Angeles—Directories.
I. Charlton, Leigh. II. Title. III. Title: Glad rags 2.
IV. Title: Glad rags two.
HD9940.U5L717   1981   381'.45687'02579494
ISBN 0-87701-178-8   81-18036
                                  AACR2.

Cover and book design by Brenn Lea Pearson

Chronicle Books
870 Market
San Francisco, CA 94102

To Fred Bernstein

Photo Credits

Clothes, shoes, and accessories photographed for *Glad Rags II* were purchased or borrowed from the following stores:

The Accessory Co.
California Fashion Accessories
Chic Lingerie
Debs Factory Shoe Outlet
The Designer Room
Fantastic Designer Room
Flexatard
H. Harper's Personal Touch
Ideal Fashions
Importique
Irene Tsu
Jack and Jill
Jantzen
Jean's Star Apparel
Judy's Warehouse Sale
L. A. Woman
Lanfield's
Loehmann's
Lore Lingerie
Marshalls
Melon Patch
Ohrbach's
Patina
Repeat Performance
Samplings
Second Time Around (Long Beach, Torrance and Pasadena)
Shoes by Shirley
Standard Shoe Stores

Glad Rags II Models:

Bette Cunningham
Gretchen De Boer
Stephie Ellison
Kym Denyse Fisher
Cathryn Gates
Bethany Hale
Wesley Hudnall
Kathy Naples
Janella Robinson
Frankie Slater
Dong Su
Conrad Suhr
Annette Swanberg
Deva Tamburri
Glenda Toni
Alicia Winegarden

Acknowledgements

A special thanks goes to our "third partner," Mason Buck, for his moral and editorial support and expertise. We are grateful to our valued friend, Viki King, for her talent and inspiration as a true "Glad Ragger." Our appreciation goes to Charles Allen for contributing his graphic talents and to our families and friends for their welcome enthusiasm and educated feedback. We are grateful for the support of the many fine bookstores throughout California (and beyond) that have played such an important role in the success of *Glad Rags*. Our sincere thanks go to all the hardworking bookstore managers who kept *Glad Rags* in stock and on the shelves, especially Shelly McArthur, manager of the Arco Plaza B. Dalton/Pickwick Bookstore in Los Angeles, for giving so generously of his time and knowledge. We would also like to acknowledge the importance of consumer input from several thousand women and men we have met and spoken to since the publication of *Glad Rags*. Their avid interest has always been, and continues to be, our greatest incentive for writing. Finally, we are forever indebted to all the store owners, managers, manufacturers, and jobbers who contributed their years of experience to the creation of *Glad Rags II*.

Note: *Glad Rags* correspondence and/or requests for information on *Glad Rags* presentations available to groups should be addressed to: Glad Rags, P.O. Box 25060, Los Angeles, CA 90025.

Introduction

Two years and over thirty thousand copies of *Glad Rags* later, we're back with an updated, revised, and expanded edition. If you liked *Glad Rags,* you'll love *Glad Rags II* because there are twice as many stores to choose from. Our premise remains the same: you can *dress* rich without *being* rich. In *Glad Rags II* you'll discover over six hundred of the *best* discount stores in Los Angeles and Orange Counties offering savings of 20 to 80 percent on clothing, shoes, and accessories for the entire family. Now more than ever before, it's possible to be both fashionable *and* frugal.

Glad Rags II is new in two important ways. First, we have expanded our geographical area to include discount stores in Orange County. Listings follow the stores located in Los Angeles County in each of the ten chapters (all listings are organized alphabetically by store name). Also, consult the Orange County Index for stores with multiple locations.

Another addition is our Children's chapter. In response to overwhelming demand from the mothers we have met at talks given throughout the Los Angeles area, we have researched stores which feature clothing (and more) for infants through teens. For the complete listing of stores that carry children's apparel (including stores that carry clothing and shoes for the entire family), consult the Children's Index.

As in *Glad Rags I,* we have a Men's Index listing the nearly 250 stores that also carry men's clothing, shoes, and accessories.

No matter what your age, size, or personal style, there are stores in *Glad Rags II* that will meet your shopping needs. We have visited each store in the book and describe in detail the merchandise, shopping ambience and individual personality and background of the store owner, when we have found it interesting. We have included discount stores ranging from Beverly Hills boutiques to factory outlets. There are shopping experiences here to satisfy the beginning, intermediate, and advanced discount shopper. We've done the legwork for you in the hope of saving consumers not only money, but also time and gasoline. (In speaking to groups during the last eighteen months, we have learned that these three factors are nearly equal in today's economic equation.)

How to Use This Book

The sheer number and variety of discount stores in Southern California is exhilarating. *Glad Rags II* is divided into ten chapters by Type of Store. We have grouped stores of similar clothing together—for instance, stores that carry designer clothing are distinguished from manufacturers' outlets, shoe stores, antique, and second-hand shops, children's boutiques, and so forth. Our system is convenient, but not perfect. Many stores qualify in more than one area and we've had to use our best judgement in ascribing them to a chapter. Stores, like women, refuse to be stereotyped.

This is where a working knowledge of the Indexes becomes invaluable. We have seven separate Indexes: Alphabetical, Geographical, Type of Store, Type of Merchandise, Children's, Orange County, and Men's. The Type of Merchandise Index is especially helpful. Whether you're looking for silk lingerie, tailored suits, an evening gown, children's clothing, shoes, a leather coat, or any other item of apparel or accessory, we've listed the stores that carry the best selection in this category. Without the aid of this Index, you would have to look through over five hundred entries to zero in on the dozen or so best stores to buy a certain article.

Use this Index as a starting point. Naturally, inventories change and we couldn't begin to list each item carried in every single store. *Glad Rags II* is intended as a guide, but no endorsement is implied. The stores included are personal selections and no kindnesses or gratuities were given us to insure their inclusion in our book.

Each entry begins with vital statistics: address, phone number, hours of operation, parking, and whether the store has a mailing list to notify customers of special sales. Many stores accept credit cards and we've abbreviated them as follows: MC (Master Charge), VISA (Bankamericard-Visa), AE (American Express), Diner's (Diner's Club), and Carte Blanche. Checks are accepted if we note "cks," and cash is understood unless the policy is cash-and-checks, or cash only, which is stated. All stores have individual dressing rooms unless otherwise indicated.

We recommend calling ahead before visiting a store for the first time to confirm hours of operation and location. We have included only stores with a proven track record to avoid fly-by-night operations, but the retail business is constantly evolving and changing. Calling ahead is always advisable. Prices quoted reflect those seen during our visit and are meant to give the reader a reference point only.

Sizing

Next to the cost of clothing, the unpredictable nature of sizing is the most common complaint we hear from consumers. Manufacturers are starting to pay attention and we're pleased to report that more discount stores are offering petite, large, and half-sizes.

We note the size ranges available in each store so it is important to understand the fashion terminology. Women's clothes are manufactured in five basic size ranges. (Unfortunately, there is no industry-wide size measurement guideline, so a size 10 in one line may be a size 8 in another. Whenever possible, try on clothes before making a purchase to avoid disappointment later.) Sizes are defined as follows: **Missy** (or *Misses*)—a well-proportioned, "Miss America" figure, average height 5′5″–5′6″, sizes 4–20, but most commonly 6–16: clothes are cut with a fuller bust and hip measurement than Junior. **Junior:** these clothes fit a more youthful figure that has a shorter neck-to-waist measurement and a higher bust placement than Missy, average height 5′4″–5′5″, sizes 3–15 (Junior is a size, not an age, and style and cut can vary considerably among manufacturers). **Half-Size:** a fully developed figure with a short back-to-waist measurement and a low bustline, waist and hips are larger in proportion to the bust, average height 5′2″–5′3″, sizes 10½–24½. **Women's** (or Large Sizes): a large-framed, taller woman with a fully mature figure, average height 5′5″–5′6″, sizes 38–50 or 36–52, (but may go as high as size 60). **Petite:** a proportion as well as a size, petite fashions are scaled for the woman 5′4″, and below, weighing 85 to 135 pounds, sizes 0–3 and misses (4P–12P) and junior sizes cut proportionally shorter and smaller. Sizes in the Children's chapter are— **Infants:** newborn to twenty-four months; **Toddler:** 1–4; **Children's:** 4–6x, 7–14; **Student:** 14–22 (boys only); **Girl's Preteen:** 8–14.

Advice to the Bargain Hunter and
Commonly Used Terms

By doing away with ritzy addresses, mood lighting, and advertising, discount stores can offer the same clothes available in department stores and boutiques at incredible savings. Merchandise is in perfect condition (what is termed *first quality* in the trade) or it is required to be marked and sold as *irregular* (which is merchandise with minor flaws). Why are they able to sell it so cheaply? This is the first question a shrewd shopper should ask. In most instances, we've answered that question in our discussion of each store, but a few generalities might be helpful.

The proliferation of discount stores is in direct proportion to the growth of the garment industry in Southern California. The L.A. area is now second only to New York's Seventh Avenue as a center of production and commerce. Merchandise in discount stores is simply the overflow from a multi-billion dollar industry. The majority of the clothes come from local factories but the buyers also frequent New York and San Francisco, as well as other American and European cities.

Discount buying is usually done *in-season,* which means discounters will visit factories and warehouses and purchase merchandise that is old to the manufacturer (they work at least six months in advance of the new season), but is still new to the public. Discounters have the flexibility of purchasing manufacturers' close-outs and discontinued lines (a product that is no longer being manufactured) at the lowest price and passing a savings along to the consumer. Don't be fooled by the low prices; the *caveat emptor* rule still applies.

As one successful discounter explained, it's like going to see a movie on the last night it plays in Westwood for $5 or waiting an extra day and seeing it at a neighborhood theatre for $3. It's a matter of split-second timing from the discounter's standpoint. A small local store might buy its merchandise a day after a major national chain receives its order, but that will still be weeks before the consumer sees them. Manufacturers also run into trouble trying to meet production deadlines set six months in advance. A snag anywhere along the line (such as a delay in fabric delivery) may force the cancellation of an entire order and the manufacturer looks to the discounter to buy the finished garments.

Briefly, other terms you'll encounter include:

Jobber: a person who buys goods in quantity from manufacturers or importers and sells them to dealers.

Job lot: goods, often of various sorts, brought together for sale as one quantity.

Liquidated stock: a company in financial trouble sells the stock it has on hand to merchandisers—often by the lot—at prices much below retail in order to convert assets into cash.

Odd-lots: a relatively small quantity of unsold merchandise that remains after an order has been filled.

Open stock: merchandise sold in sets, the individual pieces of which are kept in stock as replacements.

Overcuts, over-orders, overruns, and overstocks: generally garments manufactured in excess of what a company has orders to sell. This merchandise is made available to discounters, or is frequently sold through factory outlets.

Past-season: anything manufactured for a previous season.

Retail: to sell directly to the consumer. In *Glad Rags,* retail is also used as a price reference, which is generally twice the wholesale price.

Returns: orders that are refused by retail stores because they do not arrive on time and are returned to the manufacturer. This is lost income unless the manufacturer can turn around and sell them to someone else. Enter the discounter who buys the garments at cost or below and sells them at or slightly above wholesale.

Seconds: merchandise with more than minor flaws which may be noticeable and affect the aesthetic appeal and performance of the item.

Sample: an item shown by the manufacturer's representative (or salesman) to the prospective merchandiser/buyer for the purpose of selling the product. Samples are frequently sold at a discount after they have been used to generate sales. Display samples are similar except they may be used exclusively on models and/or mannequins.

Wholesale: the selling of goods in relatively large quantities, especially the sale of such goods to retailers who sell them to the consumer. Wholesale price refers to the cost of goods to the retailer, except in discount shopping when consumers can buy at or near this price.

Now that you are armed with these few facts and the list of stores, we hope you have a happy bargain hunting and that you'll discover, as we did, that beating the system is the only way to shop.

Table of Contents

Designer

The discriminating and fashion-conscious bargain hunter has more stores than ever before to meet her exacting demands for quality *and* savings. Since writing *Glad Rags I,* we've watched with delight as many more designer labels become available in discount stores. This is the "high end" of discount shopping. At these stores you'll find the most expensive clothes described in the book, but the prices still represent a considerable savings over what you might expect to pay. The merchandise in the designer category is usually sold in the best Beverly Hills or Newport Beach boutiques and better department and specialty stores across the country. Many of the garments are imported—often from France and Italy—and some are European-sized. The higher prices reflect the import duties, elegant fabrics, quality construction, fine workmanship, and/or a designer's name, reputation, and unmistakable talent. A few of these stores are outlets for a specific local designer—an exciting discovery. Please consult the **Type of Store Index** for additional sources for designer clothing. Many stores carry a broad range of merchandise and fall into more than one category.

ℒ𝒜 𝒞ounty

Carol Anderson

719 S. Los Angeles St., Suite 910, Los Angeles. (213) 623-5100.
Hours: Vary with each special sale.
Purchases: MC, and cash. All sales final.
Parking: Street and area lots. Mailing list.

Most of the time Carol Anderson fans can find her things at better specialty and department stores such as Nordstroms, Neiman-Marcus, Saks Fifth Avenue, and Bloomingdale's. The line's styling appeals to women who like a fashionable look and who are willing to spend from $75–$125 retail. Now for the good news. Twice a year the factory holds special sales to liquidate samples, overruns, discontinued styles from seasons past and seconds—all for only $9–$30. Since the sale is by invitation only, the people at Carol Anderson request that you *call* them (don't visit the office) and ask to be put on the mailing list in order to receive flyers announcing each sale. Besides the Carol Anderson dress line, the firm's Jaff separates label is also available in blouses, pants, and skirts. Principal Jan Janura describes the sale as "total chaos with absolutely the best deals ever." Sizes run from 4–14, samples in size 10. There are no dressing rooms at the sale so you'll have to leave your modesty at home and just be prepared to try things on in the aisles between racks like everyone else. (We wear leotards for just this reason).

Le Chateau

314 N. Beverly Dr., Beverly Hills. (213) 271-9801.
Hours: Mon.–Sat. 10–7.
Purchases: MC, VISA, AE, cks. Returns and exchanges. Layaway.
Parking: Street and area lots. Mailing list.

"In the heart of Beverly Hills you get downtown prices," say the folks at Le Chateau. It's a treat to walk the boutique-lined streets of one of America's richest shopping areas and find an attractive store that offers savings of 30 to 50 percent on clothing, shoes, and accessories for men and women. Styles are classic to casual, with a deep selection of dresses, suits, blouses, slacks, and jeans. Since *Glad Rags I*, Le Chateau has added shoes from Charles Jourdan, Anne Klein, Yves St. Laurent, Nickels, Garolini, and more. Casual and dressy styles in sizes 5–10 average $22–$75. Men's shoes average $45–$65. Women's clothes are sized 4–14 and carry labels such as Jack Mulqueen, St. Piel, Diane Von Furstenberg, and the Le Chateau house label (designed and made in Europe). Silk dresses average $75 and suits in wool gabardine or linen start about $145. A linen-like suit made of rayon and cotton paired with a Jack Mulqueen silk blouse purchased for and worn on the *AM Los Angeles* show has served us well through many guest appearances and speaking engagements. Excellent customer service includes fittings and alterations done on the premises.

d'Crenza Couture

8855 Santa Monica Blvd., West Hollywood. (213) 659-4000, 657-4263.
Clothes shown by appointment only. Call during business hours: Mon.–Fri. 8–4:30.
Purchases: Cash or cks. All sales final.
Parking: Street and area lot.

"We're the only salon over a saloon in town—just like in Europe," says owner Lea d'Crenza. For fourteen years, his well-established couture line has been found in expensive boutiques and specialty stores across the country—including oil-rich Texas. The missy-sized line encompasses award- and opening-night gowns, city suits, dresses, jacket dresses, cocktail clothes, and coat ensembles. The chic woman of means will be able to meet most of her wardrobe needs here. Retail prices for d'Crenza start at $800 and climb to $6000, but by buying directly from the salon, you'll save 50 percent and more on samples and one-of-a-kind items. Since this is a couture line, there are no overcuts, closeouts, or irregulars. Samples from d'Crenza are custom-fit on the spot to accom-

modate sizes 6–14, with larger sizes available by special order—also at wholesale. Mr. d'Crenza designs one line per year in pure fibers for trans-seasonal dressing. A note for those who like to dress uniquely: the d'Crenza line is not sold anywhere else in Los Angeles.

Evy's

13549 Ventura Blvd., Sherman Oaks. (213) 990-1074.
Hours: Mon.–Sat. 10–5.
Purchases: MC, VISA, cks. Exchanges. Layaway.
Parking: Street. Mailing list.

Here's yet another interesting discount-store operation. Evy's in Sherman Oaks is the permanent sale location for the regular retail Evy's boutique in Beverly Hills. When you think about it, it's a winner in two ways. Evy's Beverly Hills customers get to choose from new merchandise constantly because the things that don't sell are moved to Sherman Oaks after two months. Shrewd shoppers know thay can always find better and designer dresses and sportswear for 20–70 percent off at the Valley store. While some of the labels are removed by the time they reach the sale store, we did see Mollie Parnis, Adele Simpson, and Harvé Benard. A mature clientele shops here for values in conservative styles, sizes 6–14, that can be worn for several years to come. Quality-conscious women will be pleased to find lots of lovely natural fabrics like silk, wool, linen, and cashmere. We also feel the evening gown, cocktail dress, and accessories selection is particularly noteworthy.

French Connection

8214 Santa Monica Blvd, Los Angeles. (213) 654-9393.
Hours: Mon.–Fri. 10–7, Sat. 10–6.
Purchases: MC, VISA, AE, cks. Exchanges.
Parking: Street and local lots. Mailing list.

Imported and designer clothing at hard-to-beat prices has attracted loyal customers from all over the world to these stores. We discovered French Connection researching *Glad*

Rags I, and are pleased to say that it is every bit as good as we first reported. The stores' strengths remain in their emphasis on pure fabrics such as silk, wool, cashmere, and cotton and in their range of casual to dressy sportswear and separates for men and women. Labels include Daniel Hechter, Calvin Klein, Ted Lapidus, Cacharel, Kenar, Tahari, Marc D'Alcy and more, all discounted 40–70 percent. There is an excellent selection of designer jeans, silk blouses, pants, dresses, skirts, blazers and suits in sizes 4–14. An Anne Klein classically styled wool gabardine skirt purchased from French Connection two years ago for $60 remains a staple in the *Glad Rags* wardrobe. Quality, taste in fashion, and customer service from professionals are further recommendations. Many of the studios maintain running accounts to costume films and television shows—an endorsement from those in the business of making people look good.

Ideal Fashions

9218 W. Pico Blvd., Los Angeles. (213) 550-7091.
Hours: Mon.–Sat. 10–6.
Purchases: MC, VISA, cks. All sales final.
Parking: Street. Mailing list.

Ideal Fashions is hard to beat for convenient shopping (right next to Beverly Hills), experienced sales help, and a broad range of better merchandise. Labels seen and purchased here include Regina Kravitz, Halston, Givenchy, Oscar de la Renta, Giorgio Sant' Angelo, Pinky and Diane for Private Label, Calvin Klein, Anne Klein, Liz Claiborne, Jag, Norman Todd, Morton Myles, Daniel Hechter, St. Gillian, and more. Top designers from both coasts and Europe are well represented and affordable at 25–60 percent below retail. Sizes range from 2–18 and styles include a complete wardrobe of sport, casual and dress apparel as well as coats and jackets. Ideal has a new discount membership club that offers an additional 10-percent savings to members who pay a one-time fee of $40. Unfortunately, this extra discount does not apply to sale merchandise during their January and July clearance sales, or to purchases from the handbag department. It helps to know retail prices before shopping at Ideal—these are not

bargain basement prices . . . or goods. Even though the store is large, the personalized service and free fashion consultation make shopping a breeze.

Importique

16733 Ventura Blvd., Encino Fashion Center, Encino.
  (213) 990-4733.
Hours: Mon.–Sat. 10–6, Thurs. 10–9.
Purchases: MC, VISA, cks. Exchanges or credit.
Parking: Free lot.

After visiting every store in the Designer chapter of *Glad Rags I* a fashion aesthete friend of ours settled on Importique as her favorite. The reason, as she explained, is that Importique consistently offers designer quality at affordable prices. Selection, fine fabrics, and the latest forward-fashion styles, plus timeless classics at 30–60 percent discount are also reasons she has become a loyal customer. One among many, we might add, as witnessed by Importique's expansion over the last two years. Our friend relies on Importique's 100-percent wool, Italian gabardine slacks for $69–$90 (retail $150–$190) and silk blouses which sell for $19–$95 (retail to $175) for her executive wardrobe needs. Suits range from $100–$150 (retail $300–$400) and silk dresses average $50–$80. The store is owned and run by the Gould family, and Judy Gould offered us some insights into how buying patterns have shifted in recent years: "We do better with high-end merchandise. A $200 sweater will sell faster than one for $19, because women are buying quality now rather than quantity. We used to sell fifteen pairs of pants at a time, but now a woman will come in wearing a two-year-old pair of slacks and ask us to help her find a blouse to go with them." Importique carries casual sportswear to dressy evening separates. It stays on top (sometimes even ahead) of fashion trends. Merchandise is both domestic and imported with the scale tipping towards the former. All clothing is first quality and the Goulds don't buy closeouts, so the styles are current. Shipments arrive three times a week in women's sizes 4–12. Men's shirts and slacks are also available. We've been asked not to mention labels, but most are found in boutiques and specialty stores. You'll see two exclusive New York designer lines not discounted elsewhere, as well as Missoni-like Italian knits. Accessories, including scarves, belts, purses, and small leather goods are also good value.

distinguish herself from the crowd. Sizes are 4–12 and prices average $24–$80 for silk tops, $50–$120 for hand-painted silk dresses, $40–$60 for 100-percent cotton separates and dresses, and $10–$25 for Lycra spandex pieces. Call first for an appointment and, for the best selection, shop just after new merchandise has been shipped to stores and boutiques. Try-ons are allowed, but dressing facilities are limited.

Jerry Piller's

8163 Santa Monica Blvd., West Hollywood. (213) 654-3038.
Hours: Mon.–Sat. 11:30–6.
Purchases: MC, VISA, cks. All sales final.
Parking: Free lot behind store. Mailing list.

Jerry Piller is a legend in the discount business. His motto is: "Imitated but Never Duplicated," and after fifty years in the business he helped create, he continues to lead the way. Jerry Piller's prefers to be known as a *sale* store, rather than a *discount* store. Whatever the terminology, the savings of 50 to 75 percent on exciting high-quality, forward-fashion, designer clothing and shoes purchased from the most exclusive boutiques and manufacturers all over the country make news. The West Hollywood store specializes in small-size dresses, sportswear, and evening wear, as well as thousands of pairs of exquisite shoes from designers like Maud Frizon, Charles Jourdan, Andrea Pfister, Ferragamo, Shoe Biz, and more—including many narrow sizes. Jerry Piller's in Pasadena features men's designer clothing and shoes as well as women's. Shoes and boots are always at least half off the original price. The store security policy is the same as when we wrote *Glad Rags I*—customers are asked to leave their purses with a guard at the door and their shoes in a bag before entering the shoe room. Customers must accept these protective measures as part of the challenge of shopping at Jerry Piller's. It's not a place for the faint-hearted, and we recommend setting aside enough time for a leisurely browse—especially if it's your first visit. You'll discover an eclectic hodgepodge of bargain basement chic mixed in with the finest designer duds. Shoes are stacked floor-to-ceiling—an overwhelming selection for those with discriminating taste. For our San Francisco friends, Jerry's daughter Donna has a similar store called

Irene Tsu Studio

607 N. Huntley Dr., Los Angeles. (213) 652-7184 or 271-5190.
Hours: Mon.–Fri. 10:30–6.
Purchases: Cash or cks. All sales final.
Parking: Street and small lot.

Irene Tsu designs luxe, hand-painted silk separates and dresses under the Irene Tsu label and casual sportswear (some in Lycra spandex) for The It Company. Both lines are available at wholesale prices from her small West Hollywood design studio. We have been shopping here since researching *Glad Rags I*. We never fail to receive compliments on purchases such as a mandarin-collared, long-sleeved copper silk tunic dress with an airbrushed design that looks like calligraphy that costs us only $90. The classic silhouettes and understated elegance of Ms. Tsu's designs make them investment purchases for the contemporary woman who likes to

Donna Piller's at 12 Clement Street. A mailing list notifies customers of special sales in the fall and spring.

St. Laurence Paris

8208 Santa Monica Blvd., West Hollywood. (213) 656-8089.
Hours: Mon.–Sat. 10–7.
Purchases: MC, VISA, AE, cks. Returns for store credit and exchanges. Layaway.
Parking: Lot behind store. Mailing list.

If you detect some similarity between St. Laurence Paris and Le Chateau, you're right: these two stores are under the same ownership. Each is independently run and unique to its area and clientele. St. Laurence Paris, for example, now carries lingerie on its second floor at the same 30–50 percent discount that has always been available on imported and designer clothing for men and women. There are no shoes at this location. Casual separates, including silk blouses ($38–$70), skirts, jeans and pants, as well as sweaters, blazers, and sportswear comprise the bulk of the inventory. Labels are the same found at Le Chateau, including Guy Laroche, Daniel Hechter, Tahari, Daniel Laurent, Kenar, Ted Lapidus, and Chiori. Current merchandise in the latest fashions arrive every six weeks from buyers in New York and Europe. Prices have remained remarkably stable since Glad Rags I—men's wool gabardine suits with the St. Laurence Paris label are still $188, women's suits range from $149–$165 and silk dresses average $69–$79. Manager Solange Bouganim stresses her store's reputation for service and on-the-premises alterations. There are always sale racks to browse where discounts can be 80 percent off and special store-wide sales are held in July and December.

35 Below

1911 Westwood Blvd., Los Angeles. (213) 470-1577.
Hours: Mon.–Fri. 10-7, Sat. 10-6, Sun. 12-5.
Purchases: MC, VISA, cks. Credit or exchange within two weeks.
Parking: Free lot in rear. Mailing list.

Owner Gregg Fiene used to be a buyer for Alandales in Westwood. He's brought his buying savvy and sense of classic, tailored fashion south on the same street and lowered the prices by 35 percent. Men and women will enjoy shopping together in this classy little boutique. Clothes are neatly displayed and arranged so that you can go immediately to the wall of cubes containing blouses and sweaters, or head for the racks of skirts, suits, and jackets. Pure wool gabardine slacks by Saint Raymond Paris are $79 and regularly sell for $100–$125. Mastroianni U.S.A., an Italian-cut, American-made pant in cotton for spring was $40 the day of our visit. Lines carried include Cacharel, John Henry (tailored shirts $24–$26), Stanley Blacker Sport, French Connection (jumpsuits $46 and $55), and Gerard Martin. Lee Rider straight-leg jeans are $20 and they also carry Chemin de Fer and bon jour. Women's sizes are 4–12. Men will enjoy the same discount on a tasteful selection of European-cut suits, sportswear, jackets, and shirts.

Werle Originals

626 N. Robertson Blvd., Los Angeles. (213) 652-4871.
Hours: Mon.–Fri. 10–3:30.
Purchases: MC, VISA, cks. All sales final.
Parking: Street.

Lovely Werle evening gowns, cocktail, afternoon and all-occasion dresses and suits have been popular for more than a quarter of a century. Werle is sold in better department stores and boutiques across the country and dresses retail for $400 and up. Samples in sizes 6, 8, and 10, as well as end-of-season closeouts, overcuts, and some slight irregulars in misses sizes to 14 are sold at the factory for 50 percent below retail. Werle Originals are fashioned from dressy fabrics such as chiffon, lace, satin, wool, crepe, silk, and jersey. These exclusive designer fabrics, imported from France and Italy where they are custom-woven to Werle's specifications, are also sold at wholesale prices. Fabrics include many French laces, matte jerseys, sheer wools, silks, imported polyesters, and others not found in fabric stores. Call first for an appointment to view the dresses and fabrics, especially if you are not a sample size. There are dressing facilities, and try-ons are allowed.

Orange County

Designer Corner

3910 E. Chapman Ave., Orange. (714) 771-2184.
Hours: Mon.–Sat. 10–6.
Purchases: MC, VISA, cks. Exchanges only. Layaway.
Parking: Free lot. Mailing list.

This store came highly recommended and one visit told us why: the New York, French and Italian designer labels with their 25–50 percent off price tags. Labels include Anne Klein, Calvin Klein, Halston, Adolfo, Pierre Cardin, Charlotte Ford, Tahari, and Harvé Benard in missy sizes 4–14. All of the practical-yet-fashionable clothing is first quality and on sale at exactly the same time you'll see it for straight retail prices at other stores. Most of the fabrications are pure wool, cotton, linen, cashmere, and natural silk, in suits, dresses (work and cocktail), separates and coordinate groups. Many of the styles can easily go from day to evening and work well twelve months a year. While owner Mary Iiams focuses the merchandise on classic and classy sportswear, she does offer some slinky silk separates for evening wear. We even found a fun white feather boa. When we asked Mary what she felt is most important in her store, she summed it up in a word: service. There were several helpful (but not pushy) saleswomen assisting a dozen customers the afternoon of our visit. Wardrobe coordination down to the last accessory is a specialty of the store and customers are notified the minute their favorite labels and looks hit the store.

The Stockroom

1673 Irvine Ave., Suite L, Costa Mesa. (714) 645-4529.
Hours: Tues.–Sat. 10–5:30.
Purchases: MC, VISA, cks. All sales final. Layaway.
Parking: Free lot. Mailing list.

The young owners of this small boutique are as stylish as their inventory. Accustomed to quality clothing and in search of a way to support their clothes-buying habits, Phyllis King and Marilyn Vinci opened The Stockroom to serve women like themselves with a taste and appreciation for quality. You'll find casual and elegant dresses, suits, silk blouses and separates, dressy sportswear, blazers and cocktail dresses at the holiday season. Designer and better lines such as Paul Stanley, Albert Nipon, Norman Todd, Charlotte Ford, Regina Porter, Baron Peters, Alan Abel, S. Howard Hirsch, Simplice, Levanté, and Adolfo can be found here for 20–50 percent below retail. Don't miss the "last chance" rack where gems can be picked up for below cost. On the day of our visit, we were tempted by a Bonnie Strauss two-piece black polyester cocktail dress and jacket which retails for $185 on sale for $25! "Clothes have to *move*," explains Mrs. Vinci gesturing around the neatly arranged racks, "because this *is* the stockroom." A mailing list notifies customers of special sales. Sizes are 4–14 with Evan Picone and Anne Klein samples in sizes 8 and 10.

Two Gals Hi-Fashion Boutique

1968 N. Tustin Ave., Orange. (714) 637-7580.
Hours: Mon.–Fri. 10–5:30, Sat. 10–5.
Purchases: MC, VISA, cks. Exchanges only. Layaway.
Parking: Free lot.

If you like fashionable clothes, you might just find yourself doing more and more of your shopping at Two Gals. Owner Molly Fishman doesn't advertise her forward looks from some of the more talented designers, but then she doesn't have to. Much of her business comes from repeat customers she's developed over ten years. Even customers who move away remain loyal—they come in to shop when they're back in the area for a visit. It was a delight to find labels here you don't often see in other discount shops. Lines such as Bis,

Norman Todd, Winks, Leon Max, Max & Lulu, Something Special by Dorothy Schoelen, and Strawberry Plant are discounted 25–50 percent. During our visit we found a whole rack of the most current Leon Max sporty pieces for $17–$40, including an irresistible jumpsuit we couldn't live without. Any clotheshorse will appreciate the Bonnie Strauss assortment for $80–$110 (retail to $150) and the David Hayes suits for $175–$225 (retailing $225–$400). Molly offers a complete line of Bijou silk blouses, dresses, jumpsuits, and pants. The comprehensive inventory includes casual sportswear and jeans, dressy separates, suits, coats, and evening dresses. New arrivals and evening clothes are displayed in the front of the store, while the back houses the "double discount" racks. It was here we discovered a David Hayes suit for only $80. There are size 6, 8, and 10 samples from all lines sprinkled throughout the store. The most current pieces (all slightly irregular) from the Patty Woodard line can be found at Two Gals for only $15 each.

Neighborhood

2

These days, saving time and gasoline is equivalent to saving money. We think you'll be pleasantly surprised at the number and variety of shopping options near where you live and/or work. Check the Geographical Index for discount stores in your neighborhood that are listed in other chapters. You may be right around the corner from a fabulous resale boutique, shoe store, manufacturer's outlet, or children's shop.

Convenience is the key and savings is the bonus. Neighborhood stores carry a broad range of merchandise geared to meet the needs of the fashion season and the tastes of their clientele. Each store is unique and we've tried to characterize the merchandise mix, target customer and general shopping ambiance to help you pinpoint those you might be interested in exploring first. The Type of Merchandise Index will also help you locate specific items available in neighborhood discount stores. Get to know the shops in your area and take advantage of the personal service and wardrobe coordination offered by many boutique-like discount stores.

LA County

Bell Studio
106 W. Third St., Third Floor, Los Angeles. (213) 628-8426.
Hours: Mon.–Sat. 9–5, Sun. 9–1.
Purchases: Cash or cks. Returns and refunds. Layaway.
Parking: Validated parking with purchase.

George and Anne Applebaum take the Most-Unusual Discount Store Award for their warehouse teeming with men and women intently searching for bargains. Amenities are nil—racks are tightly packed from floor-to-ceiling with every wardrobe need imaginable. Still, the Applebaums must be doing something right since they've been in business in the same location since 1952. The secret is low prices—discounts of 50 percent on blouses, suits, coats, nightgowns, robes, evening gowns, pants, skirts, dresses, and now jeans. Size range is also a drawing card. Junior sizes 3–15, misses 6–20, half-sizes 12½–24½ and a growing selection of petite dresses and pants will guarantee a fit. The Applebaums offer great value by purchasing job-lot closeouts and manufacturers' overruns from all over the country and by turning merchandise over quickly. Everything is first quality from lines such as Loubella, Act III, Gloria Vanderbilt, Paul of California, Don Loper (neckties $1–$2!) and many more. The dressing area is rudimentary, but the values are full-fledged.

Bell's Fashion Studio
3908 Wilshire Blvd., Los Angeles. (213) 389-1672.
Hours: Mon.–Fri. 10–5, Sat. 10–4.
Purchases: Cash or cks. Refunds and exchanges. Layaway.
Parking: Free lot behind building.

When a great-aunt from Santa Barbara requested a guided shopping tour of Los Angeles in search of suits and knit dresses, there was no question where to head first—and *last*, we might add, because after going to Bell's there was no need to look further. The selection of one- and two-piece dresses, two- and three-piece suits, pants suits, blouses, sweaters, skirts, and blazers more than met her needs. Discounts are 40 percent and more on quality lines such as Butte Knit, R & K Originals, Leslie Fay, Loubella, Dorce, Royce, Leroy, Jonathan Logan, California Girl, Gloria Vanderbilt, H.I.S. for Her, and Ship 'n Shore. The store is divided into missy (sizes 4–20) and junior (sizes 3–15) areas for convenience. Sizes, including petites, are clearly marked on racks and clothes are neatly arranged and hung. This is an efficient, though not fancy, store with a large group dressing room and lots of first-quality merchandise to choose from. There are always sale racks.

Bella's Fashions
1888 Century Park E., Suite 219, Century City. (213) 556-0540.
Hours: Mon.–Fri. 10:30–5, Thurs. 10:30–7, Sun. 12–3.
6399 Wilshire Blvd., Suite 120 (in the lobby), Los Angeles.
  (213) 655-5756.
Hours: Mon.–Fri. 10–6.
Purchases: MC, VISA, cks. Exchanges. Layaway.
Parking: Building lots. Mailing list.

With shopping time for working women at a premium, Bella Rubin has the right idea in opening stores in office buildings. She brings bargains (such as $120 silk blouses for $36) close to the women who need them most. Bella's is known for its extensive selection of suits in sizes 1–20. The stores carry Sir for Her, Devon Hall, Loubella, Kirkland Hall, Condor, Jordache and Sasson suits, jackets and separates, as well as Albert Nipon and Diane Von Furstenberg dresses. Calvin Klein, Gloria Vanderbilt and Sergio Valente jeans are $32. Prices are generally 30–50 percent below retail, but sometimes you can find brgains for below wholesale. New merchandise arrives daily and Bella stresses the professional wardrobe advice her stores offer customers. There's a broad selection—including blouses, sweaters, lingerie, and accessories—to choose from.

C.H.L. Casual Clothing

15600 Roscoe Blvd., Van Nuys. (213) 988-5920.
Hours: Mon.–Thurs. 10–5:30, Fri. 10–6, Sat. 10–5, Sun. 10–4.
Purchases: MC, VISA, cks. Refunds and exchanges. Layaway.
Parking: Free lot.

In the four years C.H.L. has been in business, it has built up a loyal word-of-mouth following about the good quality offered at low prices. Indeed, the weekday afternoon of our visit, we ran into two dozen men and women shopping among the racks and racks of casual and sporty separates for both sexes. Discounts vary depending on the kind of deal the owners strike with local manufacturers. If they happen upon an especially good buy, they pass the savings along to their customers. Most of the women's jeans, tops, blouses, blazers, sweaters, rompers, jackets, and shorts are in junior sizes 1–15 with some of the stock 4–16 missy. There's a wide variety of color and size to choose from in first-quality merchandise.

Clothes Encounters

8364 W. 3rd St., Los Angeles. (213) 651-5999.
Hours: Mon.–Sat. 10–6.
Purchases: MC, VISA, cks. Exchanges only. Layaway.
Parking: Street. Mailing list.

Even though proprietress Ellen Singer's nifty little shop has been open only a short time, she seems to be onto something. Her concept of selling current, fashionable goods at the lowest possible prices is a sure winner. She asked if we'd seen cheaper price tags on the same items anywhere else and we had to say no. It's hard to spend more than $39 in the store (unless you bought a blazer). Sweatshirts, handknit sweaters, dresses, blouses, and jeans sell for $8–$34. The $3 rack intrigued us most, though. Ellen had such terrific buys on this permanent sale rack (obviously priced far below original wholesale) that we had to ask how she buys for Clothes Encounters. Although the store is new Ellen herself is an old hand at the clothes game. A former model and designer, she's always worked in the garment industry and buys from diversified sources in order to offer quality at low prices. We found

several of the Esprit de Corps labels, Alex Colman, Malibu Media, Marie France, and Loubella as well as some vintage Harriet Selwyn for you Fragments fans. Seeing is believing.

The Clothes Out

1607 Montana, Santa Monica. (213) 394-2614.
Hours: Mon.–Sat. 10–5.
Purchases: MC, VISA, cks. Exchanges. Layaway.
Parking: Free lot behind store. Mailing list.

"We'll bend over backwards for a sale," is the motto at The Clothes Out, but calisthenics weren't necessary to win our patronage. Savings of 30–50 percent on a classic selection of missy sportswear, coordinate groups, and activewear is reason enough. Blouses are a house forte. Styles from Lady Manhattan, Wrangler, Alice Stewart, William Kasper, Loren, and French Connection average $12–$30. Coordinated separates from Breckenridge (pants suits, skirts, and jackets) and an extensive selection of skirts, sweaters, and dresses in sizes 6–18 and small, medium, and large are also good bets. Misty Harbor trenchcoats that regularly sell for $120 were $72 and $80 the day of our visit. Pull-on pants in petite and regular

lengths for sizes 6–18 ($12.50) are always in stock. The Clothes Out carries samples in size 10 from Swirl (loungewear) and California Girl (regular and petite dresses). Jogging suits and active sportswear from White Stag and Aileen as well as jeans in the $21 range from Wrangler, Chic for H.I.S. and Ralph Lauren round out the casual wardrobe needs. January and July are special sale months.

The Company Store

921 Broxton Ave., Westwood. (213) 208-5757.
Hours: Mon.–Wed. 10–6:30, Thurs.–Sat. 10–10, Sun. 12–6.
14502 Ventura Blvd., (at Van Nuys), Sherman Oaks.
    (213) 789-6293.
Hours: Mon.–Sat. 10–6:30.
Purchases: MC, VISA, AE, cks. Exchanges. Layaway.
Parking: Street. Mailing list.

We've always enjoyed the contemporary sportswear and accessories available at The Company Store for 30–40 percent below retail. Remember our *Glad Rags I* story about the nine separates plus extras like belts and scarves for $150 that mixed and matched make eleven outfits? Well, prices have gone up a bit since then, but you can still put yourself together very reasonably and, as we've noted before, if you're not an Edith Head at wardrobe coordination, the saleswomen are more than capable. Active sportswear is a new area of strength. Jogging suits priced at $20 practically run out of the stores under their own power. There's a complete line of sportswear from Sasson and Jordache (including their jeans at one-third off), as well as labels such as Loubella, Tomboy, Collage, Condor, Calvin Klein, Gloria Vanderbilt, Tattoo, Ann Marie, Happy Legs, Jo Matthews, and Evan Picone. Prices are generally $1–$80 in junior (some missy) sizes 1–15. There are major sales after each season, as well as a continual sale rack.

Darn Near Perfict, Inc.

8246 White Oak, Northridge. (213) 996-1196.
Hours: Mon.–Sat. 10–5.
Purchases: MC, VISA, cks. Exchanges. Layaway.
Parking: Free lot. Mailing list.

It's darn near impossible to find better prices on basic casuals for the *entire* family. Discounts are 50–75 percent on Levi's and Wrangler cords, denims, wash-outs, brushed denims, shirts, blouses, tops, and shorts. Seventy-five percent of the merchandise is first quality and the rest is slightly irregular with a select group of closeouts (some designer jeans). Clothes will fit infants to elders, including large sizes. There are always racks or tables filled with extra-sale merchandise, and mailing list customers are entitled to additional discounts. All you urban cowboys and girls will like the Western styles Darn Near Perfict has been carrying since it opened in 1973.

Designer's Fashions, Inc.

29134 Roadside Dr., #101, Agoura. (213) 707-1104.
Hours: Mon.–Sat. 10–6, Sun. 11–5.
Purchases: MC, VISA, cks. Exchanges only. Layaway.
Parking: Free lot. Mailing list.

Conejo Valley working women like to shop here for casual and dressy separates and dresses for 40–70 percent off. While it

is true you will occasionally find a designer label such as Diane Von Furstenberg or Anne Klein, most of the brands are better New York and local lines such as Evan Picone, W.C.C., Tomboy, Condor, and Gerard Martin. Basic sportswear pieces are available year round with more evening clothes at holiday time and swimwear and cruise wear during the appropriate seasons. Sizes come in both junior and missy 3–14 and prices are generally in the $20–$60 range.

Diana's Corner

9551 W. Pico Blvd., Los Angeles. (213) 553-0283.
Hours: Mon.–Sat. 10:30–5:30.
Purchases: MC, VISA, cks. Exchanges. Layaway.
Parking: Street. Mailing list.

There's always a three-rack sale (dresses, jackets, and blouses and tops) in progress at Diana's, as well as discounts of up to 30 percent on junior and missy sportswear. This corner shop is light, cheerful, and filled with name-brand merchandise from California manufacturers including Tomboy and Tattoo. Prices, as a general rule, start about $10 for blouses and go up to about $70 for dresses. Sizes are 3–15/16. Mothers can look for practical suits while their daughters slip into jeans and T-shirts.

Dina's Duds

813 S. Glenoaks Blvd., Burbank. (213) 846-0210.
Hours: Mon.–Fri. 10–6, Thurs. 10–9, Sat. 10–5, Sun. 12–5.
Purchases: MC, VISA, cks. Exchanges within seven days.
    Layaway.
Parking: Rear lot and street. Mailing list.

Inside this charming white-brick building with light blue trim you'll find a junior sportswear, separates, and coordinate group boutique. Discounts of 30–50 percent are offered on lines such as First Glance, Condor, Jonathan Martin, Mr. Topper Action Wear, E-Z Street Clothing Co., Tomboy, W.C.C., Sunbow, and Roberta. Sizes are 1–13 with lots of samples in 7–9 and medium. Mothers and daughters can shop this five-year-old store together. Coordinate groups, blazers, and tailored slacks hang together in a side room and clothes are grouped on racks by style for easy browsing. Complete outfits—including accessories which are also available at Dina's—decorate the walls and spark the imagination. Count on finding current season, popular-selling merchandise from local manufacturers and importers. The day of our visit, E. Indian cotton dresses were priced from $25–$31 (regularly as much as $65), and Chemin de Fer jeans in spring pastels were $27–$28 (regularly $34–$36). Watch for seasonal and special sales for extra markdowns, as well as the sale rack that changes continually.

Downtown Clothing Co., Inc.

30313 Canwood St., Agoura. (213) 707-1120 (in the Plaza
   Reyes Adobe Shopping Center)
Hours: Mon.–Sat. 10–5:30.
Purchases: MC, VISA, cks. Exchanges only. Layaway.
Parking: Free lot. Mailing list.

Bobbie Rosenberg characterizes her store as being a boutique offering discount prices on women's and girl's clothing. She offers garment district prices in the West Valley/Agoura/Westlake area, so—she says—there's no need to travel to Downtown L.A. and pay for parking. After shopping in her store, we must agree. Tasty merchandise selection is a balance between career clothes and fashionable casual attire such as dressy warm-up suits. When she opened a year ago, Bobbie decided she wanted to run an attractive, friendly shop where women and their young daughters (sizes 3–6x, 7–14 and pre-teen) could shop together. Sizes start at 3/4 for women and go to 18 with a few XL blouses and occasional petite dresses and pants. The girls' selection is not as extensive and includes mostly pants, tops, and dresses. Customers can participate in a special punch-card discount promotion.

Dress n' Save

2139 S. Hacienda Blvd., Hacienda Heights. (213) 695-0964.

Sunshine Fashion Showroom

9664 Baseline, Alta Loma. (714) 987-7229.
Hours: Mon.–Sat. 10–6.
Purchases: MC, VISA, cks. Exchanges. Layaway.
Parking: Free lot.

"If it's expensive, smart and simply beautiful, we've got it for less," says the owner. Low prices, combined with courteous, helpful employees who have been with the company for years, make these discount stores popular with teens through matrons. Prices are below wholesale on a complete line of missy and junior sportswear, dresses, evening wear, and coats in sizes 2–16. About the only thing you can't buy here is lingerie. Merchandise is manufacturers' overruns and closeouts from suppliers in California, New York, and Florida. New, top-line garments arrive daily. Twice a year, the first week of January and July, everything is discounted an additional 20–60 percent off the already low prices.

Encore Shop

3135 Glendale Blvd., Los Angeles (Atwater area).
  (213) 663-3765.
Hours: Tues.–Sat. 10–5:30.
Purchases: MC, VISA, cks. Refunds and exchanges. Layaway.
Parking: Street. Mailing list.

Encore, which used to be a resale shop, now offers all first-quality separates and dresses in junior and missy sizes 3–18 and large sizes 30–52. One important fact hasn't changed, though. It's still the same friendly little neighborhood shop it's been for six years. Mary Lou, the owner, clips the labels from garments, but they're the same ones you'll find in retail shops. Prices are 25–50 percent off for everything in the store including all kinds of accessories. The big hit with Encore's loyal following is the semi-annual sale where every stitch is marked down another 50 percent.

Farouche

1510 Pacific Ave., Venice. (213) 392-7295.
Hours: Winter, 11–4 daily. May–Sept., 10:30–6 daily.
Purchases: MC, VISA, cks. All sales final. Layaway.
Parking: Street and public lots. Mailing list.

Farouche is an unpretentious neighborhood discount store featuring popular junior and young contemporary lines at 40–50 percent below retail. Owners Ann Margaret Vermeulen and Jean Claude Vermeulen (who is also a designer) pick up good buys from California manufacturers and jobbers. The merchandise selection includes Esprit de Corps, Made in the

Shade jeans (with their terrific fit for $19–$29), French Connection, San Francisco Shirt Works, and Wayne Rogers. Sizes go from 3–13 in sportswear, dresses, and jumpsuits that sell for $10–$45. Sometimes you'll spy a special bargain such as a two-piece Helena International silk suit for only $50. During the summer, there's an extra bargain rack out front to lure in the beach crowd and turistas.

Fashion Finds

291 S. Robertson Blvd., Beverly Hills. (213) 659-5067.
Hours: Mon.–Sat. 10–6.
Purchases: MC, VISA, cks. Returns, exchanges and refunds.
  Layaway.
Parking: Street. Mailing list.

Fashion Finds is a boutique with many handmade and hand-painted items in addition to its junior merchandise from California and New York manufacturers. The store also imports and manufactures fur coats, so there is always a good inventory and because it is owner-run, the prices are low. Clothing is discounted 50–60 percent and sizes are 1–13 in lines such as Judy Knapp, Jordache, Wayne Rogers, Fresh from California, and more. Clothes are styled for youthful and more mature tastes, so mothers and daughters can enjoy shopping here together.

The Fashion Mart

3343-½ Wilshire Blvd., Los Angeles. (213) 388-6525.

The Downey Garment Center

7930 E. Florence Ave., Downey. (213) 928-4909.
Hours: Mon.–Sat. 10–6.
Purchases: MC, VISA, cks. Exchanges. Layaway.
Parking: Street. (The Downey Garment Center has a free lot.)

The Wilshire store has been in business for fifteen years, and owner Larry Adams recently expanded his operation to Downey. Both stores feature a complete line of missy sports-

Gene's Warehouse Store

2301 E. Willow St., Signal Hill. (213) 424-9691.
Hours: Mon.–Sat. 10–6, Sun. 12–5.
Purchases: MC, VISA, cks, store charge. Exchanges.
Parking: Free lot.

If you like shopping at any of the twenty-four Gene's retail stores located in shopping centers throughout Southern California, you should know about this "disposal" store. Sportswear, dresses, coats, suits, accessories, and more are brought to this central location after the first markdown. Merchandise is from medium to better manufacturers, including Modern Jr., Campus Casuals, Pant-Her, College Town, Evan Picone, Gloria Vanderbilt, Calvin Klein, and Gunne Sax. Clothes are junior size 5–13 and misses 6–18. Styles are directed toward the career woman so you'll find coordinate groups and lots of mix-and-match separates. All prices are 30–50 percent below original retail and there are monthly sales for even greater discounts.

Hang-Up Dresses & Sportswear

920 Manhattan Ave., Manhattan Beach. (213) 372-5211.
Hours: Mon.–Sat. 10–6, Sun. 11–6.
400 W. 6th St., San Pedro. (213) 547-4775.
Hours: Mon.–Sat. 10:30–5:30.
Purchases: MC, VISA, cks. Exchanges.
Parking: Street. Mailing list.

"We specialize in trying to keep the latest fashions at discount prices, but service is our best feature," claim owners Mike and Jan Holland. "We know most people are very busy and have little time to shop, so we know all our merchandise and can be especially helpful in selecting and coordinating the snazziest, smartest outfits." The Hollands stock clothing from evening wear to sportswear, including warm-up suits and clothing for the career woman. Clothes are junior sizes 3–13 and all first-quality, name brands. They carry Irene Kasmer dresses and blouses, Ardee sweaters, tops, and pants, and designer jeans at 30–50 percent below retail. New merchandise arrives daily and there is always a sale in progress.

wear, coordinate groups, and dresses. Mr. Adams maintains his own warehouse and sells to other stores, as well as to the public in these nicely appointed shops. This means savings of 30–70 percent on name-brand, fine-quality, current goods. You'll find especially good buys on the complete line of Loubella Extendables and dresses from Julie Miller and Arabesque. Puccini blouses run $6–$20, dresses and jeans average $20, and pants, including petite proportioned lengths, are $12–$20. Jeans are size 3–15, but other clothing runs to size 20. The stores offer a wide selection of color and style in washable, easy-care fabrics fashioned for the mature woman.

Home Sweater Shop

2737 W. Manhattan Beach Blvd., Redondo Beach.
   (213) 644-6840.
Hours: Mon.–Sat. 10–5:30, Sun. 11–4.
Purchases: MC, VISA, cks. Exchanges. Layaway.
Parking: Free lot behind building.

This shop, with the ambience of a pleasant warehouse, is crammed with sweaters at spectacular savings, plus close-outs of all sorts of missy and junior sportswear, and dresses. This store has been in business thirty years and dresses women from the inside out—Exquisite Form bras to size 48 build the foundation for the broad range of fashions. Labels will vary, but Home Sweater Shop generally carries Graff, Lady Graff, Dittos (jeans priced at $16–$18) and a copy of Levi's Bendovers for $15. Sizes range from 5–42 and half-sizes can be made by on-the-spot alterations. You'll find discounts of 20–80 percent on jackets, suits, jogging suits, shorts, and, of course, sweaters ($10–$25). Name-brand swimsuits are only $10. If this sounds like an eclectic mix, it is.

There's always a sidewalk sale with a rack of items for $1–$10. Inside, the most expensive garment—a pantsuit—is $60. Most clothing is first quality and the few irregulars are clearly marked and reduced accordingly.

L.A. Clothes Distributors

5817 Uplander Way, Culver City. (213) 649-4799.
Hours: Tues.–Fri. 11–6, Sat. 10–5, Sun. 11–4.
Purchases: MC, VISA, cks. Refunds and exchanges.
Parking: Street. Mailing list.

If you're in the market for a pair of jeans, you'll find over three thousand here to choose from. And to top off your denims, there are sweaters, tops, T-shirts and blouses from well-known Los Angeles and San Francisco makers of young junior casual separates. The 30-percent discount prices apply to the men's casual sportswear and jeans selection and to boys' T-shirts, velours, sweaters, shirts, and surfer shirts. There are a few women's career separates and dresses in missy sizes, but the styles and selection are really best in the junior actionwear and casual items. We found especially good color-and-style combinations among the jogging suits, jump-

suits and shorts with matching knit tops. Prices for women's clothing start at about $5 and go up to $80 for an occasional designer-label wool blazer. Boys' items sell for $6–$19. There's a nice belt display with price tags of $2–$5. If you're looking for something new and fun to wear on weekends or want to put some pizzazz in your morning job, give L.A. Clothes Distributors a try.

Lady Malibu
259 S. Beverly Dr., Beverly Hills. (213) 273-7565.
Hours: Mon.–Sat. 9:15–6.
Purchases: MC, VISA, cks. Exchanges.
Parking: Street and area lots.

Lady Malibu knows its customer and serves her well. The Lady Malibu woman likes tailored separates, coordinate groups and suits that can be mixed and matched and worn year after year. In this era of "investment dressing" consciousness, it's worth knowing where you can buy classic, quality goods for 15–60 percent below retail. Eight or ten better East Coast lines are consistently offered, along with

California-made apparel. Labels you'll find include John Henry, David Hayes, Laurie London (dresses), JH Collectibles, Junior House, Sir for Her, and Condor. Working women will appreciate the good selection of blouses by Givenchy Sport and Anne French. Coats are in stock all year round and there is a showcase of accessories, including beautiful scarves (we bought a stunning Anne Klein silk scarf, which was regularly $30, for $15). There is always a $10 sale rack and prices can go as high as $500. Special store-wide sales are held in January and July. Sizes range from 3–16 and all styles are current.

Laney's Fashions
12204 Ventura Blvd., Studio City. (213) 877-2266, 980-5090.
Hours: Mon.–Sat. 11–6.
18539 Devonshire St., Northridge. (213) 360-9003.
Hours: Mon.–Sat. 11–6.
Purchases: MC, VISA, cks. Exchanges.
Parking: Street and lots.

Junior separates, coordinates, suits looks, activewear, jeans, and play clothes in sizes 3–13 are one-third to one-half off at Laney's. Store owner Stewart Herman spent twelve years as a sales rep for one of the country's largest and most popular junior houses before breaking into discount retailing. He has maintained the connection with his former employer and now buys his overstocks and end-of-season merchandise at substantial discount. This savings is passed along to the consumer. Laney's coordinate groups and suit looks serve the career woman well. Blazers are $30–$40 (values to $80), blouses $11–$2, pants $17–$22, and skirts $16–$20. Jordache and Sergio Valente jeans are $30 (regularly $40 and up). Sales are held five times a year, and there is always a sale rack inside.

Lanfield's

2723 Main Street, Santa Monica. (213) 396-4363.
Hours: Sun.–Wed. 10–7, Thurs.–Sat. 10–9 (later during the summer).
Purchases: MC, VISA, cks. Refunds and exchanges. Layaway.
Parking: Free lot next door. Mailing list.

When Bob Lanfield started selling clothes out of his apartment closet, he had women standing on his bed trying to get a look at themselves in his dresser mirror. From this modest beginning has emerged an elegant boutique on trend-setting Main Street. Nothing but the prices are below average. From the forest green carpet and dark wood paneling to the "sexy career woman" fashions Lanfield's specializes in, the emphasis is on style and service. "Our clientele comes here for fashion, the discount (30 to 70 percent) is gravy," Mr. Lanfield says. The merchandise is junior and contemporary in sizes 3–14 and some 16s. Popular labels include Nathan Road, Tattoo, Winks, Malibu Media, and Claudine. "We're trying to stay out of jeans—into slacks," says Mr. Lanfield, "because the jeans market is oversaturated." Lanfield's has a good selection of casual pants and classic gabardine trousers from $25–$77 which retail to $125. Blouses are another strong suit with a complete line of styles from First Glance and hand-embroidered silk blouses from Nathan One for $60 (regularly $90). Dresses are generally priced under $50, but during the holidays you'll find luxury items such as a Bonnie Strauss creation for $220 (regularly $350). Jogging suits, jumpsuits, sweaters, and jackets complete most wardrobe needs. There's a basket of

bikinis and lots of exciting accessories to choose from. One warning: you can spend more on a lizard-and-silver belt than on most of the clothes in the store, and believe us, we were tempted to.

Leonard's Fashion Fair

18946 Ventura Blvd., Tarzana. (213) 342-3151.
Hours: Mon.–Wed. and Sat. 10–6, Thurs. & Fri. 10–9, Sun. 12–5.
Purchases: MC, VISA, cks. Refunds and exchanges. Layaway.
Parking: Free lot. Mailing list.

Leonard Shapiro, known for "the fastest markdowns in Southern California," hates to see merchandise sitting around. Thus, you'll always find current-season fashions on sale for 35–40 percent below retail. Not bits and pieces, mind you, but entire racks with a wide selection of missy sportswear from top houses such as Liz Claiborne, Loubella, Evan Picone, Pendleton, St. Tropez West, Villager, Campus Casuals, Chaus, Ellen Tracy, Jordache, Gloria Vanderbilt, and Condor. (Whew!) If an item doesn't sell at full price after sixty days, it's moved to the sale rack: patience and luck count when you're a bargain hunter. Sizes are 4–16 and Leonard's carries petite sizes in pants. This is a spacious, friendly store with five full-time fashion coordinators on hand to help you pull it all together. There are semi-annual special sales—in June, and believe it or not, on December 26 starting at 7 A.M.

Lippman's

8939 W. Pico Blvd., Los Angeles. (213) 278-2200.
Hours: Mon.–Sat. 10–5:30, Sun. 12–5.
Purchases: MC, VISA, AE, cks. All sales final.
Parking: Street and free lot. Mailing list.

Your favorite junior and contemporary sportswear looks are available at Lippman's for 15 to 30 percent less than you'd expect to pay at department stores. We can't mention labels, but most of the fashions come from better New York designers and manufacturers. New merchandise arrives weekly and there's always a sale rack with super discounts. Lippman's is known for its career girl coordinate groups and casual separates like pants, tops, shirts and sweaters in forward-fashion styles. A mailing list notifies customers of private sales four times a year.

Monterey Fashions

211 S. Garfield Ave., Monterey Park. (213) 573-0316.
Hours: Mon.–Sat. 10–5:30.
Purchases: MC, VISA, cks. Exchanges. Layaway.
Parking: Street. Mailing list.

Looking for large sizes? Monterey Fashions offers a range of missy blouses, pants, pantsuits, and dresses at 25 percent below retail. Sizes run to 46 in blouses and to 38 in pants. Junior size 3–15 pants, blouses, skirts, and dresses are also available. Prices start at $4 for polyester pants and run to $30 for a Cardessa dress. There are also half-slips and *Roman Stripe* panties for sale, as well as jewelry and scarves. There's always a half-price sale rack and there are regular store-wide sales.

Ms. Fashions

3877 Pacific Coast Highway, Torrance. (213) 373-4622.
Hours: Mon.–Sat. 10–6.
Purchases: MC, VISA, cks. Store credit and exchanges.
   Layaway.
Parking: Free lot.

Discounts of 50–70 percent on junior sportswear, dresses, lingerie, handbags, shoes, and accessories have made Ms. Fashions popular with smart shoppers. The store carries merchandise from twenty to thirty top manufacturers in sizes 1–13. The clothing appeals to women of all ages—students, business women, homemakers, and senior citizens. Everything is first quality and most fashions are current season. You'll find consistently good buys in the following categories: dresses (business and dressy), $14–$50; pants and jeans, $16–$24; tops, $6–$25; shoes, $12–$25; handbags, $9–$16; jumpsuits and jogging suits, $20–$32. Special sales are held two times a year.

Ms. Fits

310 Vista Del Mar, Redondo Beach. (213) 378-6998.
Hours: Mon.–Sat. 10:30–5:30.
Purchases: MC, VISA, cks. Exchanges only. Layaway.
Parking: Street and area lots. Mailing list.

If you enjoy manifesting your own personal style and like a store that features the new and different, Ms. Fits is your kind of place. Patty Stearns and Jane Ryan have created a cozy, inviting shopping atmosphere that is complete with lots of personal service for their customers, a loyal following that has been building during the two years they've been open. The store isn't very big—you'll feel like you're walking into a closet, but don't be deceived. The selection of colors, styles, and first-rate labels make this shop bigger than it seems. You'll find the Lanz, Liz Claiborne, DeWeese, Ellen Tracy, and Claudine lines here as well as a couple of other "biggies" we can't mention. Much of Ms. Fits' frequent buying is done in New York. Prices are about one-third off for all types of classy sportswear, both in traditional and contemporary styles for sizes 3–14. Price tags show both the regular retail and Ms. Fits' discount price. All in all, this is a nifty little store and we recommend it highly.

My Place Fashions
3130 Pacific Coast Highway, Torrance. (213) 530-9992.
Hours: Mon.–Sat. 10:30–5:30.
Purchases: MC, VISA, cks. Exchanges. Layaway.
Parking: Free lot. Mailing list.

In the South Bay where many discount apparel stores thrive, owner Betty Pretty survives the competition by specializing in career women's coordinates and dresses. The store's atmosphere is that of a small boutique with its antiques and well-coordinated displays of accessorized outfits. Junior and missy labels in sizes 5/6–15/16 are Toni Todd, Vicky Vaughn, Donnkenny, and Sagamore Way coordinated separates. Jeans labels are Wrangler and Jenage. Belts, umbrellas, handbags, and hats make up the stock of accessories. Betty frequently sponsors store promotions and sends customers $5 birthday gift certificates. She periodically mails extra discount coupons to her customers, so add your name to her list.

9th Street Warehouse
1124 W. 9th St., Upland. (714) 985-5715.
Hours: Mon.–Sat. 10–6, Sun. 12–5.
Purchases: MC, VISA, cks. Exchanges.
Parking: Free lot.

The best way to evoke the immensity of the inventory is to tell you that it looks like one big happy swap meet. This comes as no surprise really, since owner Karen Martin got her start in the apparel business by selling at swap meets more than eight years ago. Actually, this store is better organized and provides a more pleasant shopping experience than do most outdoor flea markets. There's so much good stuff here, you almost can't leave without buying something. The merchandise mix is eclectic due to the fact that Karen says she just can't resist a good buy. Adjacent to the retail store are four equally large warehouses storing merchandise waiting to be sold. The side areas of this vast warehouse feature men's and women's shirts, jeans, sweaters, and jackets, as well as skirts, blouses, and jumpsuits for women. The center aisle houses thousands of pairs of children's and adults' jeans, all for under $20. Family size ranges are: women's 2–16; men's, small to extra large; and children's 7–14. Most of the stock is first quality—the seconds are clearly marked. Manager Marilynn Pretzer, Karen's sister, helps customers with their purchases. When you're in Las Vegas, stop by the family's other store, the Southwest Clothing Co.

Off Rodeo
1135 S. Beverly Dr., Los Angeles. (213) 556-5455.
Hours: Mon.–Sat. 10–5:30.
Purchases: Cks and cash. All sales final. Layaway.
Parking: Street.

Owners Irene Astrow and Sue Shaw have the right idea: they offer personalized shopping within the context of their room-sized boutique tucked away in an office building. Catering to the career and active woman, Off Rodeo prides itself on locating items to meet specific wardrobe needs. They will also special order and call customers when new merchandise arrives. All this service, as well as discounts of 30 to 70 percent on first-quality, current season merchandise is worth noting. Styles are classic to dressy. You won't find jeans, but jumpsuits and pleated trousers for work are popular items. Buying is done in California and New York and lines carried include Singer & Spicer, Carol Horn, Willi Wear, and Reminiscence. One- and two-piece silk dresses by Bijou and Chin are espe-

cially good buys. Prices range from about $27 for a polyester blouse to $190 for one-of-a-kind sweaters. Sizes are 3–14. Be sure and look at the Off Off Rodeo sales rack for drastic markdowns on current fashions.

Piller's of Eagle Rock

1800 Colorado Blvd., Eagle Rock. (213) 257-8166, 257-8167.
Hours: Fri. and Sat. 10–5:30, Sun. 12–5.
Purchases: MC, VISA, cks. All sales final.
Parking: Free lots. Mailing list.

Piller's of Eagle Rock has been in this location for over thirty years discounting moderate to better merchandise 50 to 75 percent. Good shoppers can find real values midst the long racks of sportswear, dresses, blouses, shorts, and more. The store carries shoes and apparel for men and women purchased as job lots, end-of-the-season closeouts from manufacturers and after-sale items from Rodeo Drive boutiques. Piller's may also bail out a store in financial trouble by paying cash for its merchandise at a low price and will then resell it at a discount. Women's sizes are 4–22½ in clothing styled for teens to mature women. Shoes are sizes 4½–10½ in all

widths. Two times annually, Piller's of Eagle Rock holds its "three for one" sale. Almost everything in the store is one-third the original price. Customers are notified by mail, so stop by and put yourself on their list. This family-run business closes the last weekend in July (after a big sale) and reopens in the latter part of August.

The Prism

5314 2nd St., Long Beach. (213) 434-6494.
Hours: Mon.–Sat. 10–6, Fri. 10–8, Sun. 11–5.
Purchases: MC, VISA, cks. Exchanges. Layaway.
Parking: Street. Mailing list.

This little shop, with its warm, cozy atmosphere, soft lighting, antique furniture, and hidden niches filled with accessories, is one of the most charming bargain boutiques we've visited. For those of you who discovered The Prism in *Glad Rags I,* we should add that it now carries a complete line of lingerie— sleepwear, foundations and teddies—at competitive prices in addition to the discounted better and designer sportswear and dressy separates. Owners Majken Neff and Pamela Wittes have excellent taste in merchandise and it shows in their collection of Phyllis Sues, Christine Albers, Singer & Spicer, and Willi Wear fashions. They also carry handmade, one-of-a-kind specialities, as well as lots of Irka silk garments. Silk is featured and prices are hard to beat—blouses run $28–$40 and dresses, $35–$60. Pants—from jeans to silk run $20–$40. Discounts average 30–50 percent and there are always sale items. The Prism does alterations.

Rags For Dolls

128 Glendora Ave., La Puente. (213) 330-3915.
Hours: Mon.–Sat. 10–5:30, Thurs, 10–7:30.
Purchases: MC, VISA, cks. Exchanges only. Layaway.
Parking: Free lot and street. Mailing list.

On the weekday afternoon we dropped by Rags For Dolls, there were so many women busy trying on clothes that the restroom had to be pressed into service as another dressing room. In looking around and talking to owner Pat Karvala, we got the feeling that customers don't just browse, they *buy*. That's understandable since the store carries many of the most popular missy dresses and sportswear lines (California Girl, Loubella, Mel Naftel, Sir Julian, Alex Colman, Puccini, and Goldie) at 50 percent off. In addition to the prices, the broad selection of colors and styles within each size makes this shop a real favorite among area shoppers. Sizes range from 6–20 in dresses, long and short evening gowns, and sportswear; blouses go to 46 and pants to 40 waist. Petites are included, as well. Goldie petite pants and the California Girl petite dresses are big sellers. Sweaters, pants, and blouses start at $10; dresses and pants suits are priced up to $48. Pat offers honest advice and personal service to her customers, which seems especially valuable because she herself is so stylish. The garment assortment in the store reflects shoppers' requests: Pat Karvala knows her customers and gives them exactly what they want.

The Sample Shop

1425 Wilshire Blvd., Santa Monica. (213) 393-2946.
Hours: Mon.–Sat. 9:30–6, Sun. 11–4.
Purchases: MC, VISA, cks. Exchanges. Layaway.
Parking: Street.

A fixture in Santa Monica for twenty-five years (and one of the oldest discount stores in Los Angeles), The Sample Shop serves its missy clientele well. Value, selection (everything from pajamas to parkas), and a broad size range (6–40) are three of the reasons this store has remained popular through the years. Labels are left intact, although we've been asked not to mention them. The Sample Shop specializes in coats and carries one of the largest selections in Santa Monica all year round. Prices run from $28–$150. Sweaters are another forte and there are styles to suit a young woman's taste as well as her more mature counterpart's. Dresses are $20–$80 with the majority in the $35 range. Pantsuits are a popular item and sell for anywhere from $20–$100 depending on the fabric and designer. Another big plus is the fact that this store carries half-sizes 12½–26½. Customers here set a premium on practical, wearable clothes that will not go out of fashion, so don't come looking for the avant-garde. Most of the merchandise is first quality, and irregulars are marked "as is." There are always several sale racks as new apparel arrives weekly.

Sara Fashion For Less

1135½ S. Robertson Blvd., Los Angeles. (213) 271-5030.
Hours: Mon.–Sat. 10:30–5:30.
Purchases: MC, VISA, cks. Exchanges. Layaway.
Parking: Street.

Neighborhood working women have made this cozy discount boutique one of their favorite shopping haunts. Owner Sara Shai stocks her pet brands, including Jody Tootique and Bonnie Strauss, in career separates and dresses, as well as some designer jeans by Jordache and Sasson. Price tags reflect savings of 40–50 percent. In the summer, Sara carries

Elizabeth Stewart swimsuits and short sets for about $11–$13 and an unusual line of embroidered T-shirts for $7. If you live or work near this shop, be sure to drop in.

Sareet's
3882 Crenshaw Blvd., Los Angeles. (213) 292-7070.
Hours: Mon.–Sat. 10:30–6.
Purchases: MC, VISA, cks. Exchanges. Layaway.
Parking: Free lot behind store.

Sareet's is a large store with little prices. As we mentioned in *Glad Rags I*, the store does a big business in jeans priced from $12–$35. Lines include Baccarat, Clippers, and Jordache. Sizes start with 24-inch waists—which will fit some ten-year-olds—and go to 38 inches. On the other end of the spectrum, you'll find large sizes, 38–46, in tops and slacks for $5 and $6. Dress slacks in sizes 1/2–19/20 are $6–$8 and dresses in sizes 3–16 run $15–$45. Blouses are a featured item and the most expensive style in the store the day of our visit was $12, although most blouses were in the $8 range. Nothing was priced over $40. A velveteen skirt-and-blazer suit for $38 had a retail value of $85. Polyester gabardine coordinates in sizes 8–18 were priced to move at under $20 per piece. The broad range of styles and sizes is consistent even though specific lines will vary. Discounts are up to 70 percent.

Saundra's Fashions
7940 Vicki Dr., Whittier. (213) 699-4494.
Hours: Mon.–Fri. 10–8, Sat. 10–7.
Purchases: Cash or cks. Exchanges. Layaway.
Parking: Free lot and street.

To be succinct: at Saundra's there are really good values on young, junior casual separates and dresses all neatly organized so that it's easy and pleasant to stop. Well-known labels like Warren Z, Upstairs Downstairs, D.C., and Q are available in sizes 3–15 for 40 percent below retail. A rack running the entire length of the store held $6.50 fitted polyester pants in every color. We found some nifty khaki pants for only $12 in the jeans section. T-shirts and turtlenecks start as low as $4

and you can spend up to $30 for a pair of designer jeans. Most of the store's inventory is pants and blouses and you'll find plenty of styles and colors to choose from.

7th Ave West
1216 Beryl St. (at Prospect), Redondo Beach. (213) 376-4426.
Hours: Mon.–Fri. 10–7.
Purchases: MC, VISA, cks. Exchanges. Layaway.
Parking: Free lot.

The folks at this store put a bit of extra effort into their operation. The saleswomen know their merchandise *and* how to outfit their customers. The contemporary merchandise is a cut above that found in other stores: some of the labels represented are Paul Stanley, Irka, Diane Von Furstenberg, Carole Little, and a New York sweater line, RBK. We found $120 London Fog raincoats on sale for $56. There's also a supply of popular young-junior brands like Tomboy, Jonathan Martin, Collage, and Summit Sportswear. By now you can probably figure out that this classy outlet has regular, steady customers who prefer to do most of their shopping here for savings of 30–70 percent. Sizes range from 1/2–15/16 with a few 18s. Career coordinates and weekend gear such as jeans and sweaters comprise the inventory. A few dressy items are added at the holiday season. Manager Deni Taylor advises shoppers to come in often since 7th Ave West stocks hundreds of new and different items each week.

Tenner, Inc.
11733 Victory Blvd., North Hollywood. (213) 761-5906.
Hours: Mon.–Sat. 9:30–5:30.
Purchases: MC, VISA, cks. All sales final. Layaway.
Parking: Rear lot and street. Mailing list.

It's always nice to discover a classy operation that's been in business for thirty-seven years selling better missy brands at *wholesale* prices. Furthermore, we're especially delighted to

note the particular lines Ruth Tenner offers, since they are not usually available at discount. Alas, we can't reveal the identities of these "famous labels," but, trust us, they're found in the ritziest sections of your favorite Beverly Hills specialty shops and department stores. The clothing selection includes day dresses, cocktail length and evening gowns, pants, blouses, two-piece dresses, blazers, jumpsuits and suits in sizes 4–20. Prices start at $22 for blouses and pants and go to $50 and $60 for dresses with many garments selling for around $40. Suits are a good buy—we found an especially nice $300 (retail) number for only $139. Ruth is quite proud of a particular line of very slightly irregular hand-painted silk dresses for $110 to $170, regularly sold for up to $300 retail. Due to the technique, we couldn't even tell that they were seconds. Sales held two or three times a year reflect prices marked down an additional 20–30 percent below wholesale. Don't wait for a sale to inspect this store, though. You'll always find at least one rack of specials. We discovered a $12 rack of dresses and jumpsuits the day of our visit.

V.I.G. Discount Fashions

1888 Pacific Coast Hwy., Redondo Beach. (213) 316-0658.
Hours: Mon.–Sat. 11–6, Sun. 11–4.
Purchases: MC, VISA, cks. Exchanges. Layaway.
Parking: Free lot.

Since we wrote *Glad Rags I,* V.I.G. has expanded its selection of junior sportswear, coordinate groups, sweaters, blouses, dresses and jeans. Sizes are 3–13 from moderate-priced manufacturers such as Bobbie Brooks and California Girl. Women's apparel, sizes 4–18 as well as petite pants and dresses, is still V.I.G.'s strong suit and the store is terrific for the mature shopper who prefers practical, timeless clothing. There are racks of Goldie polyester slacks in every color imaginable, including a new, nubby linen-look, for $12–$16. Pants are available in proportioned lengths. The average price for jeans (both junior and missy) is $15 and V.I.G. now carries a popular stretch denim. To accompany these pants are lots of sweaters and tops from Just Tops and Norben California at the same 30–50 percent discount. A unique feature of this store is the large collection of evening gowns. Prices range from $27–$90 (for an elaborate, sequin-encrusted creation), but most range from $40–$60. In the spring, there are styles for young prom-goers.

Vi & Gloria's Discount Fashions

14321 S. Hawthorne Blvd., Lawndale. (213) 679-6585.
Hours: Mon.–Sat. 11–6.
Purchases: MC, VISA, cks. Exchanges only. Layaway.
Parking: Free lot.

It's easy to see why local working women—from TRW, Mattel, Northrop, and Xerox—frequent this little shop for classic, traditional sportswear and dresses. Their favorite labels are sold here for 40–50 percent off retail. Vi says, "We cater to the working gal." She also admits to being an avowed clotheshorse and that's probably what got her started in the business ten years ago. Examples of the values found here: NaMa blouses for $19, Summit skirts for $17, Collage, Present Co., and Rochelle sweaters for $15–$20, Chic by H.I.S. and Wrangler Jeans for $15, and Emme dresses for only $15. If you're a size 10, check out the sample dress selection. Vi's clientele must know how to have a good time because she stocks quite an array of long and short evening dresses, some with jackets for $40–$70. The ladies at TRW enjoy the store's fashion shows put on at the company. Sales are held every three months, but you can drop by any time and see sale-tagged items sprinkled throughout the stock.

Women's Clothing Warehouse

29370 Roadside Dr., Agoura. (213) 707-1140.
Hours: Mon.–Sat. 10–6, Fri. 10–8:30.
Purchases: MC, VISA, cks. Exchanges only. Layaway.
Parking: Street and free lot. Mailing list.

It may sound a little funny, but this is actually a warehouse within a warehouse. A large building houses the warehouse-like operations of three discount clothing companies, one of which is the Women's Clothing Exchange. But don't let the

word "warehouse" scare you off. This store features lots of attractive displays with separates put together into attractive outfits, merchandise arranged neatly on racks by type, size, and color, and even colorful banners hung from the high ceiling to give the place a cheerful, upbeat feeling. It's easy and fun to shop here. Sizes go from 1–15 with a large selection of 1s and 3s. Prices range from 40 to 60 percent off for junior and missy casual sportswear, day dresses and actionwear from Tomboy, Jean St. Germain, Eclipse, Marie France, and Carole Little for St. Tropez West. New merchandise arrives every week and there are always specials marked down throughout the store, as advertised weekly in the Los Angeles Times and local newspapers.

The Yellow Balloon

2140 W. Artesia Blvd., Torrance. (213) 538-4257.
Hours: Mon.–Fri. 9:30–6:30, Sat. 9:30–6.
Purchases: MC, VISA, cks. Exchanges. Layaway.
Parking: Free lot.

You won't find two more personable discount storekeepers than Fay and Joe Goldfarb. Even if you just come in and look around, you'll have a good time at their store. The 30–50 percent savings will make your checkbook happy, too. The size range is unusually broad. Garey Petites pants and tops and blouses to size 46 make The Yellow Balloon a favorite among South Bay shoppers. Popular labels like Loubella, Teddi, Goldie, Campus Casuals, Jody Tootique, and Tomboy sell for about $10–$30, with some items—such as blazers—selling for more. Joe and Fay carry a few robes and accessories, like belts. There's always a sidewalk sale rack out in front of the store.

Orange County

CJ's Fashions

743 Baker St., Costa Mesa. (714) 754-1892.
Hours: Mon.–Fri. 10–6, Sat. 10–5.
2774 Sepulveda Blvd., Torrance. (213) 530-8701.
Hours: Mon.–Fri. 9:30–6, Sat. 10–5.
Purchases: MC, VISA, cks. Refunds and exchanges. Layaway.
Parking: Free lot. Mailing list.

Women fond of no-nonsense, classic designs in easy-care fabrics by Koret of California, Alex Colman, Teddi, Mel Naftel, Lady Arrow, and California Girl will appreciate the wide array of CJ's merchandise. Discounts run from 30 to 50 percent in missy and a few junior sizes 5–18. Larger-sized ladies can buy blouses to size 46 and pants to size 40. Petite-proportioned dresses and pants can also be found here. You'll like the per-

sonal attention—Cynthia and Jill consider it their shop's forte. Besides many local customers who frequent the shop, several Easterners save their annual buying sprees for CJ's during vacations to the Southland. One woman even sent her mother-in-law when she docked in Los Angeles during her cruise around the world. Pants and skirts start at $10 and run up to $22. The garment selection also includes blouses, sweaters, dresses, coats, raincoats, jackets, and pantsuits for up to $70. CJ's also carries robes and caftans.

De Javu

31952 Camino Capistrano (Mercado Mall), San Juan
    Capistrano. (714) 661-8511.
Hours: Mon.–Sat. 10–5.
Purchases: MC, VISA, cks. Exchanges and store credit.
Parking: Free lot.

Mix and match casual sportswear coordinates from Dana Point are discounted 20 to 50 percent. Clothes are cut to fit women size 6–18 and styled for a mature customer who has outgrown fads. Blouses, skirts, suits, and pants are manufactured in polyester and polyester blends ideal for home laundering and for travel. Styles are classic and vary little year-to-year, so women can begin to build a wardrobe and know that new pieces in seasonal colors and fabrics can be added with ease. Prices on a complete line of first-quality, current-season merchandise average $22.50–$37, for blouses, and $12.50–$40, for skirts and pants. Seasonal sales help make room for the latest styles.

Dell's Sample Shop

1294B S. Coast Hwy., Laguna Beach. (714) 494-7661.
Hours: Mon.–Sun. 10–6.
Purchases: MC, VISA, cks. Exchanges. Layaway.
Parking: Lot.

Owner Mary Odell Knowlton buys current-season, first-quality merchandise directly from local manufacturers and jobbers and saves her customers 40 to 70 percent on merchandise ranging from hats, purses, robes, and evening wear to dresses, suits, jumpsuits, blouses, and jogging suits. There isn't much you can't find at her newly expanded store. For misses, she carries Loubella Extendables, Le Roy knits, Julie Miller dresses and suits, Puccini blouses, and Dana Point jackets, to name a few. Juniors can choose from Rock Candy, City Girl, Tomboy, Cole of California, and Moonglow. Sizes range from 3–20, and petite-sized dresses. Merchandise reflects what is being made and sold for each season, so you'll find rompers in the summer and jackets in the winter.

Discount Fashions

451 N. Tustin Ave., Orange. (714) 633-3688.
Hours: Mon.–Wed., Sat. 10–6, Thurs. and Fri. 10–9, Sun. 12–5.
Purchases: MC, VISA, cks. Exchanges. Layaway.
Parking: Free lot. Mailing list.

Tracy Zelden pools her buying with two other *Glad Rags* shops—The Sampler and On the Rack—so that she can buy in quantity and thus offer missy sportswear at 25 percent off. The Campus Casuals line comprises 75 percent of the stock—other labels are Ann Marie dresses, Shirt Strings, Michael S pants, and Rae Hepburn blouses. Tracy recently added a new jeans resource: Rodeo Drive. She says the fit is one of the best she's found and that it's catching on with her customers. Sizes run from 3/4–15/16. Look for the new Campus Casuals petites line in the near future. Besides traditional career and casual coordinates, Tracy carries sportier items like warm-ups, shorts, rompers, and gauze and terry caftans. For the convenience of customers, hats, belts, and handbags are 15–25 percent off. The store will be expanding soon to the space next door where a "designer" section will hold Breckenridge, Calvin Klein, and Evan Picone at lower-than-retail prices.

Flo's Klothes

5948 Warner Ave. (Warner & Springdale), Huntington
    Beach. (714) 846-8131.
Hours: Mon.–Sat. 10–5:30, Thurs. to 8.
Purchases: MC, VISA, cks. Exchanges. Layaway.
Parking: Free lot behind Southwest Savings. Mailing list.

Flo has been in business for four years and comes from a family of successful garment manufacturers. Thus, you can always count on an extensive collection of junior sportswear from major California lines (unfortunately, we can't mention labels). Prices are at least 30 percent below retail on coordinated separates, blazers, sweaters, warm-ups, dresses, blouses, jumpsuits, shorts, pants, swimsuits, cover-ups, and tennis wear. There's always a sale rack outside with bargains under $20. Inside, you'll find the perfect mix of sportswear for the active Southern California lifestyle. Swimsuits are available all year round and the day of our visit, last year's styles (which could pass easily for this year's) were drastically reduced—a perfect time to buy. Flo's Klothes carries some clearly marked seconds in tennis outfits and warm-ups for $8–$17, as well as samples in size 9. Sizes are generally junior 3–13 (an entire rack of 3s!) with some missy sizes and small, medium, and large. Casual handbags are $7.75–$9. Flo's inexpensive accessories help pull an outfit together. Designer jeans average $23 and most items in the store are under $50. During the holiday season, Flo and her partner Shelley stock dressy dresses and jackets. Clearance sales are in January and August.

Golden Galleon

25130 Del Prado Ave., Dana Point (in the Dana Wharf
    Shopping Center). (714) 493-8521.
Hours: Mon.–Sun. 10–6.
Purchases: MC, VISA, cks. All sales final. Layaway.
Parking: Free lot.

Mary caters to what she likes to call the "beach crowd." She also serves the boating and sailing crowd, since she stocks

Half Krazie

9931 Hamilton Ave., Huntington Beach. (714) 964-3393.
Hours: Mon.–Fri. 10–9, Sat. & Sun. 10–6.
Purchases: MC, VISA, cks. Exchanges. 5-day hold.
Parking: Free lot. Mailing list.

During our visit, Krazie Katz Fashions, a fixture in Huntington Beach for seven years, was being transformed into Half Krazie. Owner Ivan Katz, who used to be a shoe buyer for veteran discounter Jerry Piller, explained that his new policy is to sell everything in the store at half of its original retail price. Garments, shoes, and accessories will no longer be double ticketed with retail/discount prices. Customers will simply pay half of what it says on the price tag. The merchandise is aimed at the working gal 17-years-old and up. Sizes are 3–18 in junior and contemporary missy styles. You'll find good buys on Wrangler Jr. jeans ($18) and poly gabardine slacks ($12) as well as pants by A. Smile and Rose Hips. Dresses by Sweet Inspiration, Jody Tootique, Infinity, and Rage of California are $25 and under (biggest selection in spring and summer). Tops range from $5 for regular T-shirts to $16 for long-sleeved blouses. Seasonal sportswear such as shorts and bathing suits are good buys. Bikinis and maillots by Eenie Meenie, High Tide, Daffy and Britt average $12. Warm-ups will be available all year 'round. Mr. Katz buys after sale shoes from all over the country—a small, eclectic selection.

J & J Discount Fashions

602 W. Chapman Ave., Suite F, Placentia. (714) 996-2501.
Hours: Mon.–Sat. 10–5:30.
Purchases: MC, VISA, cks. All sales final. Layaway.
Parking: Free lot. Mailing list.

Jane Jackson carries a nice selection of missy separates available for 30–50 percent below retail. We can't mention all the labels, but you will find first-quality, current-season pants, tops, blouses, blazers, shorts, and sweaters from such

everything imaginable for all kinds of surf-and-sand activities. Customers rave about the huge selection of swimsuits and the outerwear collection of jackets and windbreakers. Styles appeal to the more mature women—lots of customers come from nearby Leisure World. Sizes 6–22 are available in coordinates and sportswear from Aileen, Designers Originals, Weather Tamer, Personal, and Frank Lee. A couple of examples of Mary's large-size selection: swimsuits to size 48 and Le Roy sweaters to 46. Mary also carries Gilda regular- and petite-proportioned pants in sizes 8–20. Accessories include canvas beach bags, socks, pantyhose, and beach thongs. Prices generally fall in the $10–$30 range for swimsuits, blouses, pants, jackets, and skirts, with T-shirts, sweatshirts, and tops a little less. Merchandise is marked 20–30 percent below retail and there's always a sales rack. You can save an additional 10-percent off all new things coming into the store. We've seen lots of sales at the end of a season, but at the beginning, too? What an idea!

makers as DeWeese and Goldie. She even carries a few large size and petite pants and blouses. Prices average $19 for pants ($29 retail) and $25 for blouses ($42 retail). The blazer jackets and pants are from the same manufacturer so you can coordinate a pantsuit and easily find a pretty print blouse to complete the outfit. While Jane's shop is small, she carries lots of colors and styles in each size. She's built up a steady, loyal clientele during her six years in business and takes good care of customers by calling frequently when new items come in and notifying them of special sales. For hungry shoppers, J & J is located next to an interesting little Mexican/Chinese cafe called Kelly's Taco Suey. The $1.95 luncheon special is a real *Glad Rags* value—and tasty, too.

Labels For Less Fashions

5454 La Palma Ave., La Palma. (714) 826-0620.
Hours: Tues.–Sat. 10–6, Thurs. 10–6:30.
Purchases: MC, VISA, cks. Exchanges only. Layaway.
Parking: Free lot. Mailing list.

It's impossible to spend more than $30 for any one item here. As a matter of fact, on the sales racks—where there's always a good selection—a *complete outfit* might be $30. Designer jeans, pants, blouses, and tops are the store's bread-and-butter. Well-known-and-liked missy polyester pants that sell for $26 retail are only $19 here, and are available in eleven colors. If you can't find your particular size or color, you can order them, also at the discount price, and they'll be available within a week. These name-brand pants are also available in petite sizes 5–16. One long wall rack features dresses at an average price of $24, including a selection of petite sizes. Owner Steve Brodkin likes to keep his customers happy by turning over his stock quickly and continually offering new and interesting items. During our visit we discovered some stylish new jeans with side-seam details that were just beginning to hit the retail fashion scene. Labels For Less also carries a good selection of jumpsuits, blazers, and two-piece warm-up suits.

Notre Place

170 E. 17th St., Costa Mesa. (714) 548-3035.
Hours: Mon.–Fri. 10–2:30. Call for a Saturday appointment.
Purchases: MC, VISA, cks. Exchanges only.
Parking: Street. Mailing list.

Joan Lippman and Lynne Koffler's office-suite boutique can best be described as a haven for "discount investment dressing." While specific labels can't be mentioned, we must say that you'll find tastefully styled, better separates and coordinates for 20 percent below the prices in retail boutiques and department stores. While most of the styles are fairly conservative (even some *de riguer* preppy lines), Joan and Lynne offer a few sportier and more casual pieces in actionwear and gauze. Notre Place has developed a loyal clientele during its four years of operation thanks to all the service they offer. The proprietors order items for customers, coordinate wardrobes, and even suggest other stores for that special something to complete an outfit. The mailing list is used to notify customers of the January and June sales when everything is sold at wholesale (50-percent off), and also to announce the arrival of new seasonal merchandise. If your own style tends toward classic sportswear and your closet holds some better New York labels, you owe it to yourself to stop by Notre Place.

Patti's Casual World

23354 El Toro Rd., El Toro. (714) 581-8740.
Hours: Mon.–Fri. 10–6, Sat. 10–5.
Purchases: MC, VISA, cks. Exchanges and store credit.
   Layaway.
Parking: Free lot. Mailing list.

Edith Guio was a Patti's customer until she bought the store two years ago. Loyalty like this is common among the women who appreciate buying name-brand clothing at a savings of one-third and more. Even though labels have been removed, you'll recognize the large selection of famous manufacturer proportioned pants, pantsuits and blouses. Petites, as well as large and half-sizes will find clothing to fit. Sizes are 5–16 in both missy and petite and Patti's carries blouses to size 44 and pants with waist sizes to 34. Styles are casual to dressy. Dresses rarely are priced over $40 and long, cotton-blend, embroidered caftans and hostess gowns from the Phillippines are $40–$50. Formals are available all year round for under $60. All merchandise is first quality and Edith stresses the friendly atmosphere and service her store is famous for. Coffee and wine are always available, and husbands and boyfriends are welcome to sit and enjoy the hospitality while the women shop. Customers (mostly women in their late thirties and older) come from all over the world, including one woman from Saudi Arabia who flies in monthly on her husband's private plane to do her buying.

The Price Tag

27601 Forbes Rd., Laguna Niguel (in the Three Flags Center). (714) 831-2420.
Hours: Mon.–Fri. 10–5:30, Sat. 10–4.
Purchases: MC, VISA, cks. Refunds and exchanges. Layaway.
Parking: Free lot. Mailing list.

We might as well begin with the most important information— the labels: well-known junior and missy lines such as Pant-Her, Loubella, West Coast Connection (W.C.C.), White Stag, Jantzen, High Tide, and Rose Marie Reed are available here at one-third off. We got *really* excited when we learned that during frequent sales everything in the store is reduced another 50 percent. Watch the local *Pennysaver* and *Saddleback Valley News* for sales announcements and get yourself on their mailing list. The fashions include casual sportswear like swimsuits and You Babes wrap shorts for $9 and $10, Pant-Her, and W.C.C. dressy coordinates for $20–$50 and day dresses for $15–$19. Store manager Virginia and one of the co-owners shop long and hard for the very best buys. At holiday time, there's a nice grouping of long dresses. Virginia says the one thing she likes best about the store is the down-to-earth, relaxed atmosphere. No high pressure sales tactics here—just good values in a very pleasant store.

Rosie 'N Me

515 W. Commonwealth Ave., Fullerton. (714) 879-9421.
Hours: Tues–Sat. 10–5:30.
745 N. Tustin Ave., Orange. (714) 997-1830.
Hours: Mon.–Sat. 10–5:30.
Purchases: MC, VISA, cks. Exchanges only. Layaway.
Parking: Street. Mailing list.

Shopping at Rosie 'N Me is as pleasant and comfortable as shopping in someone's home: as a matter of fact, the Tustin store is a cozy little yellow house filled with first-quality, current goods and samples in dresses, sweaters, blouses, jeans, pants, skirts, and warm-up suits. The dining and living rooms hold missy and junior sportswear in sizes 3–18. The bedrooms have been transformed into dressing rooms, and, on the day of our visit, the kitchen housed the sale racks with savings of 60 and more percent off. We found several pairs of 100-percent silk Clovis Ruffin pants for only $12. Garments are clearly displayed by type and size, and both retail and discount prices are marked on every tag. Labels include Organically Grown, Alex Colman, Carole Little, Ellen Tracy, Liz Claiborne, and Nell Flowers. You'll also find lots of samples from a very famous San Francisco manufacturer of denim jeans and sportswear and a popular line of missy polyester fitted and pull-on pants for only $19, regularly $34 retail. Prices range from $15 for a cotton shirt to about $75 for a $150 blazer or a $110 dress. Rosie does a lot of shopping at retail stores on her days off to stay informed on prices and it shows in these two stores. Shop here for good value and lots of selection.

The She Shop

621 E. 17th St., Costa Mesa. (714) 645-1665.
Hours: Mon.–Sat. 10–6.
Purchases: MC, VISA, cks. Exchanges. Layaway.
Parking: Free lot. Mailing list.

Teens to grandmothers shop here for casual and dressy sportswear in sizes 3–16. Most labels have been removed, but we saw Rochelle sweaters and purchased one on sale for $35 that was regularly $175. The average discount is 50–75

percent and special buys the day of our visit included Jean St. Germain jumpsuits for $34 and jeans for $20. Dresses range from $20–$36, blouses are $6 or less, and belts are priced under $9. Gift certificates may be purchased at any time and clearance sales are held three times a year.

Shipley's

2201 Main, Seacliff Village, Huntington Beach.
  (714) 536-4700.
Hours: Mon.–Fri. 10–8, Sat. and Sun. 10–6.

The Joint Warehouse

247 Pine, Long Beach. (213) 432-4278.
Hours: Mon.–Sun. 10–6. No checks accepted.
Purchases: MC, VISA, cks. Exchanges. Layaway.
Parking: Free lot. Mailing list.

Casual sportswear for the entire family is available at Shipley's two locations. The Huntington Beach store services its beach-community clientele with name brands such as Lightning Bolt, Ocean Pacific, Kennington Blue, Alex Colman, Wrangler, Levi Strauss, and a full range of designer jeans. Women's sizes are 1/2–18, boys are 8–18, girls 7–14 and men's range from small to extra large in shirts and from waist size 28-44 in pants. The Long Beach store also offers clothes for children (toddlers and up) at their 25 percent discount. Name brands are not as prevalent here, but prices are even lower. Pants and jeans are the biggest sellers in both locations. If you can't find a pair to fit you among the hundreds of styles, you just aren't trying. There are always special purchases and extra-discount sales. Racks are clearly marked with price and size and arranged by style. The day of our visit, there was a large rack of current Danskin styles at $3 below retail. Shipley's buys closeouts, bucket lots, and some irregular merchandise, which is clearly marked.

The Shore Shop
The Villager Shoes
2117 Main St., Huntington Beach (in the Seacliff Village
  Shopping Center). (714) 536-4600.
321 Seal Beach Blvd., Seal Beach. (213) 594-8928.
Hours: Mon.–Thurs., Sat. 9–6, Fri. 9–8, Sun. 11–5.
Purchases: MC, VISA, cks. Exchanges. Layaway.
Parking: Free lot. Mailing list.

Sportswear and beachwear for the whole family at 20–60 percent off attracts shoppers from all over. Men can shop for pool
wear and leisure wear, while women browse through the
junior and missy-sized separates and swimsuits. The boys
assortment is equally good in jeans and popular casual tops
and jackets in sizes 8–20. Labels are clipped, but the popular
lines include Ocean Pacific, Off Shore, Brittania, Campus,
Sweet Baby Jane, Loubella, Jantzen, White Stag, Hang Ten,
and Levi Strauss. Sizes range from 3–20 for women. All the
merchandise is first-quality.

Conveniently located within each store is The Villager
Shoes featuring men's and women's footwear for 30–40 percent below retail. Women's sizes run 5–10 from popular
casual makers such as 9 West, Bass, Sperry Top-Siders,
Cherokee, and Street Cars. Prices run about $20–$40 and
you'll always find a sale table with final markdowns.

Sunshine Fashions
144 W. Lincoln Blvd., Anaheim. (714) 535-8288.
14333 Inglewood Ave., Hawthorne. (213) 973-1334.
Hours: Mon.–Sat. 10–6:30.
Purchases: MC, VISA, cks. Exchanges only. Layaway.
Parking: Free lot.

Owner Ha Sook Kim and her two daughters are their own best
advertisements for these little neighborhood discount shops.
A more well-groomed and better-dressed mother-and-
daughter team you won't find. The Kims sell junior and missy
dressy sportswear pieces, jeans and dresses for 25–35
percent off. We liked the well-organized store layout that
made it easy to find exactly what we were looking for. There

were whole walls full of $15–$22 sale blouses. Another long
rack stretching the length of the store held $6 and $7 polyester fitted pants. Some of the brands featured are Cardessa,
Clipper, Three Girls, Vivian, and Cheeks. Sizes run from 1–16,
with a few large size blouses up to 42. The store also carries
sweaters, dresses, and real and fake-fur jackets and coats.
Career women will like the convenient assortment of attache
cases, along with the handbags and other accessories.

Chains

3

Many neighborhood discount stores in *Glad Rags I* have grown into chains for *Glad Rags II.* The little are getting big and the big are getting bigger as discount retailing grows by 20 to 30 percent each year compared to a 3- to 4-percent growth in regular retailing. We define a chain as a store with three or more locations. Generally, all stores have the same name, but there are exceptions and these are noted. You'll find a broad range of merchandise offered at these stores. As Eastern discount chains move Westward, we see more New York lines, and there is the ever-growing West Coast apparel market, as well as merchandise from other manufacturing centers such as Dallas, Miami, and Chicago. Several discount chains started out many years ago with one store in the garment district and have grown gradually. Others have sprung up overnight and continue to expand, spreading the discount message throughout Southern California. Shoe store chains are listed in the Shoes and Accessories chapter.

LA County

Beno's

1500 Santee St., Los Angeles. (213) 748-2222.
142 Oregon St., El Segundo. (213) 322-6477.
12233 S. Norwalk Blvd., Norwalk. (213) 594-0840.
1255 Bixby Dr., City of Industry. (213) 336-4632.
15000 La Miranda Blvd. (La Miranda Mall), La Miranda.
   (714) 994-3552.
17162 'A' Murphy Ave., Irvine. (714) 549-8521.
1101 S. Cyprus St., La Habra. (714) 992- 6771.
1981 E. Wright Circle, Anaheim. (714) 634-3749.
1149 Los Angeles Ave., Simi Valley. (805) 526-5845.
6815 E. Washington, City of Commerce. (213) 724-0755.
6500 Platt Ave., Canoga Park. (213) 710-8258.
11282 Los Alamitos Blvd., Los Alamitos. (213) 594-0840.
Hours: Mon.–Sat. 10--8, Sat. 10–6, Sun. 12–5.
2579 Pacific Coast Hwy., Torrance. (213) 530-1344.
Hours: Mon.–Sat. 10–6. Sun. 12–5.
7280 Bellaire Ave., N. Hollywood. (213) 982-7749.
Hours: Mon.–Sat. 9–5.
870 Carson Mall, Carson. (213) 327-8663.
Hours: Mon.–Fri. 10–9, Sat. 10–7, Sun. 12–5.
Purchases: Cash or cks. Refunds and exchanges.
Parking: Free lots.

Beno's operates sixty-three stores in California, fifteen of which are discount stores, with one in San Diego. The stores look like giant supermarkets for men's, women's, and children's clothing. They specialize in casual sportswear for the entire family—from infants through large sizes for both men and women. The selection of coordinate groups and separates in women's junior and missy sizes has been expanded since we wrote *Glad Rags I*. The range of merchandise remains broad—hosiery, pants, bras, slips, and nightgowns to dresses, suits and coats. It's the jeans selection, however, that brings people back to Beno's. You'll find first-quality jeans in all styles and brands arranged by size and color. Discounts are 20 percent and more throughout the store.

Bob's Sportswear

807 S. Los Angeles. St., Los Angeles (213) 622-8871.
Hours: Mon.–Sat. 9:30–5:30.
229 E. 9th St. (at Santee), Los Angeles. (213) 622-1530.
Hours: Mon.–Sat. 9–5.
16573 Ventura Blvd., Encino. (213) 789-9191.
Hours: Mon.–Sat. 9:30–6.
3002½ Sepulveda Blvd. (in the National and Sepulveda
   Shopping Center), Palms. (213) 477-0165.
Hours: Mon. and Tues. 10:30–7, Wed. 10:30–8, Thurs.
   10:30–9, Fri. 10:30–8:30, Sat. 9.30–6, Sun. 11:30–5:30.

B and B Sportswear

10669 W. Pico Blvd., West Los Angeles. (213) 475-3107.
Hours: Mon.–Thurs. and Sat. 9:30–5:30, Fri. 9:30–6.
860 S. Los Angeles St., 4th Floor, Los Angeles.
   (213) 623-8543.
Hours: Mon.–Sat. 9:30–5.
Purchases: MC, VISA, cks. All sales final. Layaway.
Parking: Street and area lots. Mailing list.

Sale racks of current merchandise (priced at only $5.75 and $6.75 the day of our visit), as well as everyday discounts of 40–60 percent on better lines make Bob's worth a visit. The owners buy exclusively from manufacturers so you'll be able to buy the same fashions you see advertised by department stores. Lines carried include Esprit de Corps, East Side Clothing Co., Happy Legs, Paul Stanley, and Irene Kasmer. Sizes are junior 3–13 and contemporary missy 4–14. You can always find lots of blouses ranging in price from $7 up to $50 for silk. Dressy and casual separates comprise the majority of the inventory—clothes for work and play. The downtown stores have large gang dressing rooms.

Fantastic Factory Outlet

11146 S. Downey Ave., Downey. (213) 923-2404.
12803 Valley View Ave., La Mirada. (213) 921-3919.
6035 E. Florence Ave., Bell Gardens. (213) 771-3463.
3428 Tweedy Blvd., South Gate. (213) 564-9566.
1265 W. Central Ave., Brea. (213) 691-8880.
Hours: Mon.–Thurs. 10–7, Fri. 10–9, Sat. 10–6, Sun. 11–5.
Bell Gardens and South Gate stores are closed on Sunday
   and Monday.
Purchases: MC, VISA, cks. Exchanges. Layaway.
Parking: Free lots. Mailing list.

Ruby Kuchera's chain of discount fashion stores reminds us of comfortable neighborhood dress shops popular twenty years ago. Missy and junior styles are well displayed in a kind of old-fashioned atmosphere that fits with the values of 40–70 percent savings on all kinds of separates and dresses, as well as nightgowns and peignoir sets. Specialties include mix-and-match separates (blazers, pants, blouses, and skirts) and dresses, including cocktail styles during the holidays. All clothing comes from better manufacturers, but you can still find a good dress for under $40. There is a Junior Corner with lots of jeans and tops to complement the full missy selection. Sizes are 3–18. Watch for special "two-for-one" sales, as well as the semi-annual "champagne sales" which feature store-wide "bubbly good buys."

Fashion Corner

200 E. 9th St., Los Angeles. (213) 489-3730.
Hours: Mon.–Sat. 9:30–5:30.
242 N. Market St., Inglewood. (213) 672-3198.
Hours: Mon.–Sat. 10–6.
321 Main St., El Segundo. (213) 322-5981,
Hours: Mon.–Sat. 10–6, Fri. 11–7.
8827 S. Sepulveda Blvd., Westchester. (213) 641-3584.
Hours: Mon–Sat. 9:30–6, Fri. 10–7.
Purchases: MC, VISA, cks. All sales final. Layaway.
Parking: Street and area lots.

"We've grown up with our customers" explains co-owner and buyer Joyce Harris. "We're less bubble-gum junior now—and more sophisticated. We have a contemporary look that works for young girls and working women." Here you'll find jeans to chiffon dresses discounted 40 percent and more. New merchandise arrives daily from California and New York manufacturers. Sizes are 3-15 in all the current styles of the season. Special discount racks offer extra savings on popular items. The gang dressing rooms—comfortable and mirrored —are perhaps the largest in L.A.

Harpers Ladies Wholesale Jobbers

331 E. 12th St. (at Maple), Los Angeles. (213) 747-5441.
Hours: Mon.–Sat. 9–5.
8588 W. Washington Blvd., Culver City. (213) 839-8507.
Hours: Mon.–Sat. 10-6, Fri. 10–8.
22766 Ventura Blvd., Woodland Hills. (213) 347-3633.
15616 Ventura Blvd., Encino. (213) 789-5837.
Hours: Mon.–Sat. 10–6, Thurs. 10–8.
Purchases: MC, VISA, cks. All sales final. Layaway.
Parking: Street and free lots.

"We're still the only one that sells *below* wholesale," Harpers boasts, and our experience bears this out. It's hard to beat Harpers' day-to-day discounts of 50–80 percent on name brand merchandise in sizes 1–16 (junior and missy). Their sale racks are legend. On one of many visits, we found a designer-made wool jersey skirt for $5 and a forward-fashion strapless jumpsuit in cotton sweatshirting for $10. We can't begin to list the labels, because almost all moderate to better lines are represented; twenty-five are designers. The range of merchandise is equally broad—from outerwear to swimwear. Dresses are strong, as are sportswear, coodinated separates and anything currently trendy. New merchandise arrives con-

stantly. There are large group dressing rooms. Watch for two stores opening in Orange County.

Headlines

20556 Hawthorne Blvd., Torrance. (213) 371-4332.
16672 Beach Blvd., Huntington Beach. (714) 848-1098.
28138 S. Western Ave., San Pedro. (213) 548-6277.
Hours: Mon.–Fri. 11-8, Sat. 10–6, Sun. 12–5.
3759 Wilshire Blvd., Los Angeles. (213) 383-6633.
3146 Wilshire Blvd., Los Angeles. (213) 738-1922.
Hours: Mon.–Sat. 10–6.
Purchases: MC, VISA, cks. Refunds and exchanges. Layaway.
Parking: Street, free and area lots. Mailing list.

The principals of this chain of stores also manufacture the very popular line of junior separates that make up most of the merchandise selection at Headlines. Hence, the savings of 30–40 percent on the latest first-quality Judy Knapp, Swat, Western Connection, and Jordache in sizes 3-13. Merchandise is turned over quickly; new items arrive each Thursday. Prices start at $9 for pants and tops, and go to $26 for jumpsuits. Besides sportswear items and a few dresses for

$20–$23, you'll find some snazzy warm-up suits in velour for $15 per piece and other sets for $21. We like the values, especially one long rack of eye-catching pants in every color for only $11. There are always several sales racks in the store. If a young junior look is your style, Headlines is your store.

Judy Brown's

766 S. Los Angeles St., Los Angeles. (213) 622-5820.
Hours: Mon.–Sat. 9:30–6.
20148 Hawthorne Blvd., (Best Plaza), Torrance.
  (213) 371-0939.
Hours: Mon.–Fri. 11–9, Sat. 11–7, Sun. 11–6.
2573 W. Via Campo (Montebello Plaza), Montebello.
  (213) 722-5626.
Hours: Mon.–Sat. 10:30–8.
Purchases: MC, VISA, cks. Exchanges. Layaway.
Parking: Street (downtown) and free lots.

Judy Brown's is a factory outlet for a manufacturer of polyester dresses and blouses. Dresses, pants, tops, and skirts average $10–$20 and are popular with mature women and office workers. Judy Brown's also carries silk blouses, dresses, and other sportswear at wholesale prices which range from $20–$80. They advertise all the popular designer jeans at competitive discount prices averaging $30. Sizes are junior and missy 3–20.

Loehmann's

6220 W. Third St., Los Angeles (Fairfax Area). (213) 933-5675.
19839 Victory Blvd., Reseda. (213) 873-1155.
130 Laguna Rd., Fullerton. (714) 879-8665.
Hours: All locations, Mon.–Sat. 10–5:30, Wed. 10–9:30.
Purchases: Cash or cks. All sales final.
Parking: Free lots.

Loehmann's—the name is synonymous with designer fashions at discount prices. Founded in 1921 in Brooklyn by Frieda Loehmann, the nation-wide chain now encompasses fifty-two stores (up from thirty-eight when we wrote *Glad Rags I*). The grandame of discount clothes retailing, Loehmann's remains a leader in its field. "Ours is one store not affected by inflation," says a Loehmann's spokeswoman. "Women *still* have to buy clothes, and when they can buy quality for less here, that makes our business better than ever." Discounts at Loehmann's are guaranteed to be at least one-third below retail, with many items half-off. All merchandise is first quality, and new shipments arrive *daily*. Any dedicated Loehmann's shopper will tell you it pays to shop frequently. Clothes are marked down three times until they are sold or sent back to New York. Prices can get ridiculously low—a $50 dress marked down to $4 for example. Sizes are 4–18 in a complete range of wardrobe needs, with the exceptions of shoes and lingerie. There isn't much you can't find at Loehmann's, but the store prides itself on stocking complete outfits so that a woman can put herself together in one location. Each store has an accessory boutique where hats, bags, scarves, sunglasses, and small leather goods are also discounted. All major designers will be represented, although labels are removed in some cases. Prices run the gamut—from $1.49 for a blouse to $850 for an Yves St. Laurent cocktail dress that would retail for $1500 or more. Twice annually, the Park LaBrea store hosts a "fur event." Major design houses bring in their mink, fox, beaver, and other fine fur creations. An example of the savings is a Russian sable coat priced at $25,000 that sold at Loehmann's for $12,000. Watch for the "Fall Event" held for one day in September. The stores bring in totally new merchandise to introduce the new fashion season. There are several spacious group dressing rooms.

MGM

1347 N. Lake Ave., Pasadena. (213) 791-1012.
3090 N. Lincoln Ave., Altadena. (213) 794-4664.
20761-A S. Avalon Blvd., Carson. (213) 515-1320.
Hours: Mon.–Sat. 11–7.
Purchases: MC, VISA, cks. Exchanges only. Layaway.
Parking: Free lots.

A broad size range and low prices distinguish this growing chain of discount stores. Girls two-years-old and up will be able to save 40 to 60 percent on dresses, sportswear, and jeans. Clothes for work and play are well mixed and there are many name brands to choose from. Jeans are a big seller and MGM carries styles for as little as $4. Designer jeans are available at wholesale prices for children through adults. Childrens' sizes are 4-20 in unisex jeans, and there are girls' dresses, blouses, and play clothes. Girls' dresses start at $6 and blouses at $3. Women's sizes are 3–24½, including petites. MGM manufactures dresses and blouses under its own label. Large and half-sized dresses are $18–$21 and blouses are $9–$16. Polyester pants in sizes 1–24½ are $5. Junior and missy dresses in polyester, rayon, silk, or double georgette manufactured by MGM start at $9 and blouses are as low as $3. New clothes arrive several times each week and there's always a sale rack of clearance items.

Marshalls

19731 Vanowen (at Corbin), Canoga Park. (213) 346-0208.
16830 San Fernando Mission Blvd., (at Balboa), Granada Hills. (213) 368-5621.
15906 E. Imperial Hwy (Green Hills Shopping Center), La Mirada. (213) 947-2811.
16672 Beach Blvd., Huntington Beach. (714) 848-9333.
Oakbrook Village on Avenida de la Carlota, Laguna Hills. (714) 855-1431.
Hours: Mon.–Sat. 9:30–9:30, Sun. 12–5.
Purchases: MC, VISA, cks. Refunds and exchanges.
Layaway.
Parking: Free lots.

At Marshalls, you'll find substantial savings on the same brand-name fashions sold in department and specialty stores. There's a complete line of menswear, misses' and juniors' fashions, lingerie and accessories, women's large-size sports-wear, infants', toddlers' and children's wear, as well as family footwear, and household items. We call Marshalls a discount department store. Merchandise is purchased all over the country and then sent to the headquarters in Massachusetts for nationwide distribution. This explains the wide variety of labels, many of which are not seen in other local discount stores. The stores are large, and it takes patience and a good eye to shop effectively—25 percent of the merchandise is irregular. There are clearance racks for an extra 30–50 percent savings and inventory sales in August and February.

m. frederic & co.

2251 S. Sepulveda Blvd., West Los Angeles. (213) 477-3002.
Hours: Mon.–Sat. 11–7, Sun. 2–5.
11701 Wilshire Blvd., West Los Angeles. (213) 820-8383.
Hours: Mon. and Tues. 10–6, Wed.–Sat. 10–9, Sun. 2–8.
572 Washington St., Marina del Rey. (213) 822-2336.
Hours: Mon.–Fri. 117–7, Sat. 10–6, Sun. 12–6.
229½ S. Beverly Dr., Beverly Hills. (213) 273-4716.
Hours: Mon.–Sat. 10–6.
Purchases: MC, VISA, cks. Exchanges only.
Parking: Street, free and pay lots. Mailing list.

If we were going to design a discount store, the kind of cheerful neighborly little shop you like to have right around the corner from your home or office, it would probably look just like m. frederic & co. There's nothing fancy here, just all our favorite junior labels at 40 percent off, plus the very latest, complete Jag sportswear line for almost half off. Owner Phyllis Levine, along with her son and daughter, stocks a comprehensive assortment of career and casual separates in all three stores. Thus, it's easy to see why m. frederic's is so busy during lunch hours. Phyllis & co. started carrying selected men's clothing to keep the men busy while their wives and girlfriends were shopping; the Beverly Hills store has the biggest selection. Besides stylish Jag coordinates, MacKeen, French Connection, and Jean St. Germain are represented in all types of separates and actionwear including vests, jumpsuits, and bodysuits. If you like sweaters, you'll appreciate the unusually large array of styles and colors at m. frederic. Since almost everything in the store is priced under $20, you can easily get all decked out for about $50. All three of the Levines like to *move* clothes and turn their stock over frequently. Don't be surprised if you receive lots of announcements of sales and special promotions once you put yourself on the mailing list.

Ohrbachs's

6060 Wilshire Blvd., Los Angeles. (213) 933-8111.
14650 Parthenia Blvd., Panorama City. (213) 894-7181.
Colorado at Central (Glendale Galleria), Glendale.
   (213) 240-8850.
3555 Carson (Del Amo Shopping Center), Torrance.
   (213) 542-7711.
200 Los Cerritos Mall, Cerritos. (213) 860-0501.
6600 Topanga Canyon Blvd. (Topanga Plaza), Canoga Park.
   (213) 704-6404.
Hours: (individual stores may vary slightly): Mon.–Fri. 10–9,
   Sat. 10–6, Sun. 12–5.
Purchases: MC, VISA, AE, store charge, cks. Refunds and
   exchanges. Layaway.
Parking: Free lots.

When we queried a good friend and ace shopper about her latest shopping spree to Ohrbach's, she responded, "You know how it is: you *look* everywhere else, but you *find* it at Ohrbach's." She proudly displayed an acrylic sweater that looked hand-knit that she'd purchased for $6. We've found that by watching newspaper ads announcing special purchases and sales, and dropping in occasionally for a recreational browse, it's possible to get a handle on Ohrbach's. Merchandise changes continually, which makes each visit a new experience, so get to know the departments that carry your style. Our first stop is always the shoe department where we've picked up some fabulous values. Another favorite is the junior sportswear and separates department. Sweatsuits in bright colors are unbeatably priced and there's always a good selection of fashion pants, tops, and skirts. We got lucky one day and purchased unstructured jackets for $16. They were such a hit and so versatile, we went back for more, but the stock was sold out. Good buys don't stay around long. Ohrbach's makes no bones about being a copy store. "We may not have it first, but we'll be a close second," the management says. You can usually find the latest fashion trends priced about 20 percent below other department stores. This applies to men's, boys', children's and infants' apparel also. Clothing for the entire family, including large sizes and maternity wear is priced at least 10 percent below other deparment stores. We recommend trying on clothing before making a purchase because cuts and sizes are erratic (a common complaint at any price, but particularly in budget clothing). Accessories (especially purses and totes), hosiery, underwear for the whole family, scarves, and hats and gloves are also worth a look.

The Original Large & Half Size Factory Outlet

910 S. Santee St., Los Angeles. (213) 623-3390.
Hours: Mon.–Fri. 9–5:30, Sat. 9–4.
6586 Van Nuys Blvd., Van Nuys. (213) 997-1673.
Hours: Mon.–Sat. 10–5:30.
663 Second St. (Mervyn Center), San Bernardino. (714) 381-1027.
Hours: Mon.–Fri. 10–7, Sat. 10–6, Sun. 12–5.
1700 S. Central Ave., Los Angeles. (213) 749-4760.
Hours: Tues.–Sat. 9–4:30.
Purchases: MC, VISA, cks. Exchanges. Layaway.
Parking: Street and lots. Mailing list.

Next to the *price* of clothes, the most common complaint we get is about the lack of *special-sized* clothing. Women tell us they will pay almost any price to find something that fits, is flattering and well-made, so it's doubly good news to know that you can have all this and more at *discount*. Buying here is done directly from manufacturers and savings is 25–50 percent on quality lines such as Pendleton, Liz Sophisticates, Herald Place, Mr. Alex, Koret, Levi-Echo II, and Peggy Lou. Blouses are sizes 30–46 with some 48s, pants 30–42 and caftans, sleepwear, and lingerie run to size 48. You'll also find coats and evening dresses. There are racks of last season's fashions priced under $10. Watch for a new store opening in Orange County.

Pant Store With No Name

10813 Zelzah Ave., (Granada Village Center), Granada Hills. (213) 363-0715.
Hours: Mon.–Fri. 10–8, Sat. 10–6, Sun. 12–5.
9075 Woodman Ave., Arleta. (213) 893-2257.
19401 Victory Blvd., (Loehmann's Plaza), Reseda. (213) 344-1260.
Hours: Mon.–Sat. 10–6, Wed. 10–8, Sun. 12–5.
2807 E. Cochran (Sycamore Square), Simi. (805) 527-6888.
193 N. Moorpark Rd., (Janss Mall), Thousand Oaks. (805) 495-4733.
Hours: Mon.–Fri. 10–9, Sat. 10–6, Sun. 12–5.
Purchases: MC, VISA, cks. Exchanges.
Parking: Free lots. Mailing lists.

Owner Andy Myers half seriously refers to himself as "the Jerry Piller of girls' clothing." His discount chain offers 60 percent toddler through girls' size 14 casual wear and 40 percent junior jeans and tops. Primary labels are Jordache, Chemin de Fer, and Sergio Valente jeans, and a wide selection of tops, including sweaters, T-shirts, and blouses. Junior sizes are 1–13 (waist sizes 26–32). Women size four and up will be able to save 15–50 percent on everyday clothing needs.

Sacks SFO

8 Horizon Ave., Venice. (213) 399-8890.
Hours: Mon. & Tues. 11–6, Wed.–Fri. 11–8, Sat. & Sun. 10–7.
16740 Ventura Blvd., Encino. (213) 981-8625.
Hours: Mon.–Sun. 10–6, Thurs. 10–8.
1734 Newport Blvd., Costa Mesa. (714) 646-7835.
Hours: Sat.–Tues. 11–6, Wed.–Fri. 11–8.
Purchases: MC, VISA, cks. All sales final (exchanges on gifts). Layaway.
Parking: Venice, lot one block south; Encino, rear lot; Costa Mesa, adjacent lot. Mailing list.

To *Glad Rags I* readers, Sacks SFO will always be affectionately known as Sacks Fifth Off (guess who couldn't take a joke?). But whatever the sign outside says, the discounts in-

and men's pants are waist-sized 28–40. Sweaters, shirts, jackets, and activewear are available for both men and women. There is always a large selection of silk and other natural fibers. Many items are priced under $30 and spot sales and store-wide clearance sales in January and August are further incentives to spend and save.

The Sampler

947 E. Main St., Alhambra. (213) 289-5281.
1031 S. Baldwin Ave., Arcadia. (213) 447-0951.
129 La Mirada Mall, La Mirada. (714) 994-0842.
308 E. Broadway, Glendale. (213) 247-3570.
2212 W. Beverly, Montebello. (213) 728-4219.
965 E. Green St., Pasadena. (213) 795-7639.
16123 E. Whittier Blvd., Whittier. (213) 943-2276.
1207 Los Angeles Ave., (Larwin Sq.) Simi Valley.
   (805) 526-7377.
Hours: Mon.–Sat. 10–5:15, Sun. 12–4:45. Arcadia,
   Montebello, Whittier, and Glendale: Fri. 10–8:45.
Hours: (Simi Valley) Mon.–Fri. 10–8, Sat. 10–6, Sun. 12–5.
Hours: (La Mirada) Mon.–Fri. 10–9, Sat. 10–6, Sun. 12–5.
Purchases: MC, VISA, cks. Exchanges and store credit.
   Layaway.
Parking: Free lots. Mailing list.

This chain of manufacturer's outlet stores has been in business for twelve years. The stores are very large, and stock a range of junior and missy apparel sizes 1–18 and half-sizes. Merchandise from over four hundred manufacturers is represented; you will find everything from super-inexpensive cotton tops to better-quality dresses, coats, cocktail dresses, and evening gowns (during the holidays and prom season), coordinate groups, sportswear, jeans, and activewear. Almost all of the labels are removed, so some knowledge of various lines, along with attention to construction and details, helps. The mailing list notifies customers of the semi-annual "bonus time" sale when the entire stock is discounted another 50–75 percent below their regular discount prices.

side are still an honest 40–70 percent below retail. For consistently exciting new fashions from top East and West Coast designers, it's hard to top Sacks. These stores could just as easily be included in our Designer chapter. We're pleased to report that since our first visit (and we've been loyal customers ever since), Sacks in Venice has been remodeled and expanded. It's still bumper-to-bumper shopping at times as clothes-conscious men and women look for ways to save money without sacrificing style or quality. Sportswear suited to the California lifestyle is Sacks' strong point. Owner David Sacks buys clothes you live and work in. Merchandise is always current season and first quality. Women's sizes are 2–16

Taking Advantage
942 S. Los Angeles St., Los Angeles. (213) 689-1582.
Hours: Mon.–Sat. 8:30–5.
24291 Avenida de la Carlota, Unit P-7 (Oakbrook Village),
   Laguna Hills. (714) 855-4661.
Hours: Mon.–Wed. 10–7, Thurs. & Fri. 10–9, Sat. 9–6,
   Sun. 12–5.

Julie Jones
20054 Hawthorne Blvd., Torrance. (213) 542-5503.
Hours: Mon.–Fri. 10–7, Sat. 9–6, Sun. 12–5.
Purchases: MC, VISA, cks. Exchanges.
Parking: Downtown, street and area lots; Laguna Hills and
   Torrance, free shopping-center lots. Mailing list.

The Taking Advantage of *Glad Rags I* has grown out of its office suite into three spacious stores filled with designer names such as Anne Klein, Calvin Klein, Gloria Vanderbilt, Liz Claiborne, Ellen Tracy, and Evan Picone. You'll also find better California sportswear manufacturers, such as West Coast Connection, well represented. All clothing is discounted 40–60 percent and is first-quality, current-season merchandise. Coordinate groups, sportswear and separates in sizes 3–15 (juniors), 4–16 (missy), is popular with women who make their careers inside and outside the home. At the downtown store only, there are Left Bank shirts for boys in sizes 8–20 and men's small–extra large. The range of merchandise is impressive. Blouses, including silks, crepe de chine and georgette, start at $15; dressy sweaters and sweater jackets in angora, hand-knits, wool, and blends are $12–$90. Blazers and jackets that can be coordinated with lined and belted trousers (from $20) average $30–$90. There are lots of pants in all fabrications (depending on the time of the year), as well as T-shirts, jeans, and activewear. There is one large dressing room at the downtown location and individual ones at the other two. Outfits are color–coordinated and displayed so that complete ensembles can easily be selected. Saleswomen are courteous and helpful, but never pushy.

Orange County

Allison's Place

Over twenty-five locations in Los Angeles and Orange counties. Check your telephone White Pages for the store nearest you.
Hours: Mon.–Fri. 10–8, Sat. 10–6, Sun. 11–5.
Purchases: MC, VISA, cks. No cash refunds. Layaway.
Parking: Street and free lots. Mailing list.

Allison's Place has grown from three stores to over twenty-five and hasn't stopped yet. With the growth has come a new sales policy; nothing in any of the stores is over $10! In fact, at ten of the smaller stores, nothing is over $5. Obviously, volume has a lot to do with the low prices. Owner Ben Goldstein buys clothing by the *tonnage*, "throws away the dross, and sells the cream," as he puts it. The cream can be a sweet bargain like a name-brand dress which sells for $25 in a mall store, available at Allison's for $5. Sizes are 1/2–15/16, with blouses up to large-size 46. "Whenever good merchandise comes along at the right price, we'll go after it," the owner explains, adding that at times you can find men's shirts, as well as clothing for teens and juniors. Accessories, including earrings, bracelets and belts are $1–$3. "I've always wanted to try this concept of one-price retailing," Mr. Goldstein adds. "It's not a new idea. I grew up with it and saw it work in New York. The secret is low prices and a broad range of merchandise. Ninety-nine out of a hundred people will buy something once they come into the store." Watch for stores opening in San Diego, Ontario, and in the San Gabriel Valley.

Clothes Time

Sixty locations in Southern California. Consult your telephone directory for the store nearest you.
Hours: Mon.–Fri. 10–9, Sat. 10–8, Sun. 11–6.
Purchases: MC, VISA, cks. Refunds and exchanges.
    Layaway.
Parking: Free lot and street. Mailing list.

The atmosphere at these junior sportswear shops is decidedly no-nonsense. As one of the store managers explained, "We're selling clothing, not ambience." The light, open, self-service arrangement does make for pleasant, efficient shopping, and there are enough locations to be convenient to every bargain shopper. Well-known makers like Esprit de Corps, San Francisco Shirt Works, Barbara Barbara, and

Irene Kasmer manufacture the sporty and career separates in sizes 1–13 sold here for 40–70 percent off. Volume buying and sales are the keys to this four-year-old chain's success. New items arrive in each store constantly to replenish the stock of goods. A garment lasts on the racks an average of just two weeks before it's sold. In other words, if you like it, you'd better buy it, because it probably won't be there when you come back.

The Garment District

2952 W. Lincoln Ave., Anaheim. (714) 761-2031.
Hours: Mon.–Fri. 10–6:30, Sat. 10–6, Sun. 12–5.
2431 N. Tustin Ave., Santa Ana. (714) 547-2227.
Hours: Mon.–Fri. 10–6, Sat. 10–5:30.
171A 17th St., Costa Mesa. (714) 642-0051.
Hours: Mon.–Thurs. 10–6:30, Fri. 10–7, Sat. 10–6, Sun. 12–5.
25280 Marguerite Parkway, Mission Viejo.
 (714) 586-6582.
Hours: Mon.–Fri. 9:30–9, Sat. 9:30–6, Sun. 12–5.
1027 N. Coast Hwy., Laguna Beach. (714) 497-2262.
Hours: Mon.–Sun. 10–6.

The Ferry Stop

506 Bay Front, Balboa Island. (714) 673-2188.
Hours: Tues.–Sat. 11–5.30, Sun. 12–5.
Purchases: MC, VISA, cks. Exchanges. Layaway.
Parking: Free lots. Mailing list.

A chain of thirty-three stores has grown from the original Balboa Island location. The secret is a central buying office which picks up overruns and samples from over three thousand California manufacturers and designers. All of the junior and missy merchandise in sizes 3–16 is first quality and stores receive new shipments three to four times *per week*. Thus, The Garment District is a new store each time you shop. Discounts are 40 to 70 percent on all types of garments—activewear to evening gowns. Buying is done in season, so you'll be sure to find wool suits in the winter and cotton sundresses in the summer. There's always a good selection of jeans (designer $30, others $12–$16), blouses, fun accessories, and inexpensive handbags. Women with contemporary to classic tastes will find clothes to please them. Labels carried include Diane Von Furstenberg, Frances Henaghan, William Kasper, Act III, Plum Tree, KoKo Knits, Albert Nipon, and much more. Prices are as wide ranging as the lines represented. Each store is individually owned and therefore unique. In the Santa Ana shop, you'll also find better jewelry—estate pieces averaging $100–$200 and 14K gold on consignment. The entire family can shop in the Mission Viejo location. One-third of its business is in discounted children's clothes (infants to size 14, boys to size 20). There is also a selection of men's tops size small to extra large.

It's Fantastic

1037 Pacific Coast Highway, Seal Beach. (213) 594-0490.
5701 E. Santa Ana Canyon Rd., (Canyon Plaza Shopping
 Center), Anaheim Hills. (714) 974-1780.
369 Seventeenth St., Costa Mesa. (714) 642-9380.
24320 Swartz Dr., El Toro. (714) 951-9312.
Purchases: MC, VISA, cks. Exchanges only. Layaway.
Hours: Mon.–Sat. 10–6, Fri. 10–7, Sun. 12–5.
Parking: Free lot.

Carole Little for St. Tropez West is this five-store chain's specialty, although you'll find other contemporary junior and missy lines like Condor, West Coast Connection, Albert Nipon, Jones New York, Evan Picone, Chenault, Broadway Directions, John Richard, Irene Kasmer, Jag, and Organically Grown in sizes 1/2–13/14. Dressy separates in silk, wool, and linen, along with day dresses and suits comprise the bulk of the inventory. Your weekend and off-hours shopping needs can be met at any one of these locations, too. Sporty separates and jeans sell for about $20. The broad price range goes from $15 blouses to $65 wool blazers to $85 silk dresses and more for suits and some designer dresses. Professional women make up the majority of the store's clientele. There is a specially proportioned dress line available to fit petite-sized women. Everyday savings are 50-percent below retail and there are lots of specials. There are frequent sales at the Seal Beach store, the "outlet" for the other locations. Everything here is marked down another 25 percent and manager Lori Preusch is always moving clothing onto sidewalk sale racks.

Roberta's Discount-ique

25351 Alicia Parkway, Laguna Hills. (714) 768-2965.
31931 Camino Capistrano, San Juan Capistrano.
   (714) 493-3464.
Hours: Mon.–Fri. 10–5:30, Sat. 10–5. (The San Juan
   Capistrano store opens at 9:30, Mon.–Fri.)
357 S. Coast Hwy., Laguna Beach. (714) 494-1134.
Hours: Mon.–Thurs. 10–6, Fri. & Sat. 10–9, Sun. 11–5.
Purchases: MC, VISA, cks. Exchanges within seven days, all
   sales final on sale merchandise. Layaway.
Parking: Free lots. Mailing list.

Owner Bob Margolis "retired" into discount retailing after more than twenty years in the garment industry and his knowledge and connections are evident in the quality of designer and brand-name sportswear and coordinated separates he buys in New York and Los Angeles. Shoppers will find a broad range of merchandise. The Laguna Hills store is half a block from Laguna Hills High School and a half mile from Leisure World and it serves both communities admirably. The merchandise mix is 25 percent junior and 75 percent missy. Sizes are 3–15 and 4–20, as well as small to extra large. For the petite woman, Roberta's offers Levi Strauss and Jantzen proportioned pants and jeans in sizes 4–18. The San Juan Capistrano store has recently added a discount Western boutique. On our visit, we noted unusual and beautiful handknit sweaters by Nannell which regularly sell for $112 and were on sale for $56. Other strengths include suits from Alex Colman and Alan Abel at 25 percent below retail and a good selection of long- and short- sleeved blouses for under $25. The active woman will find a good selection of sports clothes, including jogging suits and short sets. The average discount at Roberta's Discount-ique is 30–50 percent, but there is always a sale in progress, and an additional sale rack. Cash customers are given an additional 5 percent discount and after spending $200 you become eligible for a prize drawing. Sign the mailing list to be notified of special sales throughout the year.

The Store

9038 Adams Ave., Huntington Beach. (714) 963-2221.
12546 Valley View St., Garden Grove. (714) 893-2772.
2239 N. Tustin Ave., Santa Ana. (714) 835-3787.
29129 S. Western Ave., San Pedro. (213) 547-3095.
Hours: Mon.–Sat. 10–6.
Purchases: MC, VISA, cks. Refunds and exchanges. Layaway.
Parking: Free lots. Mailing list.

Two-thirds of each store is stocked with missy and junior sportswear, coordinated separates, and dresses at strictly retail prices. The remaining third always features sales and special markdowns. Clothes are marked down one-third after thirty days and one-half after sixty, so there's always a good selection of discounted merchandise. Over twenty-thousand (!) customers are also notified by mail of sales at least four times a year. The Store caters to the professional working woman of all ages. Merchandise is stylish, but not trendy, from better manufacturers such as Jantzen, Campus Casuals, Ship 'n Shore, Loubella, Aileen, Koret, and Hang Ten. Sizes are missy 6–18 and junior 5–13. A new department at all locations is the "Petite Boutique." Petite-proportioned clothing in sizes 4–16 will include dresses from Melissa Petites and Matthew Love Petites, as well as blouses and separates from Aladdin, Devon, and Personal.

Garment District

4

We visited nearly one hundred and fifty stores in the Garment District to select the best sixty-eight or so for this chapter. Nowhere is the growth in discount retailing more apparent than in this concentrated area downtown along Los Angeles, Main, Santee, Broadway, Hill, Eighth, Ninth, Twelfth Streets, and the surrounding area. This is a microcosm for the discount retailing business as a whole. You'll find low- to high-end merchandise and everything in between. We've tried to do the leg-work and much of the guesswork for you.

To best describe Los Angeles' exploding and exhilarating Garment District, we've divided the area into six geographical regions, by street, blocks, or in some cases by individual buildings. Because the physical area covered by the Garment District is so vast, we felt that this would help you get a handle on the various kinds of shopping offered.

Based on our experience in this wonderland of sensory overload for the clothes conscious, we recommend visiting the Garment District early in the day on a weekday if at all possible. Park in a lot (lots on Maple and Santee are less expensive than those on Los Angeles Street) and walk to as many stores as possible. Shopping requires time and patience because of the stores' large inventories. Service ranges from excellent to nonexistent, and that goes for try-on facilities as well. There are stores, warehouses, and outlets to suit the beginning, intermediate, and advanced discount shopper. Read on and see where you fit in. This is a bustling shopping area with more bargains per square foot than anywhere else in Los Angeles or Orange County—so don't miss it.

Los Angeles

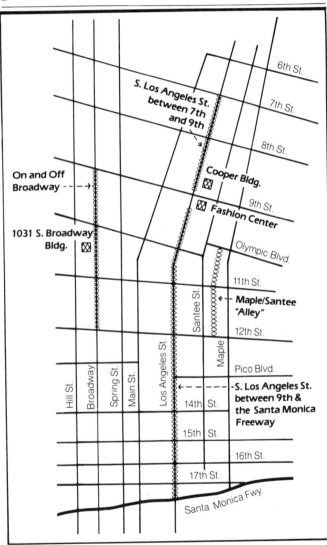

Map labels:
6th St.
7th St.
8th St.
S. Los Angeles St. between 7th and 9th
Cooper Bldg.
On and Off Broadway
9th St.
Fashion Center
1031 S. Broadway Bldg.
Olympic Blvd.
11th St.
Maple/Santee "Alley"
12th St.
Pico Blvd.
Hill St.
Broadway
Spring St.
Main St.
Los Angeles St.
Santee St.
Maple
S. Los Angeles St. between 9th & the Santa Monica Freeway
14th St.
15th St.
16th St.
17th St.
Santa Monica Fwy.

ON AND OFF BROADWAY

A more eclectic mix of discount stores exists nowhere else in the garment district than right here on 8th, 9th, 12th, Main, Hill, and especially, Broadway. We've tried to describe the gems for you. You'll enjoy shopping this area if you're an adventurous type since there is a great variety of unique shops with extra-special bargains. You can find everything from the $5-tops-and-bottoms store (Mambo) to the special rising-star (like Van-Martin Rowe and Christine Albers) designers' sample sales at 1031 S. Broadway. You might visit the stores we've recommended first and then venture into some of the others. Occasionally you'll see some older merchandise or encounter a salesperson who doesn't speak English very well, but shopping in this area is worth the extra effort. Parking, unless otherwise indicated, is street or area lots.

Amko
1051 S. Broadway, Los Angeles. (213) 489-3694.
6223 Pacific Blvd., Huntington Park. (213) 581-2402.
2534 Daly St., Lincoln Heights. (213) 221-8110.

Amko Pants
1059 S. Broadway, Los Angeles. (213) 748-3866.
Hours: Mon.–Sat. 9:30–6.
Purchases: Cash only. All sales final.

We recommend this store for its no-nonsense approach to self-service shopping for women's separates. In a large, open space you can easily find the racks of blouses, sweaters, jeans, or jackets you're looking for. Each section is clearly marked with its price from $4.80 up to $19.80. Name brands such as Tomboy, Daniel Laurent, Diane Von Furstenberg, Organically Grown, to name a few, fill the shelves. The pants-only store down the street is just that—pants and jeans in casual styles for $7.80–$14.80 in many different colors. There are other stores in downtown Los Angeles offering some of these lines at discount prices, but nobody beats Mr. Kim for his concept of wide selection, good values, and easy shopping.

Amko (Children's)
956 S. Broadway, Los Angeles. (213) 489-3694.
Hours: Mon.–Sat. 9:30–6.
Purchases: Cash only. All sales final.

Leonard Kim has expanded his successful merchandising concept to include children's wear in infants through size 14 for boys and girls. Over forty labels are represented, about half of which come from New York makers. Mr. Kim runs a large wholesaling operation in children's wear at this location. Several discounters in Los Angeles and Orange County told us they buy some of their merchandise from Amko. Nothing is over $17.80. Infants' items start at $1.90, with the bulk of the inventory selling for up to $7.80 for all types of school, play, and dressy clothes from Little Laura, Evy of California, Tracy Lynn, Mike's Girl, Candy Kiss, and Polly Flinders.

Black & White Wholesalers
1250 S. Broadway, Los Angeles. (213) 746-5841.
Hours: Mon.–Sat. 9:30–6:30.
20012 Ventura Blvd., Woodland Hills. (213) 465-6573.
Hours: Mon.–Sat. 10:30–6.
Purchases: MC, VISA, cks. All sales final. Layaway.
Parking: Free lot.

If you're downtown, have only enough time or the inclination to shop at one store and you're a junior size, this could be your store—all eight thousand square feet of it. We like the way the casual and career separates are displayed in the main area while the better things are featured in the art deco designer room—which is frankly the best reason to shop here. Better New York and California lines, such as Charlotte Ford, Mercedes and Adrienne, Joy Stevens, Jeremiah, A.J. Lowell, Karen Kane, Bill France, and Kenar all go for 50–70 percent below retail as does everything else in the store. There's lots to choose from in the designer room, especially in silk. Clothes here go for $20–$60, while they are $3–$35 throughout the store's main area. We liked the racks and racks of jumpsuits and the permanent Saturday sales. Sizes are 3–13.

H. Harper's Personal Touch Design Center
929 S. Broadway, S. 1010, Los Angeles. (213) 624-5896.
Hours: Mon.–Fri. 10–6, Sat. 10–3.
Purchases: Cash or cks. All sales final. Layaway.
Parking: Street and area lots. Mailing list.

Harriette Harper has moved her base of operations from the Vermont Avenue store listed in *Glad Rags I* to a new downtown location in the heart of the Garment District. The geographical shift reflects a business shift as well. Harriette now manufactures under two labels. H. Harper Designs is her better ladies ready-to-wear and loungewear featuring caftans, two-piece coordinates, unconstructed jackets, better blouses, and pants. These garments are made from a variety of crepes, satins, silks and lightweight woolens, challises, and imported cottons and priced from $40–$100. The Personal Touch label includes play clothes and separate skirts, blouses, pants and budget loungewear in the $15–$35 range. Clothes are missy-sized 8, 10 and 12. The loungewear and caftans are one-size-fits-all and will easily accommodate the proportions of the full-figured woman. Mailing list customers are eligible for the "birthday registry" which entitles you to a special discount during the month of your birthday. Also, Harriette plans on sending out a quarterly newsletter with information about new H. Harper creations, and eventually, a catalog for home ordering.

Hi-Teens
941 S. Broadway, Los Angeles. (213) 622-8382.
Hours: Mon.–Sat. 10–6:30.
Purchases: Cash only. Exchanges.

Children's sizes 3–6x and 7–14 sell in this light, pleasant shop for 30-percent off. While there is more selection for girls, you'll find everything but underwear and shoes for all the kids you buy for. The merchandise includes a few more interesting things that you don't see everyday in other stores. We found African shirts, girls' jumpsuits, boys' white sport jackets, lots of fancy, frilly girls' dresses, and children's jogging suits. Price tags range from $1.80–$29.80 for boys' suits, with the vast majority in the $5 category. We recommend Hi-Teens for a broad selection of up-to-the-minute merchandise in a pleasant shopping atmosphere.

Mambo
1011 S. Hill St., Los Angeles. (213) 747-3332.
Hours: Mon.–Fri. 10–6, Sat. 10–5. Closed Wed.
Purchases: Cash or cks. Refunds and exchanges.

Mambo gets the *Glad Rags* award for stability. Nothing about the store has changed in over two years—including the values and the prices. It's still a light, clean little shop selling tops and bottoms, period. Polyester pull-on and fitted slacks as well as all kinds of tops and blouses sell for $1.88–$4.80. The most popular designs are displayed on the walls. Mambo does a brisk business and it's easy to see why. At these prices, you simply can't beat the values.

Timmy Woods
718 S. Hill St., 3rd floor, Los Angeles. (213) 689-1380.
Hours: Fri. 12–5.
Purchases: Cash or cks. All sales final.

Anyone familiar with Timmy Woods' tasty, sophisticated handbags and belts will want to take advantage of her Friday factory sales when end-of-the-season merchandise and cancelled orders are sold at wholesale prices. Ms. Woods works with quality materials and designs for the woman who has risen above the ordinary and appreciates what she calls "the best designed-and-made bags in California." Leather belts are $10–$30 and bags in painted snakes, suede, canvas and suede combinations, and leather are $30–$150. Styles are casual to dressy and some of the larger bags double as attaches.

1031 S. BROADWAY BUILDING, Los Angeles.

This building houses major California designers and manufacturers. A few of them sell directly to the public on a regular basis or during invitation-only sales. We recommend calling before visiting, as these are work-rooms and warehouses with demanding schedules. (Lord help the unsuspecting shopper who arrives un-announced on a day when a new line is being shipped.) Park in an area lot and wear a leotard to facilitate try-ons as there are no dressing rooms. Sales are cash-only unless otherwise stated, and all sales are final.

Christine Albers
Suite 912. (213) 748-1708.

Seasonal sales are held four times a year to clear out end-of-season merchandise and samples. Customers are notified by mail so you must call to be put on the mailing list. Don't even *think* about buying at any other time. Christine Albers designs high-end, forward-fashion sportswear, dresses, and sepa-rates. Her fabrics are the finest European wools, cotton, and baby lamb leather. Prices for these designer-quality goods in sizes 4–12 are steep. First-quality merchandise is sold at wholesale and damaged goods are less.

Van-Martin
Suite 906. (213) 748-9542.

Designer Van-Martin Rowe has put himself on the fashion map with his "ambisexual" sportswear and activewear for men and women. Sizes run extra small to large and his "jock couture" is both practical and fashionable—a unique mixture that must be the essence of California living. Sample sales are held once a month by invitation, and appointments can be made to buy from the factory after regular working hours. The first step is to get yourself on the mailing list. Your Master-charge and VISA are welcome here.

Screamers/Drennen
Suite 957. (213) 742-0381.
Hours: Mon.–Fri. 9–5:30.

Sandy Drennen designs both lines of knitwear. Screamers is better junior sportswear and activewear and Drennen is her young designer contemporary-sportswear-and-dress line. Sizes run petite to large in both. Clothing is sold at wholesale and below by appointment. Styles are forward fashion leaning toward avant garde. Cotton interlock, wool jersey and fleece are some of the fabrics used.

B. C. Sportswear, Inc.
Suite 550. (213) 746-4848.
Hours: Mon.–Fri. 10–4.

Customers are allowed to shop in the warehouse as long as the company is not shipping an order. Call first to make certain you're welcome then go see the designer samples and over-cuts on current and last season's merchandise. Damaged goods (that can be easily repaired) are sold for $3–$5. First-quality dresses, tops, and bottoms in sizes 3–13 and petite to large sell for wholesale or below. B.C. manufactures junior sportswear for several companies and styles will reflect cur-rent fashion trends. The day of our visit, there was a tempting selection of cotton gauze dresses.

860 SOUTH LOS ANGELES STREET
(the Cooper Building)

Known to bargain-hunters for decades as The Cooper Building, 860 has become in the last two years the hub of off-price retailing in the Garment District. Busloads of shoppers now swarm through the stores and jam the elevators where only a few hearty souls used to tread. All this new shopping blood has inspired a rash of Grand Openings and breathed life into the whole area. On the other hand, women who have quietly patronized long-time merchants such as MJB and Ernest of California shudder at all the commotion and attendant price hikes. Still, most of us are delighted to discover that one building is now a veritable shopping center for discount clothes. Because the tenor of 860 is changing so rapidly, we will discuss stores with a reputable track record as well as those that offer good value and look promising. The best news is the selection of merchandise—you can afford to be picky.

Unless otherwise noted, stores accept MC, VISA, and checks; all sales are final except on gift items. There are layaways and gang dressing rooms. Mailing lists notify customers of special sales at least two times a year. We've started at the top floor and worked our way down.

Designers at Large
Room 440. (213) 623-4836.
Hours: Mon.–Sat. 9–4:30.

The owners of Fashion Reflections opened this cheerful, spacious store for large- and half-size fashions. Its specialty is sizes 36–46 and 12–24½, but there is a complete range of large- and half-sizes starting at 16 plus 1x, 2x and 3x, 16/18, 20/22 and 24/26. A handy wall chart explains pants and skirt sizes by waist and hip measurement. Designers at Large carries a full complement of wardrobe needs, excluding lingerie. Women who complain about the lack of style consciousness in large sizes should look here. These are not camouflage clothes, but attractive, flattering styles from lines such as Givenchy for Tomorrow's Dream, Rejoice, Chaus, Leslie Fay, Diane Von Furstenberg, Outlander, and Levi Strauss. Discounts range from 30–70 percent and there are individual dressing rooms.

The Accessory Co.
Fourth floor. (213) 622-6022.
Hours: Mon.–Sat. 9–4:30.

Accessories and active sportswear may seem like an odd mix, but it all works together in Gloria Binder's small shop. This is also the only store that carries clothing for men, women, and children. The merchandise mix includes totes, handbags, shoulder bags, clutches, belts, socks, children's jogging suits, men's shirts, sweaters, and shorts, women's short sets and warm-ups, as well as blouses, loungewear, and other odds and ends. Clothes are sized petite through large and 4–14. Discounts are 30 percent and more on quality lines such as Wendy Gray and Patti Cappalli. There are sale racks to browse and individual dressing rooms.

Lingerie Collections
Room 416. (213) 623-2389.
Hours: Mon.–Fri. 10–4:30, Sat. 9–5.

For lingerie, camisoles, robes, and peignoir sets, try Lingerie Collections. Merchandise includes underwear, sleepwear, and loungewear in sizes petite to extra large. Sexy fashions predominate, but Miss Modesty will also be able to save 30–50 percent on lines such as Diane Von Furstenberg and Patti Cappalli.

Joanna Footwear

Room 420. (213) 623-8788.
Hours: Mon.–Fri. 10–4:30, Sat. 9–5.

Women's daytime and evening shoes (no sport shoes) from manufacturers such as Garolini, Amalfi, Andrew Geller, Nickels, Joyce, Beene Bag, and Palizzio are here discounted 30–70 percent. Merchandise comes from "anybody we can get a break on the price from," says owner Bruce Sklar. There is a wide choice of styles—some from past seasons. The range of sizes is impressive—4–11 AAA to wide. There were lots of repeat customers in the store looking at pumps in the $20–$65 range and casual shoes under $30.

The Designer Room

3rd Floor (213) 626-3281.
Hours: Mon.–Sat. 9–5.

Wherever we go to talk about discount shopping, women have heard about The Designer Room as the outlet for Carole Little for St. Tropez West silk dresses and sportswear. Dis-counts are 40 percent on current-season items up to 60 percent and more on closeouts and damaged goods. The store carries Carole Little's complete line in sizes 2–14 and it has added designers such as Albert Nipon. There are plenty of capable salespeople to coordinate outfits from the vast inventory. Inside The Designer Room are two new departments:

Le Club Handbags

(213) 623-8709.

Owner Bill Reich came to our attention during *Glad Rags I*. He moved his operation from his home to a large corner in The Designer Room, but still offers discounts of 25–75 percent on designer and "main-floor department store" brand handbags. Family connections in the handbag business give him an edge. Meyers Handbags makes up special bags for Le Club and Bill buys Theodore seconds. Prices range from $14 for a leather clutch to $600 for a snakeskin designer bag. The selection includes sporty and evening styles of all sizes, shapes, and colors.

Opera Shoes

(213) 689-9656.

The rear of The Designer Room now houses an independently operated shoe store. Run by the father-daughter team of Max and Carole Palant, Opera Shoes carries comtemporary styles for sport, work, and dress. Traditional and avant garde footwear peacefully coexist on neatly arranged racks and displays. Max promises a consistently good selection of boots—especially fine Italian leathers. The size range is 5–10 in medium and narrow widths. Brands include Andrew Geller, HipOppo'Tamus, Zodiac, Apache, Roseta, 9 West, Martini Osvaldo, and Julianelli.

Gallery Sportique

3rd Floor (213) 622-2723.
Hours: Mon.–Sat. 9–5.

Offering career sportswear and dressy separates from well-known designers at 40 percent savings, Gallery Sportique attracts working women to celebrities. Sportswear and coordinate group lines carried in depth include Liz Claiborne, Ellen Tracy, Paul Stanley, Anne Klein, Adolfo Sport, and Overture sweaters. All merchandise is first quality and current season in sizes 4–14 (some 16s). Buying trips to New York are made monthly so new merchandise is constantly being added. Both the owner and store manager have extensive retail experience and stress customer service as well as value.

Room 310 Fashions

3rd Floor. (213) 488-9666.
Hours: Mon.–Fri. 9:30–4:30, Sat. 9–3:45.

This is the Lou Louis California outlet for sportswear geared toward the mature customer in sizes 6–16 and junior sizes 5/6–15/16. You'll find wholesale prices and lots of denim and corduroy pantsuits, jeans, jeans skirts, vests, and jackets. A two-piece set (jacket and skirt or pants) was only $16 the day of our visit. There are always sale racks and uniformly low prices.

MJB

2nd Floor. (213) 628-1604.
Hours: Mon.–Fri. 9–5, Sat. 9–4.

MJB is the Patty Woodard factory outlet and has been in this location for years. Manufacturers' overstocks in coordinated separates from the current season are sold at nearly wholesale prices. Blazers, pants, skirts, vests, blouses, shorts, and tunics are available in quantity. Sizes and color choices are broad and most items are priced under $50.

Ernest of California

Room 211. (213) 622-2297.
Hours: Mon.–Sat. 9–4:30.

This store has been in this location for thirty-two years and has been under the same ownership for the last ten. A loyal following appreciates savings of 30 percent on classic sportswear, coordinated separates, dresses, blouses, suits, and knits. Owner-and-buyer Janine Cassidy doesn't buy off-price merchandise, but works on a lower markup and counts on low overhead and volume sales to make up the difference. She carries quality lines that appeal especially to the career woman in sizes 3–18, and petite sizes 3–12. Labels include Evan Picone, Loubella, Daniel Hechter, Wilroy Knits, Century, Charlotte Ford, Diane Von Furstenberg, Applause for Rave Reviews, Stuart Lang, and California Girl. There are individual dressing rooms and customers are put together by expert hands.

International Designer's Outlet

Lobby. (213) 489–2142.

Fantastic Designer Room

Room 220. (213) 627-4536.

St. Ives

Room 201. (213) 627-4536.
Hours: (all three stores) Mon.–Sat. 9–4:30.

Fantastic is strong in better sportswear, suits for business-women, dresses, and jeans. Discounts average 40 percent on casual separates and activewear from New York and California manufacturers. There's also a discount perfume counter where your favorite scents can be purchased for less than retail. The owners of Fantastic also opened St. Ives where they feature high-end designer clothing at discount prices. Besides name designers, such as Beged-Or, Christian Dior and Pierre Cardin, St. Ives will carry a line of its own design in silk separates. Imported belts, handbags, and related accessories complement the French- and Italian-made clothing. The size range in both stores is 2–14. The lobby store is the outlet for leftover merchandise. Markdowns will be drastic—70 percent off a broad selection of labels. A Filene's basement concept for 860.

Fashion Reflections

Mezzanine. (213) 689–9256.
Hours: Mon.–Sat. 9–5.

"Glad Rags inspired me to go into business," says owner Gabe Levy. He read volume one on a flight to New York and decided to open up his own discount store. The response has been overwhelming. Gabe claims that he has more brands in one location than any other store. We didn't stop to count, but did notice labels such as Cathy Hardwick, Kasper, Jerry Silverman, Geoffrey Beene, Anne Klein, Jack Mulqueen, Ralph Lauren, Bill Blass, and Fenn, Wright & Manson. Blouses and dresses are particularly strong, but you'll find a complete range of merchandise from jeans and casual sportswear to dressy suits and evening wear, as well as shoes. Sizes are junior 3–13 and missy 4–14. Petites are sometimes available. Discounts start at 30 percent and there are twenty-four individual dressing rooms.

Sportables

Mezzanine. (213) 627-6601.

Cache International

Second floor. (213) 614-0868.
Hours: (both stores) Mon.–Sat. 9–4:30.

Both stores are under the same management, but Sportables was still setting up racks when we visited. The focus is on silk and dressy fabrics such as georgette. The stores carry Michel Laurent for Cachet silk dresses and separates, as well as clothing from other name designers (Charlotte Ford and Bonnie Strauss dresses, and Bill Haire for Friedricks Sport suits when we were there). Sportables will be adding a "casual corner" for jeans and sportswear and shoe department. Discounts are promised to be 50 percent and clothes are size 4–14.

FASHION CENTER

This year-old structure—located at 210 East 9th Street—looks like it was built to capitalize on the rapidly increasing numbers of Garment District shoppers and especially to draw business from nearby S. Los Angeles Street and the Cooper Building. Convenience is the key here since the building is so new, light, and airy. It is only three-stories tall and holds a manageable number (ten or so) of stores. If you're not up to wading through crowded racks or sorting through the Cooper Building's twenty-five shops, you might save yourself some effort and start at the Fashion Center. An additional, not-so-minor point—there are plenty of public restrooms here. Men and women shop for clothes and shoes from a variety of moderate to better quality all the way up to top European designer pieces. All Fashion Center shops accept Master Charge, Visa, and checks. Purchase policies vary so check to make sure whether things can be returned. We'll start our shopping tour on the ground floor and work our way up.

Triomphe Fashions
Ground floor. (213) 623-8799.
Hours: Mon.–Sat. 10–5.

Fine-quality fabrics and top designer labels attract clotheshorses *cum* bargain hunters to this new shop. Imported knits from Israel and Italy, and European designer pieces are the store's specialty. If you're looking for something different (especially after looking through so many California-made garments at other nearby shops) or if you need a special evening look, you'll like browsing through Triomphe. We've been asked not to mention labels, but they are among the best quality. Think of the very top French male designer and you'll have the identity of one of the Rive Gauche lines found here.

Summer and winter things are available year round. Owner Charles Cohen says, "There's no season in my place." You won't always find complete size ranges in a particular garment. Sweaters, blouses, suits, dresses, leathers, and suedes, and evening things sell at 50–70 percent below wholesale. Prices start at $20 and go up to $200.

The Party Dress
Ground floor. (213) 624-3818.

The Candy Store
724 S. Los Angeles St., Los Angeles. (213) 623-5687.
Hours: (both stores) Mon.–Sat. 9–5.

Irwin Schwartz aptly titled his Fashion Center store—it is full of hundreds of cocktail dresses and long gowns. You won't find a better assortment of party dresses anywhere else in the Garment District. While we can't mention labels, you will find them readily displayed in the store. Savings are about 25 percent off missy sizes 4–20. Besides the fancy things, you can conveniently shop for classic separates like blouses, suits, and day dresses. The party section of the inventory sells for $50–$200, while the separates start at $20 and go to $150 for suits from well-known New York makers. The Candy Store down the block features the same lines and labels as the Party Store, and better junior dresses and more separates. One of the store's specialties is the $8.75 fitted poly pants in twenty-two colors, regularly retailing for $17. Markdowns wind up on the $11 rack.

Kardin's
Second floor. (213) 623-2987.
Hours: Mon.–Sat. 9–5:15.

Kardin's offers 20–30 percent discounts on men's and women's casual and dressy footwear. The center part of the store houses displays with the latest designs from Kimel, Palizzio, Sbicca, Impo, Cherokee, Famolare, Mushrooms,

Crayons, and Nike for ladies in sizes 5–10 narrows and mediums. The perpetual upright sale racks at one end of the store offer final markdowns to $6–$20. You'll probably find a pair of shoes you like from the broad selection here. Manager Scott Stein told us that working women especially like the dressy pumps. The women's leather and suede handbags and valise prices of $7–$72 reflect savings of 20–40 percent. Men can shop here, too, for their favorite brands: Bally, Freeman Shriner, and Bass.

Quality Dress Shop

Ground floor (Fashion Center). (213) 623-9167.
772 S. Los Angeles St., (at 8th St.), Los Angeles. (213) 622-6804.
Hours: Mon.–Sat. 9–5.

Garment District shoppers from Newport Beach to Santa Barbara single out this shop for their classic suits and separates purchases. Clothes are neatly hung in coordinated outfits for easy shopping. Discounts on Pant-Her start at 25 percent; you can save as much as half on Roth-Le Cover. Other quality dress staples: Norman Gayle, Denby, Breckenridge, Gaylord, and Haberdashery by Personal. You can plan on helpful saleswomen to assist you in pulling together your purchases from all types of separates and knits. Sales run frequently. We took advantage of the $15 sweater markdowns at the time of our visit.

Champs Elysees

Second floor. (213) 623-5921.
Hours: Mon.–Sat. 9:30–4:45.

Silks, men's and women's activewear, and great bargains on racks of irregulars make this store an interesting stop on your Garment District tour. We bought an $85 designer-made wool jersey dress for $12 with a minor flaw on the hem which was easily repaired.

MAPLE, SANTEE AND AREA

Businesses in this area are concentrated in the alley between Maple and Santee Streets between 12th and Olympic—a backdoor shopping area often referred to as "the alley." While there are a few shops of note close by, most of the action is centered in the alley. There's a great similarity among these forty or so jobber-merchants. While they wholesale to smaller retailers only during the week, they welcome the general public with open arms on Saturdays. (Most shops state Saturday-only hours, but rest assured they won't turn away a sale from anyone at any time during the week.) Much of the merchandise is identical from store to store, especially the jeans. Prices are usually lower than those found on South Los Angeles Street between 7th and 9th or at the Cooper Building. However, most places won't let you try anything on. If you know your size in a particular label or if you're buying something like a sweater where exact fit isn't critical, you'll do okay. Otherwise, good luck—you're on your own.

The Saturday shopping experience here resembles the Orchard-Delancey Street free-for-all in New York. You shop early (come at 8:30 or 9), in a good mood, and armed with cash since most places only accept the green folding kind of money. There's a real swap meet air as people drift from jobber to jobber, occasionally stopping for a snack at the ubiquitous catering trucks.

Clothes for the whole family can be found here. For women we've seen labels like Alan Abell, Norman Todd, Patty Woodard, Bis, Campus Casuals, and the whole Esprit de Corp line. The buys here can be especially good. As one jobber we chatted with said, "We're the clean-up people of the industry." Garments are samples, discontinued styles, overruns, seconds, and items from several seasons past. We've recommended the stores that stand out. The rest are so completely similar that we couldn't describe one without calling to mind forty others.

California Fashion Accessories, Inc.
1106 S. Santee St., (Maple/Santee Alley), Los Angeles. (213) 749-9494.

S.A.J. Jewelry Inc.
1336 S. Los Angeles St., Los Angeles. (213) 749-6261.
Hours: (both stores) Sat. 8:30–3:30.
Purchases: Cks, cash. All sales final.

If you're into fun, colorful costume jewelry (as we are), you'll go nuts in here. Bangles, beads, earrings, hair ornaments, flowers, pins, you-name-it, all come in a complete rainbow of pretty brights and pastels. Most prices ring up at 50¢–$2. And most items are sold by the piece although a few things come in lots of a dozen since both locations act primarily as wholesalers. Besides women's and little girls' jewelry, there are all manner of belts, wallets, and handbags. The purse selection is especially good. We picked up a tan leather shoulder bag for only $10. The general price range is $7.50–$42 with occasional $3 specials. Near the counter at the front of the store, there are also sale bins full of markdowns. The Los Angeles Street location features mostly jewelry and hair items in some interesting styles and is somewhat different from the Maple/Santee Alley store.

Casa Abraham Too

1317 S. Santee St., Los Angeles. (213) 748-6608.
Hours: Sat. 8:30–2.
Purchases: Cks, cash. All sales final.

The best buys are found here in children's wear but the rest of the family can save on casual sports items, such as jeans, jackets, and tops. This is a true warehouse operation with no-frills, self-service shopping, but you'll appreciate the fact that the merchandise is organized by size and garment type. The store's central area holds jeans of every style and color—Casa Abraham distributes Billy the Kid jeans, too. Most things sell for $4–$28. Sizes start at infants and go up to extra large for men. On the day of our visit, girls' dresses were selling, one for $4.50, two for $8.50, and three for $12. That's a

Glad Rags buy if we ever saw one. Billy the Kid shirts were going for $6.50 and $7.50. This is the McDonald's of kids' clothes stores: you could buy complete outfits for two children and get back change from a $20 bill!

S. LOS ANGELES ST. between 7th and 9th Streets and immediate area

Of all the areas in the Garment District, this two-block concentration of shops best typifies the energy and excitement of apparel trade in Los Angeles. It's also the oldest and best-known area. To the many people who are not familiar with the larger, more diverse nature of the Garmet District, this particular section *is* the Garment District and it is still one of the single best locations in all of Southern California for values at wholesale prices. We especially recommend starting your shopping itinerary here if you're not familiar with the District. One visit to any of the following merchants and you'll see why. Many of these stores have been in business for thirty or forty years and, as we all know, a good reputation over a long haul speaks for a lot, especially in discount apparel. Everybody knows everybody else along the street, so, if one proprietor doesn't have what you want, he or she will recommend another shop to you. As in other parts of downtown L.A., shopping volume has increased dramatically within the past year. On a typical Saturday, it's sometimes so crowded that it looks like Times Square at rush hour. Shop during the week if possible. Parking for all stores is street or area lots.

Sassons on L.A.

852 S. Los Angeles St., Los Angeles. (213) 489-3619.
Hours: Mon.–Sat. 9:30–5.

Harry's Wearabouts

300 E. 9th St. (at Santee), Los Angeles. (213) 689-0848.
Hours: Mon.–Sat. 9:30–5.
Purchases: MC, VISA, cks. All sales final. Layaway.
Mailing list.

We've included these two shops because the merchandise assortment stocked in both stores by owner Harry Sasson seems a bit more selective and the styles more with it than in some similar shops in the same area. The owner says his pants and tops (blouses and sweaters) assortment are the store's strong points. Wholesale prices are routine on all types of junior (sizes 1–15) and missy (4–16) dresses and separates from quality lines such as Joy Stevens, Roth-Le Cover, Marc Phillipe, Calvin Klein, and Jean St. Germain. You can also find fancy party dresses among the racks of cocktail and long gowns.

Ladies Apparel

840 S. Los Angeles St., Los Angeles. (213) 627-6861.
Hours: Mon.–Sat. 9–5.
Purchases: MC, VISA, cks. All sales final. Layaway.

Forty-seven years as one of Los Angeles' single most popular and reputable discounters sums up Ladies Apparel. We continue to recommend this store without hesitation to any women desiring value and selection in better dresses, coats, and suits. Proprietor Jules Eisenberg and his son cater to an unusually loyal following. You'll become a dedicated Ladies Apparel shopper, too, once you start saving half on your purchases. Another plus is the range of sizes: missy, 4–20 and petite, 4–14. Besides well-known West Coast makers, a number of better New York lines are also represented in the stock of over twelve thousand garments. Mr. Eisenberg asked us not to print any actual label names, but you should know

you'll find your favorites here. Don't miss the store's second level full of many different types of coats for about $60–$100. On the day of our visit, Jules showed us a $160 dressy Qiana raincoat that he was selling for only $70. Day dresses sell for $30–$90 (with cocktail dresses sometimes a little more); suits sell for $79–$110. Blazers and skirts can be purchased separately to make your own suit look.

Kids' Hang Ups

831 S. Los Angeles St., Los Angeles. (213) 623-6191.
Hours: Mon.–Fri. 9:30–5, Sat. 9:30–5:30.
Purchases: MC, VISA, cks. Exchanges. Layaway.

Like its counterpart (David Children's Wear down the street), Kids' Hang Ups has been catering to shrewd shopping mothers for a long time. Discounts consistently run 20 percent below retail for boys' and girls' apparel for infants through boys' 30-inch waist jeans and girls size 14 (no pre-teens). Everything is first quality except for some seconds in baby underwear. The selections in sizes 4–6x and 7–14 are the strongest. Quality lines represented are Aileen, Sasson, Levi Strauss, Russ Girl, and Health-tex.

B. H. Clarke Shoe Co.
818 S. Los Angeles St., Los Angeles. (213) 627-9149.
Hours: Mon.–Sat. 9–5.
Purchases: MC, VISA, cks. Exchanges. Layaway.

Since we first interviewed the folks at B.H. Clarke for *Glad Rags I,* they're carrying even better brands in order to serve discerning Garment District shoppers. Current-season women's shoes are displayed in a broad spectrum of colors. Casual footwear is available, but the dressy selection is larger and more intriguing. Sizes go from 4–10 in mostly medium (though there are some narrow widths). Prices run $20–$100, including those in our favorite section—the permanent sale racks. The man in your life can shop for his shoes here, too. Purses start at $15 and go to $60.

Schenley's Wholesale Clothing Co.
753 S. Los Angeles St., Los Angeles. (213) 623-2696.
Hours: Mon.–Sat. 9:15–5.
Purchases: MC, VISA, AE, cks. All sales final. Layaway.

Schenley's distinguishes itself from the rest of the leather stores in the District by its consistently higher-quality merchandise in a broad assortment of men's and women's leathers and furs. We've added Schenley purchases to our wardrobes on several occasions over the years since we first discovered the store. This is Sam Schenley's "outlet" in that he sells his own leather designs in addition to imports. Classic stylings come in neutral tones and in some interesting shades, such as green or pearl grey. Jackets and full-length coats in suede and leather start at about $90 for women.

Ladies 7/8 length shearling jackets sell for $225. Fox collars start at $80, fur jackets sell for $80–$135 and fox jackets for $500. Leather vests and all-weather reversible jackets are available, too. Men like to shop Schenley's because they can find a *complete* selection of leathers and suedes, as well as an added suit and sport jacket department.

Suzanne's Ladies Wear
708 S. Los Angeles St., Los Angeles. (213) 622-2400.
Hours: Mon.–Sat. 9:30–5:30.
Purchases: MC, VISA, AE, cks. Exchanges only. Layaway.

Here's another store which has distinguished itself from the rest of the crowd for a couple of reasons. The extensive coat selection ranges from jackets to full-length wool, all-weather, and raincoat styles, in addition to those made with synthetic furs, blue fox, and mink collars. Prices begin at $28 and go up to $150. The other half of the story is *half*-sizes. Women who wear this size range are always grateful to find it at discount. Suzanne's experiences a loyal, repeat clientele because of the 12½–26½ section in coats, blouses, day dresses, and long gowns. Other sizes are junior 3–13 and missy 6–26. Prices are wholesale throughout the store for coats, long gowns, dresses, separates, and pants and skirt suits. The store is family-run so if you're interested in a little friendly horse-trading, you're invited to negotiate the final purchase price.

Gerson's
327 E. 9th St., Los Angeles. (213) 622-6885.
Hours: Mon.–Fri. 9–5, Sat. 9–4.

Take 2
15272 Golden West St., Westminster. (714) 891-6047.
Hours: Mon.–Thurs. 11–6:30, Fri. 11–7, Sat. 10–6.
Purchases: MC, VISA, cks. All sales final. Layaway.

Marc Litt comes by the success of his two popular discount stores naturally: his father, sister, and uncle have also been in the rag trade for years. Marc carries a broad range of Condor

tailored pieces, Warren Z dresses and New York makers, such as Pronto and Garland. Sizes run from 1–13 in casual and dressy apparel and include an especially good assortment of coats, sweaters, and sweater coats. Prices start at $10 and go up to about $40.

The Robe Outlet

216 E. 9th St., Los Angeles. (213) 627-3549.
1022 Santee St., Los Angeles. (213) 747-5938.
Hours: Mon.–Fri. 9–5, Sat. 9–4:30.
Purchases: Cash and cks. All sales final. Layaway.

These two shops sell first-quality overruns for the Gary of California robe and loungewear lines (which are found at all kinds of department stores, including Broadway and Wards). The merchandise assortment includes the David Brown label, as well as some others clipped out of the garments. Sportswear has been deleted from both locations so you'll find extensive color and design choices among loungewear, caftans,

rompers, coverups, and jumpsuits in addition to robes. We like the fact that you can buy winter or summer fashions all year round for only $3–$40, in petite to extra-large sizes.

David's Children's Wear

712 S. Los Angeles St., Los Angeles. (213) 623-5078.
Hours: Mon.–Sat. 9:30–5:30.
La Cienega Blvd. at Centinela Ave. (Ladera Center),
    Los Angeles. (213) 645-7155.
18712 Ventura Blvd., Tarzana. (213) 343-0143.
Hours: Mon.–Sat. 10–6.
Purchases: MC, VISA, cks. Exchanges only. Layaway.
Parking: Area lots, street. Mailing list.

Owner Marty Dusig describes his store as "the most complete children's store in Los Angeles where you can buy everything from Levis to Pierre Cardin suits." Mothers shop here for underwear, pj's, socks, dresses, jeans, jumpsuits, jackets, and coats for infants through student size 22 for boys and through preteen 14 for girls. Price tags reflect 10–30 percent discounts on all famous children's brands like Health-tex, Billy the Kid, Youngland, Nannette, Kaynee, Kennington, and

Lightning Bolt, to name a few. Besides the basics like undies and school/play apparel, David's has one of the most extensive dress-up clothes departments for kids we've seen. Little girls can have any kind of frilly or fancy dress that their hearts desire and little boys can find their suits for Easter, graduation, or their Bar Mitzvah from among hundreds of spiffy two- and three-piece outfits from Johnny Carson, John Weitz, or Pierre Cardin. The suits come in slim, regular and husky cuts in even and odd sizes.

S. LOS ANGELES STREET between 9th and the Freeway, Los Angeles

This area is now filled with discount retail stores. Most have opened to the public since we wrote *Glad Rags I,* but some have been in business for years. Convenient metered street parking makes the area easy to shop, but the stores are iffy: many don't stay in business long enough to build a following and there is an abundance of low-end merchandise, as well as a lot of duplication in what you find. Still, we predict this area will continue to grow and to improve as rents up the street climb and merchants look for alternatives. Consider yourself an explorer when you're shopping here and you'll have fun. What we've done is to give you some starting points.

Palace Wholesalers

1034 S. Los Angeles St., (213) 747-9025.
Hours: Mon.–Sat. 9–4:30.
Purchases: MC, VISA, cks. Exchanges.

Palace is a manufacturer and jobber specializing in good-quality suits and jackets for men and women. The store carries Bert Newman suits from size 3–22, including petite-

proportioned sizes and Jordache sportcoats and blazers. Prices are wholesale or below and there are individual dressing rooms.

Baccarat Clothing Co.

1112 S. Los Angeles St., (213) 749-6302.
Hours: Mon.–Sat. 9–5.
Purchases: MC, VISA, cks. All sales final.

As long as designer jeans are popular, you might as well buy them as cheaply as possible. Baccarat specializes in jeans and its extensive selection of denims, cottons, corduroys, and other fashion fabrics makes this a place to comparison shop. Sizes are: women's, 26–34; children's, 2–16; and men's 28–38.

Ropole Company

1416 S. Los Angeles St., (213) 749-0078.
Hours: Mon.–Sat. 9–5.
Purchases: MC, VISA, cash. Exchanges.

Stop in here for warm-up suits with manufacturer's Rene Robaire label. These two-piece joggers for men and women are priced between $18 and $30 and come in many colors of cotton interlock, terry, fleece, and velour. Sizes are small, medium, and large. Designer jeans were much in evidence the day of our visit and were priced competitively at about $30, though owner Ron Schwartz predicts the "decline of the designer," and is moving into better pants and trouser looks.

Susie Q. Fashions

1424 S. Los Angeles St., (213) 748-9231.
Hours: Mon.–Sat. 8:30–4:30.
Purchases: Cash or cks. All sales final.

If you're fond of the Esprit de Corp line—including Plain Jane, Rose Hips, Jasmine Teas, Cecily, Bombacha, Esprit's Chemise, and In Good Hands—check out this store's inventory of junior sportswear and dresses. Prices are at least 40 percent below retail, but some of the merchandise is end-of-season. (But because of our temperate climate and Esprit's inventive fashion sense, this is not much of a problem: we bought season-old canvas flats for $4 per pair that are still fashionable.) Sizes are 3-13/14.

David's Clothing Co.

1425-27 S. Los Angeles St. (213) 749-0215.
Hours: Mon.–Sat. 9–4:30.
Purchases: MC, VISA, cks. Exchanges.

David's sells both wholesale and retail, and features casual sportswear for men and women at 40 percent below retail. Check the sale racks first for even greater discounts. Women will find blouses, skirts, painter's pants, dress pants, and tops. Men can choose from sport and dress shirts, sweatshirts, and T-shirts. Everyone can take advantage of savings on jeans. Women's sizes are 3–15 and jeans are waist-sized 27–38. Sweaters are small to extra large.

Outlet Store

1434-36 S. Los Angeles St., (213) 748-9971.
Hours: Mon.–Fri. 7–4, Sat. 7–3.
Purchases: Cash only. All sales final.

Lilly and Irving Cohen have been married fifty-two years and it's worth a visit to be inspired and entertained by them. They took over the Guild Lingerie factory outlet store two years ago for something to do. They like their work, and the customer gets a smile and a kind word, as well as "unbelievable prices." The store isn't fancy, but it's jammed with merchandise for women and children. Women's sizes run from petite to XXXX large. You'll find velour jumpsuits, ($10.50, even in the extra-large sizes), long and short gowns, camisoles, bras, blouses, children's nightgowns, and underwear. Sexy baby dolls in small, medium, and large are $4–$6. There are no try-ons.

Shoes and Accessories

5

This chapter probably put the biggest dent in our clothes-buying budget, because we found we couldn't resist a shoe bargain. Talk about happy feet—whether you wear a sample-size 4B, a 9 AAAA or a 12 WW, there are many stores to choose from. The entire family can save on footwear of all kinds at the stores listed here; children's shoes are included in this chapter as well. For other excellent sources for shoes, consult the Type of Merchandise Index. There are excellent stores in the Garment District, and we recommend looking in select resale and antique clothes stores as well.

The term "accessories" refers to handbags, leather goods, costume jewelry, belts, scarves, hair ornaments, and more. Again, please refer to our Index for additional sources.

5

ℒ𝒜 County

BF Shoes

5305 Torrance Blvd., Torrance. (213) 316-5553.
26626 S. Western Ave., Harbor City. (213) 325-5000.
9701 Chapman Ave., Garden Grove. (714) 636-8032.
1878 N. Placentia Ave., Placentia. (714) 993-7760.
7260 N. Rosemead Blvd., San Gabriel. (213) 287-9326.
25799 E. Highland Ave., San Bernardino. (714) 862-8150.
8427 Laurel Canyon Blvd., Sun Valley. (213) 768-4836.
528 E. First St., Tustin. (714) 731-1769.
1157 Los Angeles Ave., Simi Valley (Larwin Square).
   (805) 526-7428.
956. N. Mountain Ave., Ontario (Ontario Plaza).
   (714) 984-6311.
Rosecrans and LaMirada Blvd., (LaMirada Mall), LaMirada.
   (714) 523-5450.
Hours: Mon.–Thurs. 10–6,.Fri. 10–9, Sat. 10–6, Sun. 12–5.
Purchases: MC, VISA, cks. Exchanges and refunds.
Parking: Free lot. Mailing list.

"Name-brand designer shoes at discount prices in a nice atmosphere." That's what BF Shoes is all about, according to district manager Ernie Rauda. After finding high-fashion, current-season women's shoes for 20–50 percent off (by better shoemakers like Joan & David, DeLiso, Palizzio, Andrew Geller, Julianelli, Garolini, and Jones New York) we asked Ernie how BF does it. He explained that BF is the discount-store division of one of the nation's largest shoe (manufacturing, wholesaling, and importing) conglomerates. The nationwide discount chain of eighty stores sells all first-quality factory overruns and first markdowns from department stores all over the country. BF also offers its own labels manufactured by the parent company. Customers get the savings since all the middlemen and their markups are bypassed. Most shoes sell for $20–$32, with some up to $40. There's always a bargain section at the front of the store—we found great styles for $5, $10, and $15. In addition to the brands listed above, more traditionally styled lines such as Air Step, Naturalizer, and Life Stride are sold here, as well as popular Southern California casuals by Apache, LA Ladies, Bare Traps, and Cherokee. As you can imagine, there are lots of colors and styles to choose from in sizes 5–10. There's a wall display of handbags (mostly in vinyl) for $12–$26, and we saw a few pairs of dress and Western boots.

Bea's Shoe Nook

3505 Motor Ave., Los Angeles (Palms). (213) 559-0435.
Hours: Mon.–Fri. 11–6, Thurs. 11–8, Sat. 10–6.
Purchases: MC, VISA, cks. All sales final. Layaway.
Parking: Street.

On first visit, you'll swear you tumbled into an old-fashioned steamer trunk filled to overflowing with boots and shoes in every imaginable color and style. There's so much footwear, the store's layout almost defies description. How Bea ever got so many pairs displayed so well in such a small nook is a wonder. To get the most from shopping here, it helps if you are a dedicated bargain-hunter and enjoy putsing around. There are the usual casual and dressy styles from well-known brands, such as Sandler of Boston, Andrew Geller, Lighthouse Footwear, 9 West, Bare Traps, and Palizzio. Sizes start at 5 and go to 10 in all widths. New merchandise and special purchases are displayed at the front of the store, with especially forward-fashion evening shoes making up the window displays. The evening-shoe selection is hard to beat. You'll find color combinations and imported designer lines you simply won't see elsewhere. We almost forgot—price tags are a cool 40–80 percent below retail. We found a $90 pair of Papagallos for only $35. Lastly, all of us disheartened boot fans have finally found our discount boot heaven. Bea devotes an entire section of the Nook to a large assortment of casual, dressy, short, tall, and Western boots. We're still lusting after the silver evening ones we saw for $22. Most of the rest of the footwear sells for $15–$35.

Big Ben's Shoe Outlet

10865 W. Pico Blvd., West Los Angeles. (213) 475-3088.
Hours: Mon.–Thurs. 10–6, Fri. 10–8, Sat. 9:30–6, Sun. 11-5.
Purchases: MC, VISA, cks. Exchanges. Layaway.
Parking: Street.

Big Ben's has been around since 1937, and Elliott and Diane Snitzer have owned and operated the store for the last eleven years. The Snitzers buy first-quality goods from shoe jobbers who sell them odd lots, end-of-season merchandise, closeouts, and stock from stores going out of business. The resulting inventory at Big Ben's consists of casual and dressy styles with the emphasis on better lines. You'll recognize the brands: Nickels, Sbicca, Joyce, Nina, 9 West, HipOppo'Tamus, Famolare, and Crayons. Prices, 10–70 percent below retail, go from

$21–$25 with the maximum selling for $32. For instance, a pair of $65 Nickels sells here for $32. Women's sizes are 5–10 narrow and medium. Big Ben's carries a complete array of children's tennis shoes because, as the Snitzers say, that's mostly what kids wear. Two size groups, infants 5–12 and juniors 12–2½, sell for $11–$17 per pair. Men's shoes and boots are also available in sizes 6½–13. The $75 men's Famolares go for $39.

The "back stock" has thirty thousand pairs from the 1930s, '40s, '50s, and '60s including entire walls of alligator, lizard, snake, and even cheetah shoes, spike heels, Mary Janes, and sling backs. These well-made shoes with leather soles sell for $19; the skins go for $30. Elliott is the supplier of shoes to such television shows as "Laverne and Shirley" and "Happy Days" and film costumers continue to seek him out for just the right shoe to complete their movie wardrobes.

California Shoe Center

31283 Via Colinas, Westlake Village. (213) 991-3834.
Hours: Mon.–Sat. 10–6.

Warehouse Shoe Sales

19507 Business Center Dr., Northridge. (213) 701-6847.
Hours: Mon.–Fri. 10–6, Sat. 10–4, Sun. 12–4.
Purchases: MC, VISA, cks. Refunds and exchanges.
Parking: Street and free lot. Mailing list.

These two shoe outlets represent the retail end of Earnest Shoe Co., which also includes owner John Earnest's large shoe wholesaling operation. This explains the vast style selection, size range, and low prices. Ten thousand pairs are on display at each store, notably shoes from Bandolino, Amalfi, Anne Klein, Hana Mackler, Joan & David, Garolini, Andrew Geller, and Cherokee. You sample-size 6 Bs will be privileged to one-of-a-kind samples from Kimel, Selby, Papagallo, Footwear, Sbicca, and HipOppo'Tamus. Most of the styles are casual or sporty. There's a separate tennis shoe section and a few boots, as well as dress and career styles—but not many evening shoes. No matter what your age or personal style, you'll most likely find something to please you among the traditional to trendy fashions. The savings are 20 to 50 percent below retail for everything from moderately priced California-made casual shoes to expensive imported designer footwear retailing for $200–$300 (available here for $90–$170). Sizes are 4–12 in narrow, medium, and wide widths.

Cinderella Slipper Shop

109 N. Fairfax Ave. (Fairfax area), Los Angeles (213) 653-0860.
Hours: Mon.–Sat. 10–5:30.
Purchases: MC, VISA, cks. Refunds and exchanges. Layaway.
Parking: Street and rear lot. Mailing list.

This sample shoe outlet has been in business since 1941 and, according to manager Elaine Alfassa, some of Cinderella's customers have been coming in since the day the shop opened. Sample and small-size shoes (2B to 5B with the majority in the 4B category) are sold for $30–$64 for dressy styles and $24–$36 for casual footwear (a savings of up to 40 percent). Well-known brands include Erica, Howard Fox, Amano, John Jerro, Bare Traps, Sbicca, and Penaljo. The store derives its name from its specialty in evening shoes. We discovered unusual styles not seen in all the department stores. Add your name to their mailing list to be notified of the twice-annual sales.

Deb's Factory Shoe Outlet

3400 S. Broadway, Los Angeles (corner of Jefferson).
  (213) 749-8519.
Hours: Tues.–Sat. 9–3:15.
Purchases: MC, VISA, cks. All sales final. Layaway.
Parking: Street.

Next door to its shoe manufacturing facilities, Deb's sells samples, discontinued styles and overruns from the current season. Deb's main business is creating footwear for department and specialty stores that are sold under the house label. For instance, shoes with a Saks Fifth Avenue label were prob-

ably made here at Deb's. These very same styles, all in the same first-quality construction, sell for 20–50 percent off or about $25–$35. Casual and dressy styles fit 7–12 sized feet in medium, wides, and extra wides. There's a selection of nurses' shoes here for $25 that retail for $40. There really aren't any big sales here, but you will occasionally find racks with mark-downs to $10 or so.

Fayva

Stores at fifty locations throughout Los Angeles and Orange counties. Check your telephone Yellow Pages directory under "Shoes" for the store nearest you.
Hours: Mon.–Fri. 10–9, Sat. 9–7, Sun. 12–6.
Purchases: MC, VISA, cks. Some locations accept AE.
  Refunds and exchanges. Layaway.
Parking: Free lot.

After researching all the lower-priced discount shoe-store chains, we concluded that Fayva deserves recommendation for all round family shoe shopping. Both the current styles and consistently good quality construction separate Fayva shoes from the others. The chain is the fast-growing discount retailing arm of a long-time Eastern shoe manufacturing concern. Extra savings are available to customers since the stores feature only the parent company's brands made especially for Fayva, which competes for Kinney and Thom McAn customers. Men's, women's, and children's casual and dressy styles in a wide array of colors and fabrications are well-organized on self-service racks. One entire wall of the Culver City store holds hundreds of pairs of tennis shoes for kids and adults priced from $7–$12 for children, $9–$15 for women and $12–$20 for men. Other children's shoes run from $6–$17 for all styles. To help with often confusing children's show sizing, there are handy, easy-to-understand wall charts. Of the women's shoes, the casuals represent the biggest and best selection. There are also some dressy styles, slippers, beach thongs, sandals, and even nurses' shoes all for $10–$22. On our visit, we found the very latest stylings and hot colors. There are always special sale racks, as well as handbags, socks, and shoe-care products.

The Foot Factory

4333 Peck Rd., El Monte. (213) 443-1868.
Hours: Tues. 12–5:30, Wed.–Sat. 10–5:30.
Purchases: Cash or cks. Refunds and exchanges. Layaway.
Parking: Street and free lots.

Richard Rabolini runs a friendly little women's discount shoe operation that offers wholesale prices on most popular styles except evening: sandals, pumps, saddleshoes, flats, boots. Shoes from makers such as Impo, SRO, Bare Traps, and Cherokee fill the self-service racks at prices generally $12–$25. Samples, closeouts, and overruns make up the inventory. Sizes go from a few 4s–10s with lots in the 6B sample size. Most widths are medium, but you'll find some narrows and wides. There are two big semiannual sales in February and September and there's always a bargain table at the front of the store with markdowns to $2.50 and $5 a pair.

Foster's Shoes

2833 S. Robertson Blvd., Los Angeles. (213) 837-3771.
Hours: Mon.–Sat. 9:30–4.
Purchases: MC, VISA, cks. Exchanges. Layaway.
Parking: Free lot. Mailing list.

Foster's has been helping people save money for thirty-five years (nine at this location); it sells a full range of shoes with an emphasis on women's tailored styles, for 30–50 percent discount. The 4800 square feet of wholesale and retail space allows it to stock shoes for men and women. Shoes range in price from $20 to $90 (retail $35–$165) in sizes 4–11 AA to B, with a few wides. Foster's carries some closeouts, but most of the inventory is new merchandise. You find better brands such as Bally, Bernardo, Charles Jourdan, and Anne Klein. A mailing list reaching ten thousand customers gives advance notice of special arrivals.

Heel and Toe

22892 Ventura Blvd., Woodland Hills. (213) 703-9803.
Hours: Mon.–Fri. 9:30–6, Sat. 9:30–5, Sun. 12–4.
Purchases: MC, VISA, cks. Exchanges. Layaway.
Parking: Free lot.

You'll find Image America, Andrew Geller, Via Veneto, Palizzio, Lisa, Amalfi, Continentals, Adores, Naturalizer, Jean Rimbaud, and Etienne Aigner at 40–70 percent savings. The general price range is $15–$30 for dress shoes, wedgies, mules, and sandals. Owner Ann Lipson buys from jobbers and manufacturers and receives shipments of new merchandise each Thursday. New arrivals are in the front of this crowded store and about half of the stock is either last season's or slightly older. Sizes go from 4–11 in narrow and medium widths. The store also features a good selection of bags in leather, canvas, and macrame for $15–$35.

J & G Shoe Affair

1418 W. Beverly Blvd., Montebello. (213) 728-2829.
Hours: Tues.–Sat. 10:30–6.
Purchases: MC, VISA, cks. Exchanges. Layaway.
Parking: Free lot. Mailing list.

If a glance at your footwear wardrobe tells you that you're fond of casual shoes from Sbicca or bold, high-fashion numbers from Kimel, you need to shop at J & G. You'll like saving $5 to $20 per pair on these popular brands; you'll also find shoes by Ernest Hoffman, Elditas, and Rombardt. Shoes are sized from 4–10 in narrow, medium, and wide widths, and sell for $20–$75 (up to $115 retail). We were drawn to the permanent sale tables featuring many different styles for only $5 and $10. Owners Joe and Gloria Sotello like to promote shoe sales through home parties. The hostess sells eight pairs and receives a free pair worth up to $60. The same principle works in the store. Buy eight pairs and get the ninth one free. On the day of our visit we also found handbags, feather accessories, and knit tops. Look for Levi's in the future as the store expands into apparel.

La Bagg

9218 W. Pico Blvd., Los Angeles. (213) 278-3709.
Hours: Mon.–Sat. 10–6.
Purchases: MC, VISA, cks. All sales final.
Parking: Street. Mailing list.

Inside Ideal Fashions you'll find this classy leather concession with markdowns of 15 percent. The owner claims to have had a lifelong passion for leather which has finally been realized. She selects merchandise carefully and has an eye for quality and current styles. Buying is done directly from importers or from other stores. The selection includes handbags, shoulder bags, clutches, belts, briefcases, suitcases, and leather accessories, such as billfolds and eyeglass cases. The styles range from casual to conservative. Handbags start at $30 for fabric and leather designs and go up to $200 for various reptile skins which are the best-selling styles. The belt selection has recently been expanded: prices go from $6–$30 for all types, including evening belts.

M & J Shoes

8668 Wilshire Blvd., Beverly Hills. (213) 659-4541.
3707 E. Foothill Blvd., Pasadena. (213) 351-8948.
Hours: Mon.–Fri. 10–9, Sat. 10–7, Sun. 11–5.
1091 Broxton Ave., Westwood. (213) 478-0896.
Hours: Mon.–Thurs. 11–10, Fri. 11–Midnight, Sat.
   10–Midnight, Sun. 12–8.
Purchases: MC, VISA, cks. Exchanges. Layaway.
Parking: Street and area lots. Mailing list.

Even though M & J sells some of its men's and women's footwear at regular retail, the special promotions and continual sales fall within the perimeters of *Glad Rags*. During an interview with vice president Steve Markenson, we learned that M & J prefers to cater to forward shoe fashion customers with younger, more contemporary shoes for both sexes. You'll find more up-to-the-minute footwear here at lower prices than at almost any other shoe store. *Colors?* This place is a feast for the eyes besides being a boon to the checkbook: There are often six, eight, even ten different colors in a single style of

shoe. Our best advice is to get yourself on the mailing list. It's used to notify customers often of sales, special promotions, and new arrivals. A recent mailer alerted customers to the men's and women's $150 Urban Cowboy Brand boots for only $75 a pair. Secondly, stop by often to check out the specials and sale items. There is always a "two pairs for the price of one" sale for both women and men. The stock turns over so fast, there's a substantial amount of new inventory every week. Obviously, these people like the shoe business and they like to *move* merchandise. The Pasadena store serves as the "rack" store for the other two in the chain. As soon as there are only a few pairs left in a particular style (each style starts out with about twenty-four different sizes), they are sent to Pasadena along with other specials for liquidation. It's a permanent sale store!

Samples Only, Inc.

19367 Victory Blvd. (Loehmann's Plaza), Reseda.
  (213) 881-8621.
Hours: Mon.–Sat. 9:30–6, Sun. 10–5.
Purchases: MC, VISA, cks. All sales final.
Parking: Free lot. Mailing list.

Ah, to have sample-sized feet. At least twelve thousand women in the L.A. area must, because the mailing list holds the names of twelve thousand women who shop here. There is an abundance of new, fashionable shoes in every imaginable color and style from all the best manufacturers. While the size range is 4–7 B (no 6½s, which is not a sample size in the shoe industry), the vast majority of the store's stock is in sizes 5½ and 6. Store owner Rose Malhmood stocks four hundred different styles in each of these sizes. Rose has operated this pleasant, spacious store for nine years and gets assistance from her husband, Hy, who used to be a shoe buyer for Robinson's. The same brands carried by the best Beverly Hills department stores and boutiques are here: Charles Jourdan, Bruno Magli, Anne Klein, Halston, Mr. Seymour, Martinique, Vaneli, Sesto Meucci, Jacques Cohen, and SRO. The Malhmoods have added stock in sizes 7–10, all B widths; however, 90 percent of the inventory is still in sample-sized footwear. Discounts for all shoes are 30–60 percent at prices running from $21 to $75 for Bruno Maglis and Charles Jourdans retailing for $150.

If you're looking for a handbag, Samples Only has a terrific selection. Rose carries canvas, leather, suede, vinyl, and snakeskin purses, in addition to some of the most unusual and stunning evening bags we have ever seen. Some are samples—all are discounted and sell for $6–$236.

Sample Shoes Unlimited

1255 2nd St., Santa Monica. (213) 394-0026.
Hours: Mon.–Sat. 11-5.
Purchases: MC, VISA, cks. All sales final. Layaway.
Parking: Street and municipal lots.

"For petite feet only," the card reads: if you're lucky enough to wear a size 4–6 medium shoe, you're in for a treat. Shoes cover the floor and line the walls of this small store. Shoes here sell for $20 to $50. The selection of salesman and display samples is excellent. Brands include Palizzio, Garolini, Rinaldi, Golo, Selby, Evan Picone, Caressa, Givenchy, Sesto Meucci, Halston, and Anne Klein. There is also a selection of exquisite one-of-a-kind designer shoes made in Los Angeles—all in size 4. They receive new shipments two months ahead of the retail stores, so shop early in the season for the best selection. A pair of shoes stays in the store until someone buys it, so there is a wide style selection.

Santa Monica Shoes

419-421 Wilshire Blvd., Santa Monica. (213) 393-4734.
Hours: Mon., Thurs., Fri. 9-9, Tues., Wed., Sat. 9-6, Sun. 11-5.
Purchases: MC, VISA, cks. Refunds and exchanges. Layaway.
Parking: Street and rear lot. Mailing list.

For over thirty years, Santa Monica Shoes has been known for 30–50 percent savings on all types of men's, women's, and children's shoes. Merchandise turns over quickly since prices are only $15–$30 for women's footwear and $5–$15 for children's. Everything is first quality and represents shrewd buys in closeouts and samples from manufacturers and jobbers. Much of the ladies' inventory runs to traditional styles by Enna Jettick, Andiamo, Beacon, and Sebago, but you'll find some more forward fashions, too, all in sizes 4–12 for all widths. Children's dressy and sporty shoes in sizes 1–13 come from Stride Rite, Step Master, Mother Goose, Peaks, Pro-Keds, Converse, and Jack Purcell. There are always sale racks with especially good values and plenty of salespeople to help you with your purchases. The mailing list notifies customers of the major sales and special promotions, and there's even a special mailing list for you lucky sample size 4Bs.

Sav-Mor Shoes

16919 Devonshire St., Granada Hills. (213) 360-4488.
Hours: Mon., Thurs., Fri. 9:30-9, Tues., Wed., Sat. 9:30-6, Sun. 11-5.
Purchases: MC, VISA, cks. Refunds and exchanges. Layaway.
Parking: Free lot. Mailing list.

This family-owned and -run store has been selling current, first-quality shoes at 20–40 percent savings since 1965. The name brand shoes for the entire family include Acme, Hush Puppies, Stacy Adams, Mother Goose, Keds, Nike, Sbicca, Bare Traps, Freeman, Jarman, Jacques Cohen, Sperry Top-Siders, Bass, New Balance, Etonic, Buster Brown, and Dan Post. Good-quality leather bags by Phillipe and Cherokee are priced $6 to $12 lower than department store prices. There

on dress and tailored styles. Some of the stock includes high fashion and evening looks. Four to 12 AAA, AA, and B is the size range. (The store has discontinued its wide-shoe stock.) Prices are 40–70 percent off labels such as Charles Jourdan, Garolini, DeLiso, Caressa, Nina, Nickels, Andrew Geller, and Bandolino. Most sell for $20–$35. Recent Bruno Maglis and Andrea Pfisters retailing for up to $245 are sold here for $50. Single pairs or slow-moving styles are discounted again—as low as $5 on their "riot racks"—hard to beat for price and quality. Browse for other markdowns at $8.99 and $12.88 throughout this self-service library of shoes.

Shoe Mart

12625 W. Washington Blvd., Los Angeles. (213) 397-3440.
Hours: Mon.–Thurs. & Sat. 9–6, Fri. 9–8, Sun. 11–4.
Purchases: MC, VISA, cks. Refunds and exchanges.
    Layaway.
Parking: Street and rear lot.

This store carries many different styles and colors in lots of well-known brands including Cherokee, Nike, Delmar, Pierre, Minnetonka, Hot Foots, Beacon and Miss Boston. The prices run from $12 to $24 for sandals, heels, and wedgies; boots are in the $20 to $60 range. The styles are not the latest fashion, but you can certainly pick up some values, particularly in canvas espadrilles, wedgies, and slippers. There's also a section of sample size 6Bs; the regular stock runs from 5–10 in mediums and wides (no narrows). Check out the sale tables for super buys at $1.98 and $3.99. The 20–40 percent savings applies to children's footwear, too. Most pairs sell for $7–$20. The biggest seller is Mother Goose brand. Children's size ranges are available for infants through approximately eleven years. The handbag selection is good, too, with lots of vinyl bags in several colors and styles for $11–$15. The leather purses are also notable in a comparable style and color range for $16 to $28.

are salesmen to help you select from the thousands of pairs of shoes. Women's sizes run 5–11, in narrow, medium, and wide. Complete size ranges for children of all ages are available, along with men's sizes 5–15. Ask about their Lucky 13 Shoe Club. Over seven thousand customers have already taken advantage of this unique offer: buy twelve pairs of shoes and get the thirteenth pair free.

Shoe Bazaar

5458 Wilshire Blvd., Los Angeles. (213) 937-4075.
Hours: Mon.–Fri. 9:30–6:30, Sat. 9–6, Sun 12–5.
Purchases: MC, VISA, cks. Exchanges. Layaway.
Parking: Street. Mailing list.

New shoes that are refused orders or overruns from better manufacturers arrive here twice weekly. Since the store attracts many working women from the area, the emphasis is

Shoe Mart, Inc.

10014 Long Beach Blvd., Lynwood. (213) 569-3088.
Hours: Mon.–Sat. 9:30–6.
Purchases: MC, VISA, cks. Exchanges. Layaway.
Parking: Street.

This better-shoes-for-less store has been a favorite with local families for thirty-three years. First-quality dress, sport, and work shoes are available for every member of the family for 20–60 percent off. The women's selection includes young junior styles and more mature traditional, dressy, casual, and action styles in sizes 4–12 AAA to EE. Labels available are Enna Jetticks, D'Roma, California Debs, Continentals, and California Cobblers. The children's size ranges are infants 1–4, 1–8, 8–12, 12½–4, up to EEE widths from shoemakers such as Mother Goose, Charm Step, Easy Street, Hush Puppies, and Pro-Keds. Styles range from school and dressy to shoes for active sports like soccer, tennis, and basketball. Prices run from $10–$25 for kids' footwear and $15–$30 for women's. There's also a complete line of men's work and Western boots, sports shoes, and casual and dressy styles.

Shoe Rax

14301 Whittier Blvd., Whittier. (213) 693-2715.
12345 Hawthorne Blvd., Hawthorne. (213) 772-4712.
5577 Sepulveda Blvd., Culver City. (213) 391-6227.
8974 Warner Ave., Fountain Valley. (714) 848-5977.
18222 Sherman Way, Reseda. (213) 881-7212.
Hours: Mon.–Fri. 10–9, Sat. 10–6, Sun. 11–6.
Purchases: MC, VISA, cks. Refunds and exchanges.
Parking: Free lot.

This self-service outpost for final markdowns from Standard Shoe Stores is appropriate for tight budgets, odd sizes and/or eccentric tastes. We found a pair of $10 silver pumps that added the right touch of flash to a holiday outfit. Most shoes are $8 to $25 which represents savings of 20 to 70 percent below Standard's previous discount prices. The stock consists of special purchases from shoe manufacturers and jobbers along with markdowns from Standard Shoe Stores. Check the special racks of $3.88, $5.88 and $7.88 final, final deals. Not all styles or colors are available here in every size, but ask if you don't find what you're looking for. Many shoes aren't on display.

Shoe Warehouse Outlet

29360 Roadside Dr., Agoura. (213) 991-8079.
1226 Los Angeles Ave., Simi Valley. (805) 526-4701.
Hours: Mon.–Thurs. 10–6, Fri. 10–8, Sat.–Sun. 10–6.
Purchases: MC, VISA, cks. Refunds and exchanges.
   Layaway.
Parking: Free lot and street.

We're delighted to see more and more quality discount shoe operations opening up all over Los Angeles and Orange counties. The two-year-old Shoe Warehouse Outlet is a good example of just the trend we're talking about. Thousands of pairs of children's, women's, and men's shoes are neatly displayed on self-serve racks at prices up to 75 percent off retail. The stock comes from the firm's chain of retail shoes and as a result of special buys from shoe manufacturers. Even though they are mostly markdowns, the styles here are generally current, and range from high fashion to traditional. The best selection will be found in classic neutral and basic pumps, perfect for career women. Women's sizes go from 4½ to 12 in narrow, medium, and wide widths from popular department store brands like Papagallo, Socialites, 9 West, Selby, and Crayons. Most casual and dressy pairs sell for between $20 and $40. Stock in children's sizes 7–13½ and 12½–5 centers mainly on canvas and casual sporty styles. Tennies start at $5 with prices going all the way up to $20 for Cherokees. Other children's shoe labels are Crayons, Puma, Nike, Little Capezio, Jumping Jacks, Stride Rite, Peaks, and Super Sport. Women can shop for Western and dressy boots and there's a full men's shoe style-and-size selection.

by Shirley remains one of the best *Glad Rags* spots for shoe values. Everything sells for 40–50 percent off. Other popular labels include Andrew Geller, Jacques Cohen, Garolini, Nina, DeLiso, Barefoot, Julianelli, Beene Bag, and Famolare. Shirley really goes out of her way to stock narrows (up to AAAAA) and half-sizes. The size range is 5–12. There's always a special group of $5 and $10 closeouts for super value. We picked up two pairs of $36 Beene Bag slings for only $5. That's right, $5 for *both* or only $2.50 a pair. Sometimes Shirley runs a promotion where customers buy one pair and get the second for half price. The styles here will please women of many tastes and needs, especially those who like high fashion in footwear. Shirley also carries a wide selection of purses and belts. Canvas and fabric handbags sell for $6.50–$9.50 with leather and snakeskin styles from $20–$65. Oleg Cassini bags retailing for $110 sell here for $55 and $60. One-of-a-kind Cassini sample belts go at wholesale prices.

Stan Adler Shoes

9830 W. Pico Blvd., Los Angeles. (213) 553-9600.
1411 Wilshire Blvd., Santa Monica. (213) 394-6102.

Adler Shoes

515 W. Las Tunas Dr., San Gabriel. (213) 576-1467.
333 E. 17th St., Costa Mesa. (714) 642-5069.
464 S. Main St., Orange. (714) 542-1764.
Hours: Mon.–Fri. 10–9, Sat. 10–7, Sun. 10–5.
Purchases: MC, VISA, cks. Refunds and exchanges.
Parking: Street and area lots.

This store could be a real lifesaver if you're in last-minute need of a pair of dress shoes to accompany a special outfit. The large selection is conveniently displayed in sizes 5–11, narrow, medium, and wide, and salesmen are eager to help you. Popular brands like Sbicca, Nina, Latinas, Cherokee, Impo, and Sperry Top-Siders are discounted $3–$15 from retail. For women more interested in comfort than style, they also carry Red Cross, Air Step, Lifestride, and Naturalizer. Handsomely tooled Frye, Dan Post, and Tony Lama boots are available for $15–$20 off retail. Tennis shoes by Nike, Adidas,

Shoes By Shirley

18645 Ventura Blvd., Tarzana. (213) 788-1195.
Hours: Tues.–Sat. 10–5., Thurs. 10–7.
Purchases: MC, VISA, cks. Refunds and exchanges.
Parking: Free lot. Mailing list.

Since we first visited Shirley three years ago, her successful operation has grown. Her inventory has expanded to include more top-designer names like Charles Jourdan, Givenchy, Anne Klein and Yves St. Laurent. What hasn't changed, though, is Shirley's keen eye for picking up good buys (especially in forward looks), her specialization in narrow widths, and her willingness to pick up customers' special requests when she goes on her Monday buying trips. Shoes and Converse are also sold at a slight discount. Nurses will find a selection of regulation white work shoes. They also carry bags and belts at regular (not discounted) prices.

Standard Shoe Store
6100 Wilshire Blvd., Los Angeles. (213) 933-7211.
22840 Hawthorne Blvd., Torrance. (213) 378-9282.
1000 S. La Brea Ave., Inglewood. (213) 678-5311.
3120 E. Colorado Blvd., Pasadena. (213) 449-5111.
222 S. Euclid St., Anaheim. (714) 533-4547.
2153 Bellflower Blvd., Long Beach. (213) 597-1386.
6222 Laurel Canyon Blvd., North Hollywood.
  (213) 766-9595.
17630 Ventura Blvd., Encino. (213) 784-9627.
3077 Bristol St., Costa Mesa. (714) 540-5611.
991 Glendora Ave., West Covina. (213) 960-5577.
Hours: Mon.–Sat. 10–9, Sat. 10–6, Sun. 11–6.
Purchases: MC, VISA, cks. Returns and exchanges. Layaway.
Parking: Free lot.

Shop these stores for savings of 10–25 percent on your shoe purchases. The selection of styles and fabrication is wide ranging—there are thousands of pairs to choose from in lots of colors. Some styles are more current than others so most tastes can be satisfied. As one of the store managers told us, "We cater to everyone and everything." That goes for every kind of foot, too. Sizes go from 4–12, in narrow to extra wide. Special sale sandals start at $13 on the price scale—boots go up to $100 (retail $140). Most shoes sell in the $20–$60 range. Quality of construction and materials varies from leather to man-made materials so you may want to pay a little more for shoes you plan to wear often and save your bargain purchases for trendy styles.

Theodore of California
15401 S. Figueroa., St., Gardena. (213) 770-0442.
Hours: Mon.–Fri. 9–4.
Purchases: Cash or cks. All sales final.
Parking: Street.

For fans of those well-made and much-copied Theodore bags, here's a chance to stock up for 40–50 percent below retail. Made of canvas and vinyl in shoulder bag, clutch, satchel, and valise styles, the bags ordinarily sell for $20–$40 at dress shops and major department stores all across the country. At this factory outlet you'll find discontinued styles and slight irregulars in burgandy, navy, beige, black, and brown, as well as a few brighter shades. Occasionally special $5 tables are set up to sell off final markdowns.

Tony's Shoe Store & Repair

9139 E. Las Tunas Dr., Temple City. 286-7722.
Hours: Tues.–Fri. 9–5:30, Sat. 9–5.
Purchases: MC, VISA, cks. Refunds and exchanges.
   Layaway.
Parking: Free lot and street.

Sometimes it's kind of fun to shop at a shoe store that has a little bit of everything. You know the type—you never know *what* kind of unexpected bargain you might end up with. Since 1938, Tony's has prided itself on offering value at discount prices in men's and women's shoes and boots. Owner Vince Canzoneri buys from manufacturers and jobbers to get samples, closeouts, store liquidations, overruns . . . you name it. This explains the uncommonly varied inventory. Sizes 4–10 in all widths are well displayed for easy, self-service shopping. We especially appreciated finding some brands that are not often seen in discount shoe stores: Sperry Top-Sider, Bernardo, Old Maine Trotters, Alexander Green—even Perfect Poise nurse shoes. Stylings run the gamut from sports and tennis shoes to glittery evening numbers, all priced between $20–$30. Men can choose from an equally broad merchandise selection from Wolverine (work boots), Hush Puppies, and Sperry Top-Sider. As the store's name implies, you can have all your shoes and boots repaired here, too.

West Hollywood Hat, Bag, & Luggage Co.

7614 Santa Monica Blvd., Los Angeles. (213) 656-4647.
Hours: Mon.–Sun. 12–7.
Purchases: MC, VISA, cks. Exchanges only.
Parking: Free lot next door.

If you're in the market for hard or soft luggage, backpacks, garment bags, leather handbags, and clutches or any type of cowboy hat—stop here first. Discounts are 10 to 70 percent on items for both men and women. Full luggage sets in materials from nylon to impact-cast Samsonite range from

$85–$285. Nylon totes range from $10–$40. Cowboy hats are $8–$25 and fit both men and women. Handmade leather clutches for men that regularly sell for $155 are here for $85. Women's soft leather shoulder bags by Bartolli were $15 the day of our visit. Brands carried include Samsonite, Lancer and Yves St. Laurent. Take advantage of the weekly Super Sunday Sale when everything is discounted an additional 10 percent.

Famous Brand Shoes

10191 Valley View St., Cypress. (714) 826-4200.
24291 Avenida de la Carlotta, Suite P-8, Laguna Hills.
   (714) 855-4100.
9122 Adams Ave., Huntington Beach. (714) 962-2244.
Hours: Mon.–Thurs and Sat. 10–6, Fri. 10–8, Sun. 12–5.
Purchases: MC, VISA, cks. Refunds and exchanges.
Parking: Free lot.

It's fun to shop in this store, especially if you're an admitted shoe freak like we are. There's every style of women's shoes imaginable here for 15–50 percent below retail or from $14–$55 (with most falling between $22–$26 and $33–$39). The selection ranges from casual, including canvas deck shoes, to dressy pumps and evening sandals in sizes 4–12 in medium and narrow widths. There's even a sticker code to help you in your shopping: "W" on the sticker means wider than medium width; "S" means narrower than narrow; green means sample shoes for all you 6 mediums. Look for the "rack to the back" with specials for $7, $9, or $11 a pair. You simply have to see this rack for yourself to believe the terrific buys. You'll enjoy shopping—all the shoes are displayed on

easy-to-reach racks with handy benches between for trying on. You're welcome to browse leisurely or, if you want help, there are plenty of knowledgeable saleswomen to assist you. The stock turns over rapidly, so you'll always find new styles and colors.

Metro Shoes
1511 E. Katella Ave., Orange. (714) 639-5460, 639-1180.
Hours: Mon.–Fri. 10–7, Sat. 10–6, Sun. 11–5.
705 N. Pacific Coast Hwy., Redondo Beach. (213) 374-9151.
Hours: Mon.–Thurs., Sat. 10–6, Fri. 10–8, Sun. 11–5.
Purchases: MC, VISA, cks. Exchanges. Layaway.
Parking: Free lot.

You might find a bargain among the stock of cancellation shoes brought here after closeouts or going-out-of-business sales. All merchandise is fully guaranteed and will be repaired or replaced free of charge. Sizes run from 4½ to 11 AAA to E in an eclectic style range. Nothing is thrown out here, so you can still find '50s pointed pumps to wear with today's fashions

that recall the '40s and '50s. Prices are 20–40 percent off both women's and men's shoes. The Redondo Beach store is operated like a conventional shoe store: salespeople wait on you and fit you from the stock in the back. The newer store in Orange is set up as a self-service rack store where customers help themselves to the bargains. Prices for women's shoes run from about $10–$40 and for men's styles, $30–$70.

The Purse Place
116 Westminster Mall, Westminster. (714) 898-4654.
Hours: Mon.–Sat. 10–6, Sun. 12–5.
20032 Hawthorne Blvd., Torrance. (213) 371-1455.
Hours: Mon.–Sat. 10–6, Fri. 10–9, Sun. 12–5.
Purchases: MC, VISA, cks. Refunds and exchanges.
Parking: Free lot. Mailing list.

Bernie Goldberg of The Purse Place describes his merchandise assortment as "quality at everyday savings." It's nice to know that on any given day you can save from 10–33 percent on main floor department store brand handbags, lightweight, casual carry-on luggage, and purse accessories. Handbag fabrications include leather, vinyl, canvas, linen and other types of fabrics in styles ranging from casual to sophisticated. There's an evening selection during the holiday season. Everything offered is first-quality. The price range is $17–$60 for handbags that would retail elsewhere for $20–$80. If you use an attache case or valise for your job, you'll like the genuine leather assortment for $50–$65. The Purse Place also carries cosmetics, bags, and travel accessories.

The Shoe Horn

805 S. Harbor Blvd., Fullerton (714) 526-4758.
Hours: Mon.–Fri. 10–9, Sat. 10-6, Sun. 10–5.
Purchases: MC, VISA, cks. Refunds and exchanges.
   Layaway.
Parking: Street and free lot.

Good values in a wide assortment of year-round styles for the whole family is the key to the thirty-three year success of The Shoe Horn. You won't find any avant garde creations or off-the-wall colors, just classic styles in popular neutrals at 10–30 percent below retail. Brands for women include: Capezio, Sbicca, Nina, Naturalizer, and Christina; those for children: Mother Goose, Step Master, Converse, and Pro-Ked. Displays are set up according to color so you can quickly see all the navy or all the burgundy styles in your size, for instance. You can buy any color at any time of the year. We found lots of white pumps and sandals in the dead of winter. The assortment of classically designed pumps seemed to be The Shoe Horn's strong point for women. The children's selection is equally divided between casual/sporty and dress/school shoes selling for $10–$22. Watch the *Fullerton Tribune* and the *Santa Ana Register* for announcements of the big sales in January and July.

Van's

1212 S. Bristol St., Santa Ana (McFadden Plaza).
   (714) 957-6130.
Hours: Mon.–Fri. 9–9, Sat. 9–6, Sun. 10–5.
Purchases: MC, VISA, cks. All sales final.
Parking: Free lot.

Look no further for women's and children's canvas slip-on and oxford-style tennis shoes. This is the discount outlet for all the other retail Van's stores. Seconds, discontinued styles, and overruns of Van's own brand are liquidated (the factory is in Anaheim), along with the Phase Two brands, which is manufactured in Korea. Prices for children's quality shoes are $14 for oxford tennies, $19 for slip-ons, and $25 for high-top basketball styles. Seconds are $10 and $11 for oxfords, and $13.49 for slip-ons. The Women's sizes go from 4–12 with children's sizes 2½–12½. There are also men's styles available. One final note: you can special-order any size canvas shoe in any color Van's makes. You can even bring in a piece of fabric and have a pair of tennies whipped up to match your softball team's color scheme or to match your boat's decor—all for only $18.50 a pair.

Looking for a good buy on swimwear, leather goods, sweaters, lingerie, maternity clothes, or an entire large-sized wardrobe? These stores are a good place to start. Specialty stores carry one line or type of merchandise *in depth* and are thus able to offer you the best possible selection. If you're in need of a swimsuit, for example, it makes sense to go to a store that specializes in swimwear where you are likely to find the widest style, size and color selection—and frequently the lowest price. If you are in need of a particular item, also consult the Type of Merchandise Index for other recommended stores. This chapter and the one following on Manufacturers' Outlets have a lot of crossover—many specialty stores are outlets for their factories. The difference is mainly in our definition of terms. The stores in this chapter are generally just that—*stores,* with dressing rooms, exchange policies, and regular hours.

ℒ𝒜 𝒞ounty

Aloha Imports

6852 La Tijera Blvd., Los Angeles. (213) 641-8186/8187.
Hours: Mon.–Sat. 10–6.
Purchases: MC, VISA, cks. Returns and exchanges. Layaway.
Parking: Free lot behind store. Mailing list.

Imported clothing, shoes, gifts, and household items are sold here at about one-third less than at other import stores. Aloha Imports is both a wholesale and retail operation, and volume sales allows it to discount to the public. Imports from India, Thailand, Hong Kong, China, the Philippines, Taiwan, Korea, and France are featured. You don't have to visit the Islands to buy Hawaiian shirts and mumus for the entire family. Besides women's clothing, Aloha Imports carries shirts to extra large for men, as well as boys' and girls' clothing. Clothing for women is foreign-made, but is cut to fit the American woman. The large sizes will gracefully fit a size 20. A beige skirt and blouse set with taupe embroidery sells for $35. Short dresses average $40 and long dresses and gowns are $30–$130. Kimonos range from $22–$95 depending on the length and material (cottons to silks) used. Blouses are $15–$70 and a popular one-size-fits-all style is $27.50 and sells elsewhere for $45. You'll find batik dresses, crocheted sweaters, and lots of embroidery on blouses and jackets. Casual and dressy shoes are $10–$20.

Bea Dyke Swimwear

15620 Ventura Blvd., Encino. (213) 981-3138.
22201 Ventura Blvd., Woodland Hills. (213) 703-6171.
4644 Admiralty Way, Marina del Rey. (213) 821-8931.
9647 Reseda Blvd., Northridge. (213) 993-3540.
390 E. 17th St., Costa Mesa. (714) 548-6601.
Hours: Mon.–Sat. 10–5:30; June 1-August 31, Thurs. 10–8:30.
Purchases: MC, VISA, cks. Exchanges on everything but swimwear. Layaway.
Parking: Street or free lot.

While the discounts are not outstanding, you will find quality merchandise in a wide selection year round. And what other store will sell you a size 8 bottom with a size 10 top from regular stock? (The top and bottom must be within one size of each other, though.) However, from very special sale racks you can select any size top and bottom to fit your specially shaped body or to create your very own unique suit. You will find only top-quality lines: Cole, Catalina, DeWeese, Elizabeth Stewart, Sirena, Sandcastle, Roxanne, Gottex, Sassafras, LA Sole, Daffy, Norma Kamali, and Poppy. The average discount is 10 percent off retail per swimsuit or garment; the retail prices are marked on the tags with Bea Dyke's discount price marked in red. Those who prefer one-piece suits will find a large selection, including suits made for mature figures. Bea Dyke prides itself on its large selection of D cup suits. If you're in the market for lounge, poolside, or resort wear, you'll find all kinds of sportswear, sundresses, and terry wraps in sizes 3–18. There are always sale racks in the store. The best time to shop them is in January and February when the previous year's styles are marked down to make way for the current season's merchandise.

C'est le Jeans

15301 Ventura Blvd., Sherman Oaks. (213) 981-7810.
Hours: Mon.–Fri. 10–9, Sat. 10–6, Sun. 12–5.
Purchases: MC, VISA, cks. Exchanges. Layaway.
Parking: Street and area lots.

Jeans from several well-known designer labels sell here for 40 percent off. Prices run $25–$34 for women's sizes 26–34 and 26–38 for men. The majority of the stock is jeans, but you might find a few other sportswear items and accessories.

Creative Woman

1530 S. Myrtle Ave., Monrovia. (213) 358-6216.
Hours: Tues.–Sat. 10–6.
Purchases: MC, VISA, cks. All sales final. Layaway.
Parking: Rear lot and street.

It's rare to find a store that offers custom creations in literally any size, plus alterations, all at very reasonable prices.

Bonnie Beebe Kaufman, who runs the shop (along with her husband Ed) has been interested in sewing since she was old enough to thread a needle. This talented seamstress and designer turned her favorite hobby into a successful business six years ago. She serves all kinds of women: entertainers get one-of-a-kind costumes; large-sized ladies, and those with figure problems, especially appreciate Bonnie's ability to fit them well in flattering styles and colors. The rest of Bonnie's and Ed's clientele are those of us who just plain like to wear something different, an item or outfit not mass-produced and sold in quantity at every store in town. Bonnie will create anything your heart desires in your choice of fabric—you can bring a picture or sketch and she'll take it from there. There are racks of sample garments, mostly in Qiana, so that you can try things on to get an idea of fit and decide exactly what you want. Bonnie's own design style is not unlike that of another famous local designer, Harriet Selwyn. Their concepts are quite similar: easy, drapable, flattering styles in medium-weight Qiana ingeniously tailored into timeless, year-round styles that can be dressed up or down and go from day into evening. There are tops, blouses, skirts, pants, capes, caftans, stoles, and jumpsuits in interesting reversible stylings and color combinations. Words don't really describe the uniqueness of these garments. You'll just have to pay Bonnie and Ed a visit to see for yourself. Time is spent with each customer to help her learn all the different ways these garments can be worn and enjoyed. Prices are reasonable for all this custom work and individual attention. Pieces average $25–$40. While you're here, check the sale racks for Ed's special purchases of manufacturers' closeouts and samples. The inexpensive accessories collection is fun to browse through, too.

Factory Retail Outlet

5527 Cleon Ave., North Hollywood. (213) 980-0570.
Hours: Mon.–Sat. 9–4:30.
Purchases: MC, VISA, cks. All sales final.
Parking: Free lot.

On a small side street near Vineland and Burbank you'll find this store which carries everything for pregnant women and nursing mothers, and then some. Close-outs, samples, and irregulars of Mary Jane and Corey maternity wear and Cattani loungewear are sold in this friendly store located directly across from the factory. Coordinates in maternity styles for sizes 4–18 include pants, tunics, dresses, tops, and shorts as well as lingerie. Bras run from 32A–44F and are also available in nursing styles. Sleepwear and underpants are sized for pregnancy, too. The Cattani loungewear and hostess outfits come in sizes small through extra large and can be worn after the baby comes. Prices are 20–80 percent off —the average price tag runs only $12. Large-sized women find many of the garments to their liking, especially the blouses and caftans.

Junior Maternity

11746 E. Washington Blvd., Whittier. (213) 698-1130.
Hours: Mon.–Fri. 8–5:30, Sat. 10:30–3.
Purchases: MC, VISA, cks. All sales final. Layaway.
Parking: Free lot.

Tucked away behind Earl Scheib's is this factory outlet store for a popular line of maternity dresses and separates. The store sells overruns, closeouts and irregulars at wholesale prices or less. Much of the merchandise is in perfect condition. You can assemble a complete wardrobe, including swimsuits ($10–$15, regularly $30–$40), pants, tops, dresses, and formal wear. Prices range from $8.75–$25. There are private dressing rooms, and, for the seamstress, reasonably priced end-of-bolt fabrics. Sizes are 4–16, jeans to sizes 18 and 20. You'll also find sleepwear and pantyhose.

Kirkpatrick Sales Corp.

8592 Washington Blvd., Culver City. (213) 839-6455.
19527 Beach Blvd., Huntington Beach. (714) 960-6755.
Hours: Mon.–Sat. 10–6; March 15–September 15, Mon., Wed., Fri. 10–9.
Purchases: VISA, cks. All sales final. Layaway.
Parking: Street and free lot.

We couldn't recommend a store with a better selection of swimsuits and leisure wear: if Kirkpatrick doesn't have it, you don't need it. In business now for thirty-two years, the store continues to be a perennial favorite among Los Angelinos who want the best for less. There are separate rooms for each type of merchandise. Men's swim trunks and actionwear are in one room, and women's actionwear and separates are in another. The third room has enough different kinds of brand-name beach cover-ups and loungewear to see you through a cruise around the world. For dancing or exercising, you'll like the Danskin leotards. Then there's the swimsuit room. This is the *real* reason for making Kirkpatrick a must on your list. In this room you'll find ten thousand (at the height of the season) bikinis, one-piece maillots, and leotard-like suits by Cole, Catalina, Elizabeth Stewart, Jantzen, DeWeese, Dippers, Sandcastle, Sirena, Rose Marie Reed, and Daffy. The suits are always this season's styles, and we promise you'll have a hard time choosing the one you like best. The area you should visit first is the women's swimwear sale room. All two-pieces are $5.75 and one-piecers sell for $7.75. Sizes run from 3–52; there's a nice selection of D cup styles and suits for women who have had mastectomies.

Prices are 33–70 percent off. The small number of seconds are clearly marked on the tickets. Manager Tom Turquand buys from manufacturers, jobbers, and liquidators and passes special savings on to customers. Don't miss the every-Saturday sidewalk sale.

Lane Bryant—Final Lane

510 W. 7th St., Los Angeles. (213) 627-4824.
Hours: Tues., Thurs., Sat., 10–6, Mon., and Fri. 10–7:30.
Purchases: MC, VISA, Store Charge, cks. All sales final.
Parking: Pay lot. Mailing list.

Lane Bryant is a watchword among women who shop for large and half-sized clothing. The store specializes in sizes 14½ through 32½, J.P. 15–27 (a fuller junior cut), missy 36–52, tall sizes 10 through 22, and shoe sizes 6–12, M, W, WW, and 10–13 N,M. Final Lane is located in the basement of the downtown store. This is the final resting ground for clearance merchandise. Clothes still have their original price tags, but the amount has been slashed one, two, even three times. Clothing is usually half priced or less, but be prepared to hunt for your treasures. More designer names like Givenchy, Gloria Vanderbilt, and Joseph Picone are adding their names to the ranks of large size labels found here. Prices run from $2–$30. In addition to all types of dresses and separates, you'll find sleepwear, lingerie, bras, panties, and pantyhose.

Leather Warehouse

16415 Hawthorne Blvd., Lawndale. (213) 729-9126).
7633 Fulton Ave., North Hollywood. (213) 764-1776.
17622 Ventura Blvd., Encino. (213) 986-6062.
313 Wilshire Blvd., Santa Monica. (213) 451-8921.
Hours: Mon.–Sat. 10–6, Sun. 11–5.
Purchases: MC, VISA, Store Charge, cks. Exchanges.
   Layaway.
Parking: Street and free lot. Mailing list.

If you're in the market for any kind of leather garment, be sure to compare prices at the Leather Warehouse. Not only do these stores sell the usual tailored jackets and coats, you'll also find unique, high-style leather at their 15–20 percent discount. Nine different types of leather garments and handbags are available in a broad collection of styles and colors. As one of the store managers said, "Variety is the key." Women's sizes range from 5–24 and men's from 36–60 in labels from Andrea Michele (Leather Warehouse's own), Mirage, Avanti, Jordache, Sasson, Fantastic, Beau Geste, and Saxony. We were especially fond of the designer leather items from Joan Lober and Karen Silton. Prices for garments run from $59 up to $200. The store does a big business in special orders. If you find a color or style you like, but your size isn't on the racks, the Leather Warehouse will be happy to order it just for you.

Loré Lingerie
2228 Cotner Ave., West Los Angeles. (213) 477-0081.
Semi-annual sales.
Purchases: MC, VISA, cks. All sales final.
Parking: Street. Mailing list.

Loré manufacturers pure silk lingerie for fine stores such as Neiman Marcus and Bergdorf Goodman. If you prefer to save on luxury purchases like this rather than pay full retail, you'll be happy to know that twice a year, Loré sponsors special one-day sales. Savings range from 30–60 percent on Lore's overstocks, samples, and items with slight irregularities or "beauty marks" as factory personnel like to call them. The wide price range of $5–$200 covers bikini panties, tap pants, bras, gowns, blouses, tunics, and bed jackets. Sales are held in a factory workroom. You must forsake modesty in a storage room which serves as a communal dressing room during the one-day sale. (Part of the fun is helping others decide which of the lovely garments to splurge on). Each piece is tagged with detailed care instructions. And, yes, silk is hand-washable. Call to be added to their mailing list: Loré does not welcome drop-in customers.

Millard of California
6711 Fallbrook Ave., Canoga Park (Fallbrook Mall, North End). (213) 884-0404.
Hours: Mon.–Sat. 10–5.30, Sun. 12–5.
909 S. Broadway, 2nd floor, Los Angeles. (213) 488-0623.
Hours: Mon.–Sat. 10–3.
11028 Washington Blvd., Culver City. (213) 559-5600.
Hours: Mon.–Sat. 10:30–5:30.
Purchases: MC, VISA, cks. All sales final. Layaway.
Parking: Free lot, area lot and street. Mailing list.

Coats, jackets, raincoats, and suits are the specialty of these direct factory outlets for better California makers. You'll save 30–70 percent on two-piece suits, Qiana raincoats, and select sportswear. Prices and fabrics change with the seasons. Higher fall prices come down as the beginning of the year approaches and the coat/suit season winds down. There are several big sales held during the year. Two important ones that you may want to add to your shopping itinerary are the mid-January sale of winter items and the summer sale of samples and irregulars for the *upcoming* fall season. This one will appeal to those of you who like to get the jump on the latest styles. The folks at Millard told us they're carrying more sportswear items than ever before, especially during spring and summer. Junior and missy sizes run from 3/4–15/16 in classic, conservative styles. Working women comprise a good share of the clientele.

Norick & Co.
31149 Via Colinas, Westlake Village. (213) 991-5670.
Hours: Mon.-Sat. 10–6.
Purchases: MC, VISA, AE, cks. Exchanges only. Layaway.
Parking: Free lot and street. Mailing list.

The *Wall Street Journal* ads describe Norick & Co. as providing: "Classic clothing for the traditional woman and gentleman." (And at a nice savings, we might add.) We can't identify the labels of the classic lines carried here, but you'll be delighted to find all your favorites at less-than-retail prices

OLGA—Fashion Fabrics and other things

15750 Strathern St., Van Nuys. (213) 994-7963.
732 Moorpark Rd., Thousand Oaks. (805) 496-3963.
743 W. Baker St., Costa Mesa. (714) 957-1214.
Hours: Mon.–Sat. 10–5.
Purchases: MC, VISA, cks. All sales final.
Parking: Free lot. Mailing list.

This is one of our favorite stores: it's hard to get a better value for your dollar than you'll find here. Olga manufactures a famous line of lingerie, undergarments, and loungewear, and according to Ella Larsson, manager of all three stores, the color and style selection keeps getting better all the time. All items are marked irregular, but many are in perfect condition. The flaws are taped for easy inspection. Most of the store is help-yourself, but there are also boxes of underwear behind a counter, which you must ask for. You'll also find half and full slips, bras, girdles, leotards, pantyhose, and more. Plan to spend some time surveying the large inventory before making your selection. You won't find all sizes or colors in each style, but new merchandise arrives weekly. There is a communal dressing room for try-ons. Sizes run petite, small, medium, and large and 32–38 in bras and slips. Prices start at 25 percent off and can end up as much as 75 percent off in each store's bargain center.

Oriental Silk Co.

8377 Beverly Blvd., Los Angeles. (213) 651-2323.
Hours: Mon.–Sat. 10–6.
Purchases: Purchases: MC, VISA, cks. Exchanges. Layaway.
Parking: Street and rear lot.

Owner George Wong imports a variety of fine apparel from China and Hong Kong and wholesales it to well-known local retail shops. The good news for us bargain hunters is that he offers everything at his shop to the public for wholesale prices. He has hand-embroidered silk nightgowns for $120, long- and short-sleeved silk blouses with Chinese or sport-

when you drop by. The women's assortment runs the gamut of basic sportswear pieces, coats, raincoats, day dresses, golf skirts, and even jewelry, umbrellas, and belts. Most prices are in the $30–$70 range. The menswear selection is a bit more complete with everything from the basics (socks and underwear) to shoes and suits. Owner Paul Norick has installed quite a classy operation in what is otherwise an office complex. You have to stop and think twice to remind yourself that you're not at Abercrombie and Fitch. The salespeople, including Mrs. Norick, are most helpful. They're happy to assist you in your selections or you're free to browse to your heart's content.

shirt collars for $55–$65 ($80–$90 in fancier stores), fitted blouses made especially for the store in silk crepe de chine for $40, silk brocade jackets and robes for $40–$80 and beaded sweaters for $25. The workmanship on all garments is impeccable—covered buttons and hand-stitched hems are routine. You'll find cotton T-shirts, shawls, painted silk and chiffon scarves, and two-piece pajama sets. Dressmakers stop here first for low-priced silk yardage.

The Pant Warehouse

18500 Sherman Way, Reseda. (213) 705-9347.
6378 Van Nuys Blvd., Van Nuys. (213) 997-9527.
5259 Lankershim Blvd., North Hollywood. (213) 506-9886.
Hours: Mon.–Fri. 10–6, Sat. 9:30–7, Sun. 11–6.
Purchases: MC, VISA, AE, cks. Exchanges. Layaway.
Parking: Street and area lot. Mailing list.

This is your store for jeans. The extensive selection features women's, men's, and boys' styles for 10–50 percent off. Levi's are an especially good buy for $13.88 The rest of the

stock sells for $10–$30 and is made up of moderately priced and designer labels in sizes 24–42 and student sizes (slimmer cut) 26–30. You will also find a good selection of T-shirts, shirts, jackets, and leather jackets. The North Hollywood store acts as the final markdown center for the other stores. One room at this location houses last-ditch reductions of jeans for $3–$10 and similar values on other garments. The Pant Warehouse will also hem your jeans purchases for free.

Rosie's Discount Swimsuits

905 S. Pacific Coast Highway, Redondo Beach.
  (213) 540-2298.
Hours: Mon.–Sat. 10–5; (October–January) Thurs.–Sat. 10–5.
Purchases: Cash or cks. All sales final. Layaway.
Parking: Street.

The store's name says it all—you'll find one- and two-piece swimsuits in every color, style, and fabric, as well as coordin-

ated beach and poolside loungewear in sizes 5–24 (D cup bra sizes, too). There is also a sampling of junior dresses in terry and gauze, and sundresses with built-in bras (also available in D cups). All brands are well known and savings are 30–50 percent on samples and closeouts. There are also a few clearly marked irregulars.

Sweatsuit City

24204 Crenshaw Blvd., Torrance. (213) 539-2150.
Hours: Daily 10–6. Call for extended winter hours.
Purchases: MC, VISA, cks. Exchanges. Layaway.
Parking: Free lot.

Look no further for ski and other actionwear bargains for the whole family. Men, women, and children can save 30–70 percent on all types of ski garments: sweaters, pants, bibs, jackets, vests, stretch pants, knitted hats, gloves, and ski boots. Sizes are 6–18 for boys and girls and small through large for women and men, and extra large in jackets for men. During the summer the stock includes jogging, tennis, and

soccer attire. The store is stuffed with merchandise: on the day of our visit, the sidewalk rack held the overflow. Most prices run from $15–$40 with stretch pants, jackets, and boots a bit higher.

The Sweater Mill

265 S. Robertson Blvd., Beverly Hills. (213) 659-5765.
Hours: Wed.–Fri. 10–5, Sat. 10–3.
Purchases: MC, VISA, cks. Refunds and exchanges.
Parking: Street.

Walking into The Sweater Mill is like opening an overcrowded sweater drawer—how do you find what you need? In this case, the answers is, ask. The friendly owner/manager will help you with your knitwear purchases of all kinds: sweaters, shawls, shorts, vests, sweater sets, and evening knit outfits.

Sale items start at $4. Prices are 40–60 percent below retail. The size range runs from small to a complete selection in extra-large.

Sweater World

165 S. Fairfax Ave., Los Angeles. (213) 938-7044.
Hours: Mon.–Sat. 10–5.
Purchases: MC, VISA, cks. Exchanges. Layaway.
Parking: Street and free lot.

Sweaters, sweater jackets, sweater and slacks suits, blouses, knit tops, pants, and skirts are all discounted 40–50 percent here. You'll find top-quality knitwear by Le Roy and Dorce in a wide selection of sizes and colors. Knits are available in both wool and synthetics. Among the conservative cardigans and classic pullovers, you'll find lurex-threaded evening sweaters and glittery shawls. Solid color polyester blouses sell for $13 and knit pull-on slacks for $9–$20 (retail value $42). Sweaters average $10–$30—though you can spend up to $55 for a wool style that might retail for $100.

Thel's Clothes

4334 Sepulveda Blvd., Culver City. (213) 390-2144.
Hours: Mon.–Sat. 10–6, Sun. 12–5.
Purchases: MC, VISA, cks. Exchanges. Layaway.
Parking: Street and rear lot.

Charming Argentine Jose Tafel has operated this little jeans shop for five years and, because of his policy of offering good customer service, he's in for a long run. You know how some jeans fit great in the hips but are too big in the waist? Well, Jose and Company will nip in the waistline faster than you can say "dungarees." (Where else can you go to buy all kinds of jeans for only $13.99 and get free alterations to boot?) Designer label denims (retailing elsewhere for $45) sell here for $30. Dungarees, corduroys, and khakis come in unisex styles ranging from size 26 waist (women's size 1/2) up to 42. There's a wide variety of styles in terms of trim and leg widths. Look for the Lee Lycra stretch jean for both men and women. Blouses are 40–70 percent off in several styles, including Western for $6–$12.

VIP Leather & Suede Factory Warehouse
1543 14th St., Santa Monica. (213) 870-1542.
Hours: Mon.–Sat. 9–5; December, Sun. 10–5.
Purchases: MC, VISA, cks. Exchanges. Layaway.
Parking: Free lot and street.

This leading manufacturer's warehouse has been quietly open to the public for eleven years. Once you're past the locked door, you'll find over five thousand leather and suede coats and jackets. Garments are not individually priced, but the average is $89 for jackets and $120 for coats. This represents 40–70 percent savings over retail. Men's sizes are 36–50, women's 6–20. This is the same merchandise available in stores throughout the country. Everything is current season and first quality. The excellent style selection includes Cabretta kidskin blazers, sueded-cowhide rancher vests, and rawhide and shearling lamb jackets. There are different types, weights, and colors of leather to choose from. VIP also sells special purchases from other manufacturers and importers, especially from Israel and Egypt.

Orange County

P. F. McMullin
1530 E. Edinger Ave., Suites 8 and 9, Santa Ana.
  (714) 547-7479.
Hours: Winter, Mon.–Fri. 10–9. Sat. 10–6, Sun. 12–5.
  Summer, Mon.–Sat. 10–6.
Purchases: MC, VISA, cks. Exchanges only. Layaway.
Parking: Free lot and street.

Even though we're not skiers, we seriously considered taking up the sport after discovering this store overflowing with all types of skiwear at 40 percent off retail. Manager Todd Clark describes his store as offering a "huge selection of everything in skiwear for the entire family"—and he's right. We found labels such as Ski Skins, WigWam, Hot Finger, Jean Claude Killy, Fera, Peter Frank, Black Mfg., Allen A, and Sportiss which make ski clothes for men, women and children. Prices

range from $3 for caps, $7.25 each for thermal underwear and turtlenecks to $30, $37.50 for nylon bib overalls and $62 for stretch ski pants for adults. The children's wear selection is available in sizes 8–18 and includes Healthknit thermal underwear for $4 for tops or bottoms, nylon parkas for $25 (retail $43), ski pants for $18, and junior goggles for $8. Children's one-piece snowsuits in sizes 6–8 are $24. The store also carries down vests and down parkas for $66 and nylon styles for $38 in women's sizes. All the merchandise is carefully displayed by size and type so it's easy to find exactly what you're looking for, including gloves, hats and even suspenders. The day we visited we found a great buy on nylon wind shirts for sailing in men's and women's styles at only $9 each. Todd advises shopping during October for the best skiwear selection and invites customers to check out the tennis apparel during the summer.

Seashore Discount Swimwear

14341 Beach Blvd., Westminster. (714) 892-6839.

Atlantis Discount Swimwear

1806 N. Tustin Ave., Santa Ana. (714) 547-1552.
Hours: Mon.–Sat. 10–6. Call for winter hours.
Purchases: Cks, cash. Exchanges. Layaway.
Parking: Free lot.

Like father, like son. Robert Hargrove, of Rosie's Discount Swimsuits in Redondo Beach, has been in the business for fifteen years. His son, David, decided to go into business ten years ago and now he and his wife Ann have two successful swimsuits-for-less shops in Orange County. Since David and his dad pool their buying, the savings shows up on the price tags. But this isn't the only reason to shop here: the broad selection of styles makes this a favorite of women who wear sizes 5–20 and 38–46. All labels are snipped out of first-quality goods at 25–50 percent off. You'll like the ever-present sale rack of $4.99 bikinis and one-piece suits. The rest of the inventory consists of bikinis, one-piece, and two-piece suits for $10–$30. The larger-sized suits sell for $18–$30 (retail to $60). Both stores feature swimsuits and bikinis in D cup sizes. Besides bathing suits, long and short terry dresses, casual separates, velour warm-up suits, and cruise dresses with built-in bras (D cups, too), the store carries leather handbags.

Sousa & Lefkovits

621 South B St., Tustin. (714) 731-7151.
2251 S. Sepulveda Blvd., West Los Angeles. (213) 477-8095.
Hours: Mon.–Sat. 10–6, Sun. 12–5.
Purchases: MC, VISA, cks. Refunds and exchanges.
Parking: Street and free lot. Mailing list.

Well, Lisa Birnbach beat us to this one. She recommended Sousa & Lefkovits in *The Preppy Handbook* as one of *the* outlets to dress truly preppy without having to shop in the high-rent district. That's really it: all the *de rigueur* duds for the duck-motif set. There's a complete selection, *sans* labels, of men's and women's suits, blazers, shirts, sweaters, trousers, T-shirts, and shorts at about 35 percent off. Specifically, women's cotton and cotton/polyester broadcloth and oxford shirts go for $18 (retail $32), cashmere sweaters for $76.50 ($145 retail), and Shetland styles for $19.50 ($32 retail). You can create a suit from blazer-and-skirt coordinates in linen, madras, or wool. We found cotton plaid shirt coordinates, too. In January there's "Look, Muffy, a sale for us," so get yourself on the mailing list. (You, too, Biff and Bunny and Skip and . . .)

Manufacturers' Outlets 7

Where there's smoke, there's fire, and where there's a thriving garment industry, you'll find a wealth of factory outlets. These can be the most fun and financially rewarding stops along your discount shopping route. There's nothing better than going straight to the source to make a purchase, and there's no one who can afford to be more generous than the manufacturer. And there's the added excitement of shopping amidst the hustle and bustle of the factory. The whirr of sewing machines adds a new dimension to the shopping experience.

There are manufacturers' outlets for almost anything. The following pages will direct you to bargains for maternity wear, lingerie, dance-wear, children's clothing, sportswear, and much more. This chapter is particularly strong in women's polyester separates in regular and large sizes. Hours, purchase policies and shopping amenities such as sales-help and try-ons vary with each manufacturer. We give you that information in advance so you'll know what to expect. Again, please consult the Type of Store Index for other manufacturers' outlets in the Specialty and Garment District chapters particularly.

LA County

All Seasons Clothing Co.
8463 Melrose Ave., Los Angeles. (213) 655-2289.
Hours: Mon.–Sat. 10–6.
Purchases: MC, VISA, cks. All sales final. Layaway.
Parking: Street. Mailing list.

This new store is a company-owned outlet specializing in silk, blends and cotton high-fashion separates. The Hong Kong factory manufactures for designers the likes of Calvin Klein, and for specialty stores such as I. Magnin, Saks, and Neiman-Marcus (who put their own labels into goods). Part of the four-factory operation is set aside to make clothes exclusively for its own retail outlets. The company employs its own designers, but takes advantage of quality fabrics and skilled workmanship expected in high-end goods. Label-conscious shoppers can buy designer overcuts and irregulars, but most of the clothing carries factory labels we're unfamiliar with. Judge the quality for yourself (we were favorably impressed). There will be four lines per year designed for working women who need versatile separates that go easily day-into-evening. Sizes are 2–14 with the best selection in 4–8. Silk dresses range from $60–$80 and lined, silk suits average $110. Silk and cotton-blend sweaters were $26 the day of our visit. As a result of customer requests, more cotton goods are being manufactured. Eliminating middlemen without compromising on quality is the key. All Seasons plans to expand to Newport Beach and eventually to Santa Monica and the San Fernando Valley.

Bargain Basement
719 N. San Fernando Blvd., Burbank. (213) 849-2618.
Hours: Mon.–Sat. 9:30–5.
Purchases: MC, VISA, cks. Exchanges.
Parking: Street and free lot. Mailing list.

Though owner Kristine Lirhus also carries junior and missy sportswear, she considers her stock of first-quality and irregular one- and two-piece bathing suits, available year round, to be the store's specialty. She carries several swimsuit lines, as well as a good selection of loungewear, caftans, and terry cover-ups, all at 30–50 percent below what they cost in nearby department stores. Prices run from $5 to $38 for suits and poolside wear plus separates and dresses. Sizes go from 6–20 with blouses to 48.

Bizarre Bazaar

11251 Ventura Blvd., Studio City. (213) 506-7069.
Hours: Tues.–Sat. 11–5.
Purchases: MC, VISA, cks. All sales final. Layaway.
Parking: Free lot behind store.

The full line of New Hero 100 percent native American cotton clothing is available here for 50 to 60 percent below retail. The stock of pants, tops, jackets, vests, tunics, skirts, dresses, shorts, and jumpsuits is 70 percent women's, 20 percent men's and 10 percent children's and teens clothing, so bring the family. Women's sizes are petite (3–4) to extra large (13–14) and many of the styles will double as maternity wear. Tops are $5–$20, pants $6–$20, jumpsuits $10–$30, skirts $8–$20, shorts $5–$15, and dresses $10–$20. There are dressing rooms for try-ons and Mrs. Gold, the owner, says she'll barter for antiques and oriental rugs.

Cal Femme Sportswear

6030 Crenshaw Blvd., Los Angeles. (213) 752-3135.
Hours: Fri.–Sun. 10–5.
Purchases: MC, VISA, cks. All sales final.
Parking: Free lot. Mailing list.

This firm acts as a sewing contractor for well-known West Coast sportswear firms, We can't mention the labels you'll find here, but it's safe to say they're among the most popular. The factory showroom sells these polyester knit and gabardine separates in missy sizes 8–20 and large 36–46 at wholesale and below. Pants are $9.75–$10.75. Most merchandise is first quality, but there are some imperfects so shoppers should check all purchases carefully as there are no returns or exchanges. You won't find any dressing rooms so you'll just have to slip into potential purchases behind a rack.

California Apparel & Textile (C.A.T.)

2524 S. Hill St., Los Angeles. (213) 749-4391.
14626 Lanark St., Panorama City.
163-167 W. Cerritos Ave., Anaheim.
13132 Telegraph Rd., Santa Fe Springs.
Hours: Fri.–Sun. 10–5. Call downtown store for weekend
    sale dates.
Purchases: MC, VISA, cks. Exchanges.
Parking: Street and free lots. Mailing list.

Harvey Katz has an interesting concept here in these permanent warehouse sales where the atmosphere has been reduced to the bare minimum (there are no dressing rooms). However, the savings are so substantial that it's worth your trouble to attend. Sales are held one weekend per month; the downtown store hosts two or three monthly. Featured are Tattoo, Cal Togs, Topson Downs, Miss Tops, Kayo, Pumpernickel, and Jackie O skirts, pants, tops, blouses, and sweaters—all in the $3 to $18 price range. Current-season merchandise is first quality. Occasionally you'll find racks of irregulars. Women's sizes encompass junior 3–13, missy 4–20, and large sizes 32–38. Girls' apparel comes in 4–6x and 7–14. The selection of larger sizes is especially good.

Chic Lingerie

1126 Santee St., Los Angeles. (213) 749-2374.
Hours: Mon.–Fri. 8:30-4.
693 High Lane, Redondo Beach. (213) 372-9352.
Hours: Mon.–Fri. 8–3.30; (Call for Sat. hours).

Alley Cat

1133 Maple St., Los Angeles (in alley directly behind factory
    at 1126 Santee St.). (213) 749-2374.
Hours: Mon.–Sat. 9–4:30.
Purchases: Cash, cks. Exchanges.
Parking: Free lot, street and area lots. Mailing list.

We like this store because it's such an adventure to shop here. Nothing fancy, mind you, just rows and rows with racks and racks of every conceivable type of lingerie and lounge-

wear. Chic manufactures a wide style range for such outlets as J.C. Penney's to Frederick's of Hollywood. You'll find perfects and seconds with minor flaws selling for $2 all the way up to $22. (At these prices, how can you afford not to shop here?) Sleepwear, robes, baby dolls' and cover-ups, and dresses in sizes petite to XXXL. Fabrications include nylon tricot, fleece, quilted fabrics, and cotton/polyester blends. There are no try-ons but you can exchange anything that doesn't fit. (The Redondo Beach store is a bit tricky to find so we'll offer directions. Take 190th Street west to Phelan. Turn north, then left on Fisk, which dead ends at High Street and the Chic Lingerie factory. Drive to the north end of the factory, enter the parking lot and park on the west side of the building where you'll see a small door leading into the factory).

Cole of California

5110 Pacific Ave., Los Angeles. (213) 587-3111.
Hours: Mon.–Fri. 10–5.
Purchases: MC, VISA, cks. Exchanges only.
Parking: Free lot and street.

How can you go wrong at the only outlet store for one of America's most popular, best-selling sports and swimwear companies? After a five year hiatus, the outlet has reopened to the public so that the manufacturer can liquidate past-season goods, overruns, samples, and a few slight irregulars. A complete selection of five Cole labels is represented: Cole swimwear (missy cut), Cole Jrs. (junior swimwear), Sandcastle swimwear (full-figure fit with more mature styling), Going Places (younger styling in a full-figured junior cut), and Cole Covers sportswear coordinates. For women who have had mastectomies, there are plenty of specially designed swimsuits. Prices are generally wholesale for sizes 5–18. Most pieces run from $9–$30, but on the bargain racks you'll find really good deals for $2, $5, and $7. One of these special racks carries the designer lines—an interesting collection of ideas from the Cole designers. These are experiments in design and fabrication that don't make it to regular production, but can be special one-of-a-kind discoveries for outlet shoppers with a keen eye. There are always about 2,500 garments to choose from and customers are free to try on in private dressing rooms. The Cole Covers line encompasses knit and velour tops, skirts, jackets, shorts, and sundresses in cotton and cotton blends. The swimsuit lines include matching cover-ups, wrap skirts, pull-on tops, and tunics. Fabric and remnants are also for sale.

Con-Stan International
19501 E. Walnut Dr., City of Industry. (714) 598-1831.
Hours: Thurs. & Fri. 10–5, Sat. 12–5. Call for an
  appointment for other times.
Purchases: Cash and cks. Exchanges. Layaway.
Parking: Free lot.

Besides its extensive business in uniforms and career apparel for firms and factories all over the U.S., Con-Stan International also makes coordinated separates and dresses for sale only at its two retail outlets in the City of Industry and Honolulu. The classically styled items, (similar in look and quality to Loubella) are fashioned in woven and double-knit polyester for easy care. Sizes are missy 4–18 with some samples in 10. Almost everything is first quality—you'll occasionally find a few irregulars so indicated. Prices range from $9–$45 with most price tickets at $20–$30. New items arrive weekly. The two friendly salesladies are well known for their outfit-coordinating talents.

Daisy
119 S. Pasadena Ave., South Pasadena. (213) 254-6118.
Hours: Tues.–Sat. 9:30–5:30.
Purchases: MC, VISA, cks. Exchanges.
Parking: Free lot. Mailing list.

Due to the success of their semi-annual parking-lot sales, the people at Daisy have decided to open their own outlet store to liquidate overruns and seconds. Daisy is the sole licensee of women's Hang Ten casual sporty separates so you'll find those familiar little feet embroidered on all the women's items, which comprise 80 percent of the inventory. The balance is made up of men's, boys' and girls' sweats, tops, shorts, and T-shirts. First-quality women's items (T-shirt and tank dresses, swimwear, pants, sweatshirt warm-ups, and tops) sell for about $8–$10 (retail $20–$55). Clearly marked

slight irregulars sell for $3–$9. Children's goods sizes 3–6x go for $6–$9, (retail value to $18) and the men's things sell for $8–15 (up to $36 retail). These are mostly first quality with a few seconds available from time to time. There are plenty of private dressing rooms. The parking-lot sale fans will be relieved to hear these events will continue to be held—dates announced via the mailing list.

Flexatard
11755 Exposition Blvd., West Los Angeles. (213) 477-0418.
Annual weekend sale.
Purchases: Cash only. All sales final.
Parking: Street. Mailing list.

Write or call Flexatard and ask to be put on the mailing list for notification of their annual factory clearance sale. It's usually held in late summer or early fall—when the business manager "has the strength," as she puts it. Leotards, swimwear, bodywear, dancewear, and activewear for women in sizes petite through large are sold at wholesale and below. Girls' sizes 6–14 are also available. All items are closeouts, discontinued styles and colors, and seconds. At previous yard sales, we've purchased leotards with minor flaws for as little as $4. No try-ons. We must emphasize that this is the *only* time Flexatard sells to the public.

Greenecastle
14020 S. Shoemaker Ave., Norwalk. (213) 921-5515.
Hours: Mon.–Sat. 9–5:30.
Purchases: MC, VISA, cks. Exchanges only. Layaway.
Parking: Free lot and street. Mailing list.

Customers can save 20 percent on first-quality, current-season merchandise from this popular casual and lounge-wear manufacturer. Savings are 50 percent on closeouts and end-of-season goods, and *60* percent on seconds. Fabrics are easy-care synthetics in bright prints and solids made up into casual coordinates, robes, and caftans. Most pieces sell for $10-$25. If you're a sample size 10, you can pick up values (like $5 blouses). In general, sizes run from 6–18 with some larger sizes to 42 and 46 in tops and blouses. The caftans are one-size-fits-all. Store manager Evelyn McMillan also stocks closeouts and special purchases from other manufacturers. On our visit, we found a whole rack of men's shirts and shorts for only $6 each and some women's clothing from Garland and Lady Manhattan. You home-sewing buffs will like the super deals on yardage and notions. Finally, there's a glass display case full of inexpensive costume jewelry for under $5.

Hang Ten Co. Store

125 W. Transit St., Ontario. (714) 984-6819.
Hours: Mon.–Sat. 9–6, Sun. 12–5.
Purchases: MC, VISA, cks. Exchanges.
Parking: Street and side lot.

The vast inventory at this warehouse outlet almost defies description, but we'll give it our best shot. Golden Breed and Hang Ten casual and actionwear and Aspen skiwear for men and boys is available here by the truckload. Lest we give you the wrong impression about all this, let us hasten to add that manager Cindy Wright has created order out of what could easily have been chaos. Every garment in every size is easy to find. Almost all items are first quality with the few men's seconds in knit shirts clearly marked. Prices generally run from $7–$12 for boys sizes 6–18. Men's casual sport clothes, in small to extra large, go from about $8–$25. The skiwear is available during fall for about 30 percent off.

Hello From California

833 S. Spring St., Room 202, Los Angeles. (213) 622-0417.
Hours: Saturdays only 9–12.
Purchases: Cash only. All sales final.
Parking: Street and area lots. Mailing list.

Moderately priced junior (sizes 3–15) and missy (sizes 6–18) dresses are the house specialty. The junior line, Hello From California, is retailed through stores such as May Co., Contempo Casuals, and Rix Rack. You can buy the same styles directly from the factory at wholesale prices averaging $16–$22. Italian Dressing is the missy equivalent and is manufactured for large chains such as Sears and J. C. Penney. Prices are $13–$18.50 for dresses in seasonal fabrics. No try-ons are allowed, and all sales are definitely final, so know your size in advance. A mailing list notifies customers of special end-of-season sales with even lower prices.

Jantzen, Inc.

7835 Canoga Ave., Canoga Park. (213) 710-1033.
Hours: Mon.-Fri. 9:30–5, second Sat. of the month, 9–2.
Purchases: Cash or cks. Exchanges.
Parking: Free lot and street.

It took a bit of sleuthing to discover this particular outlet, but it was certainly worth it; the selection and values are great. Bargains for the whole family abound here in all the current Jantzen coordinated casual and active sportswear lines. Inventory is on-season, e.g., sweaters in the winter and shorts in the summer. Large signs tell shoppers whether the merchandise is factory overruns, irregulars, or discontinued items, but check purchases carefully. The prices are considerably below wholesale for items for men, women, and children. While there are not try-ons in the store itself, you can exchange anything to insure the proper fit. Leftover yardage and notions from the Jantzen lines are for sale in a large backroom.

John Fulmer Co. Outlet Store
6868 Acco St., Montebello. (213) 722-8300.
Hours: Fridays only, 11:30–1:30.
Purchases: Cash or check. Exchanges.
Parking: Free lot.

If prices of 25 to 50 percent *below wholesale* sound good to you, the range of merchandise available at this factory store will sound even better. John Fulmer Co. is a manufacturer of moderate-price clothing for girls 3–6x, 7–14 and teens, and junior, missy, and large and half sizes for women. Labels include Title IX, John Matthew, and Positive Reaction. The merchandise is sportswear including jackets, pants, skirts, and blouses. Dressing facilities are limited, but at these prices, who's complaining?

Joy Stevens
3617 Avalon Blvd., Los Angeles. (213) 232-4761.
Hours: Sat. 9–2.
Purchases: Cash or cks. All sales final.
Parking: Street and free lot. Mailing list.

All of us dedicated, long-time Joy Stevens fans finally get a chance to go right to the source and buy to our hearts' content. Go prepared for your Saturday shopping spree with the knowledge of your size in the firm's line—Joy Stevens, Directions, Collections, and J. S. Collection—since there are no try-ons. This policy is understandable when you realize that prices here are 30–40 percent below wholesale. There's a little bit of everything available: samples of each line in size 10 (some of which turn out to be closer to size 12 in fit), overruns, order cancellations, regular stock, and a few very slight irregulars, clearly marked and priced accordingly. Sizes run from 4–14, with some mother-of-the-bride gowns sized to 16. This is a real find: go and enjoy. Mention *Glad Rags* sent you.

Judy's Warehouse Sale

7710 Haskell Ave., Van Nuys. (213) 787-0300.
2850 N. Main St., Santa Ana.
Hours: Sun. only, 8–5 (semi-annually).
Purchases: MC, VISA, AE, Store charge, cks. All sales final.
Parking: Free lot. Mailing list.

If there's one single big sale in Los Angeles that everybody knows about, this must be it. This twice-yearly event draws sleep-over crowds the night before to secure their places in line. The nice folks at Judy's even serve free coffee starting at about 6 a.m. the day of the sale to all those frenzied bargain hunters. Whoever said women won't go to any extra effort to save money on clothes simply hasn't been to Judy's Warehouse Sale. Rather than finding recreational shoppers here, the term "combat shopper" comes to mind. (It's probably not a bad idea to go into training for this one). The clock is ticking down to 8 a.m., the crowd is poised on its toes, and whoosh! The flood gates open and the tide engulfs the racks and racks of final, final markdowns of everything that hasn't sold at all sixty Judy's stores in five states during the past six months. Clothes in sizes 2–14 as well as shoes, purses, costume jewelry, and gift items can be purchased at up to 80 percent off. Everything from underwear to furs goes—all labels are left in. Often the very best buys are the reductions from the "Optimum Shop," which features fine quality garments, like silk, from top designers. Final sale items from the "Gear for Guys" departments go at the same low prices. Get yourself on the mailing list—ready, set, GO!

Lanz

6150 Wilshire Blvd., Los Angeles (Fairfax Area).
  (213) 937-1400.
Sale dates: Mid-February and mid-August.
Purchases: MC, VISA, cks. All sales final.
Parking: Area lots. Mailing list.

This is *the* sale all us Lanz fans wait so patiently for. Twice-a-year the factory notifies customers via the mail of the exact dates and hours of its special sales held at the Wilshire retail store. Only first-quality overruns in Lanz Originals dresses and

sportswear, Lanz of Salzburg nightgowns and robes, and Poppy swimwear is liquidated for 65–75 percent off retail. Sizes run from 5/6–13/14.

Mainberry

123 W. 31st., Los Angeles. (213) 746-6646.
Hours: Mon.–Fri. 9–3.
Purchases: Cash only. All sales final.
Parking: Street and free lot.

Chain-store merchandise manufactured for Sears, Montgomery Wards, and Penneys is offered to the public here at wholesale prices. Polyester and poly-blend woven fabrics make up blouses, skirts, pants, tops, and dresses for three size groups: missy 8–18, large 38–52, and regular missy maternity 8–18. Everything is first quality and sells for $7 to $15. There are no try-ons.

Mode Sport

2520 Ontario St., Burbank. (213) 843-6998.
Hours: Mon.–Fri. 9–5.
Purchases: Cash or cks. All sales final.
Parking: Free lot.

This private label junior sportswear manufacturer sells its first-quality overcuts to the public for 25–40 percent below wholesale. The labels are clipped out of all these casual dresses, sundresses, tops, skirts, and coordinated pieces in cotton knit and jersey, but they're the same ones seen at well-known local specialty and department stores. Sizes are petite through large in junior cut and styling with prices from $3 to $16 for dresses. There are no try-ons.

The Outlet (Catalina)

4600 E. Pacific Coast Highway, Long Beach. (213) 434-9788.
6015 Bandini Blvd., Commerce. (213) 724-4693.
329 N. Verdugo Rd., Glendale. (213) 242-5609.
2245 W. Ball Rd., Anaheim. (714) 956-8271.
3224 N. Garey Ave., Pomona. (714) 593-6415.
9040 Balboa Blvd., Van Nuys. (213) 894-3422.
19722 Colima Rd., Rowland Heights. (714) 594-2598.
4650 E. Chapman Ave., Orange. (714) 997-1580.
Hours: Mon.–Fri. 10–6, Sat. 10–5. Bandini only, Mon.–Fri.
   10–6, Sat. 9–4.
Purchases: MC, VISA, cks. Exchanges.
Parking: Free lot and street. Mailing list.

The stores in this particular chapter represent one of our favorite categories of bargains—direct factory-to-you savings of half and more. This factory outlet is obviously popular with consumers all over Los Angeles and Orange counties since Catalina has opened four new locations in the past two years. At every store swimwear, coordinated separates, actionwear, loungewear, and lingerie are available for 40–70 percent off. Discontinued styles and seconds in all the Catalina lines comprise the inventory. Don't let these terms scare you off. The factory may officially call these garments discontinued, but in reality you'll often see things here at about the same time they're displayed in retail stores. The blue-tagged seconds, which sell for 20 percent below wholesale, are often flawed in such a minor way you can hardly find the blemish. Prices range from $10–$30 for women's blazers, jackets, tops, blouses, sweaters, skirts, slacks, and vests in color-coordinates in pure cotton, polyester, polyester/cotton, and wool blends. You'll also find an extensive selection of Catalina coordinated tennis outfits and other active sports togs. There are Dreamaway and Eté nightgowns, robes, caftans, and poolside loungewear and lots and lots of one- and two-piece swimsuits in every imaginable style for $10–$30. In addition to the Catalina brand, you will see Bay Club of California and Eté swimwear and Kayser lingerie. Sizes are junior 7–13 and missy 8–18 in the Catalina label and 38–46 (fits 18½–26½) from the Catalina Plus line. Girls' swimwear fits infants through preteen sizes for only $6–$9. Occasionally coordinating cover-ups are available, too. Finally, men's casual sportswear comes in sizes small (28) to extra large.

Outlook (Alex Colman)

2100 Figueroa St., Los Angeles. (213) 742-1700.
Hours: Mon.–Sat. 9–5.
860 S. Los Angeles St., fifth floor. (213) 623-2503.
Hours: Mon.–Sat. 9-4:30.
Purchases: MC, VISA, cks. All sales final.
Parking: Street and free lot. Mailing list.

There's simply no better way to save on the all-popular Alex Colman lines than right here at the factory outlets. The prices are the lowest and the merchandise selection is the most extensive, as you might imagine. All of the company's labels are available: Alex Colman missy coordinated separates in sizes 8–20; Mr. Alex sportswear in large sizes 30–46; the newer Makin Trax activewear pieces in small, medium, and large and Sweet Petites sizes 4–16. All the lines sell at a brisk pace since price tags are marked at wholesale on first-quality garments. Four to forty dollars covers everything. Mailings notify customers of the semi-annual sales (about four a year) where everything is reduced another 20 percent off.

La Petite Factorie

415 W. Foothill Blvd., Suite 206B, Claremont (Old School
   House Shopping Center). (714) 621-7646.
Hours: Everyday 10–5.
Purchases: Cash or traveler's cks. All sales final.
Parking: Free lot.

This Gunne Sax factory outlet sells women's and girls' long
and short dresses, skirts, vests, blouses, tops, and jackets for
5–10 percent below *wholesale*. Most clothing is first-quality,
with a few slight irregulars clearly marked. The trademark
country-styled traditional and sweet, romantic, irrepressibly
feminine styles of Gunne Sax are popular; on the weekday
morning of our visit, the place was mobbed. It took two people
at the cash register working briskly to handle the long double
line of customers. The rest of the small shop was crowded
with shoppers selecting items from many racks of clothes.
Sizes for girls in the Jeunes Filles lines run 3–6x and 7–14.
Fashions for women are currently junior size 3–13, but designer Jessica McClintock is also introducing a more sophisticated missy line. Most prices fell in the $12–$30 range. We
even found a rack of dresses marked two for $6! The back
room, which doubles as a gang dressing room, holds fabric,
trims, and collars for sale.

Ramos Manufacturing Co.

11546 S. Prairie Ave., Hawthorne. (213) 973-0580.
Hours: Mon.–Sat. 9:30–6.
15224 Hawthorne Blvd., Lawndale. (213) 973-7248.
Hours: Mon.–Sat. 10:30–6:30.
Purchases: MC, VISA, cks. Exchanges.
Parking: Street.

Of all the discount shops and outlets selling easy-care, synthetic separates, this one is hard to beat for selection and
value. (Our families rave about the purchases we've made for
them from this store.) Proprietor Eduardo Ramos has been
making these staples of women's apparel for ten years and
prides himself on quality fabrics and construction. He proudly
points out that his garments are known for good fit and that he

uses slightly stronger knits than other similar manufacturers so his garments will last longer. Customers shop here for everything from $5 shell tops to $22 two-piece pantsuits. All merchandise is first quality and includes skirts, blouses, and jackets in woven polyester and stretch gabardine, some in tailored styles. The selection of prints in blouses is extensive and the $17 long-sleeved blouse/shell sets represent a particularly good value. The rainbow of different pants shades will delight your eye as well as your checkbook. Sizes range from 4–28. Little girls' pants in sizes 1–6x sell for $2.95, sizes 7–14 for $3.95.

Sebastian

589 Venice Blvd., Venice. (213) 392-4941.
Special semi-annual sales.
Purchases: Cks, cash. All sales final.
Parking: Free lot. Mailing list.

If you wear classically styled polyester knit sportswear, this is your sale. Two or three times a year, this popular maker of missy separates holds a warehouse clearance at its manufacturing facility. The bargains were impressive. Of all the racks and racks holding all types of pants, dresses, jacket-dresses, golf skirts, tops, sleeveless shells, and sweaters, the three-piece pantsuits for $15 seemed . . . well, how could you afford *not* to buy one? Other good values included several racks of two- and three-piece pantsuits for $25, golf skirts for $6, long dresses for $13–$20, pants for $7–$9, tops for $3. Some of these same types of garments were also available for slightly higher prices depending on fabric and styling. We did see some lovely polyester/cotton two- and three-piece ensembles for $59 and $63. Sizes run 6–16 with some 18s in polyester, poly/cotton, and acrylics. All these garments could easily work year round. Colors were mostly solids in every conceivable shade with a few stripes and plaids. Watch the West Side section of the *Los Angeles Times* for the sale announcement or call to have you name added to the mailing list.

Valley Sportswear

6104 Lankershim Blvd., North Hollywood. (213) 985-6433.
Hours: Mon.–Fri. 9–4:30, Sat. 9–4.
Purchases: Cash or cks. Exchanges only.
Parking: Street and free lot.

One of the nice things about this blouse and top outlet is the wide range of choices from a single manufacturer (who must remain anonymous—we can, however, give you a hint about the maker's identity by saying that this is a very popular main-floor department-store brand). There is a style to suit almost any taste and age bracket, and new merchandise arrives weekly. Ads are pasted on the wall to show department store prices for the same merchandise. Ladies' blouses sized 8–18 and 38–44 sell at wholesale for first-quality and less for imperfects and special items. You'll find short-sleeved and sleeveless styles in polyester and nylon for about $12–$14; long-sleeved Qiana, polyester, and cotton and polyester styles for up to $12–$16; and large-size styles for $13–$16. Fabrications are mostly solids with a few prints.

Zoe

7562 Melrose, Los Angeles. (213) 653-1691.
Hours: Mon.–Sat. 11–6. Sundays for special sales.
Purchases: MC, VISA, AE, cks. All sales final on sale merchandise.
Parking: Street. Mailing list.

Elke Lesso designs and manufactures forward-fashion sportswear under the Zoe label. Four times annually, Ms. Lesso liquidates her wholesale line of women's clothing through her store on Melrose. Describing her unique position as a manufacturer with an established retail outlet, Ms. Lesso explains her end-of-season sales: "It's much nicer and more convenient for the customer to come to the store where we're set up to sell clothes. We have dressing rooms and mirrors and it's much easier to park." Customers are notified by mail to come and take advantage of the 50 percent and more savings on trans-seasonal separates such as appliqued T-shirts ($6, reg-

ularly $26), capri pants, jackets, cotton interlock warm-up pants ($10, regularly $28), fake fur coats, and evening clothes. The only thing you won't find here is the routine—Zoe's clothes are not for the timid. Women's sizes are 4–16 and selected men's styles—primarily ambisexual activewear—are 28–34. If you'd like to meet the designer, Ms. Lesso is in the store on Saturdays whether there's a sale in progress or not.

Orange County

Backdoor Boutique
14171 Chambers Rd., Tustin. (714) 544-9360.
Hours: Thurs. 12–4:30 and the second Saturday of each
    month 10–4.
Purchases: Cash or cks. All sales final.
Parking: Street and free lot.

Too bad we can't divulge the name of the well-known manufacturer that sells its overcuts, samples, and slight irregulars here at savings of 50–80 percent. But you'd recognize this label in a minute (and the labels from other West Coast lines). Backdoor Boutique is apt: you have to go around to the rear of the manufacturing plant to enter the store, a cheerful warehouse. You help yourself to the super sales racks outside and the racks and racks of current and end-of-season items inside. Sizes range from 6–18 with a few larger sizes on occasion. There's a wide variety of garments ranging from caftans, sundresses, quilted jackets, and the usual sportswear to dressy velvets and silk-like blends and satins in holiday separates. We found garments for $2 on the final markdown racks all the way up to $45 for a quilted velvet jacket retailing for $65. Most things fall in the $5–$20 range. On our visit we had great fun pawing through three racks of holiday jackets, camisoles, and pants all for only $10 each. Manager Bob Tetters told us the prices are ridiculous, and he's right. Apparel is priced to move, so you'll always find lots of new merchandise stuffed into this small warehouse space. This is your kind of store if you enjoy the hunt, as we do.

find some forward-fashion ideas among the more traditional separates. Everything is built around a mix-and-match concept and the clothes are ideal for travel. Fabrics are purchased in Los Angeles and you may find the same shirtdress made up in several fabrications. All garments can be hand- or machine-washed and there is a good balance of prints and solids. Large-size and pregnant women will appreciate the one-size caftans and sundresses. There is no charge for hems or minor alterations—a feature the hard-to-fit woman should note. We recommend taking a look first at the sale rack where clothes are reduced an additional 40 to 50 percent below their original discount price. Sizes range from 6–16 and from small to large. There are accessories on hand to help you pull together your unique look.

Laguna Junction

Village Fair Mall, Laguna Beach (714) 497-1018.
South Coast Village, Costa Mesa. (714) 557-1579.
El Paseo Village, Palm Desert. (714) 568-0590.
Hours: Mon.–Sun. 10–6 (Laguna and Palm Desert), 10–9
   Costa Mesa.
Purchases: MC, VISA, cks. Exchanges or store credit. Layaway.
Parking: Free lots.

Designer and tailor Delorus Edwards and her husband Ed manufacture a versatile line of coordinated sportswear and retail exclusively through their own boutiques at factory-direct prices. The Laguna Junction brand is found inside their blouses (average price $28), jumpsuits ($20–$40), tunics ($28), slacks ($26–$30), skirts ($28–$36), sundresses ($30), bathing suits (under $20), one-size-fits-all caftans ($47), and more. The owners travel to Europe once a year for inspiration and you'll

Resale

The phenomenon of resale shopping began about twenty-five years ago when actresses and other wealthy women who continually update their wardrobes started selling off pieces or entire closets through resale stores. Now the trend has caught on among women of all types and professions. Resale shops continue to be excellent sources for new and hardly worn clothing, shoes, and accessories. Most resale stores work on a fifty-fifty profit split, but some buy wardrobes outright. Clothing is kept on consignment for an average of sixty days during which time it may be subject to one or two markdowns before it is sold at a fraction of original retail or removed. Store owners report that in the last two years, more and more women have discovered the advantages of recycling their wardrobes. This enables the stores to be highly selective in the merchandise they accept for resale. Thus, you'll find an even better mix of fashion-forward designer looks and timeless classics. Each store develops its own personality based on the consignees' tastes and the consignors' selectivity. Resale boutiques may specialize in maternity wear, petite or large sizes, or one-of-a-kind imported and couture pieces. Several stores in Los Angeles and Orange County also buy manufacturers' closeouts and samples. Invaluable children's resale stores in the two-county area are listed in the Children's chapter.

LA County

Amazing Kate's

28317 Agoura Rd., Agoura. (213) 991-5148.
Hours: Tues.–Fri. 10:30–4:30, Sat. 10–5:30.
Purchases: MC, VISA, cks. Exchanges. Layaway.
Parking: Free lot. Mailing list.

Karen Collins, "Amazing Kate," is the sister of Pat Cheap, the proprietor of a successful Pasadena consignment shop known as Patina. Shrewd shoppers in the Conejo Valley pay one-fourth of original retail prices for children's and women's clothes of every description. Sizes 1–14, 1–10, and 1–18 for women are lovingly squeezed into this little cottage on picturesque Agoura Road. You pregnant ladies can even find recycled maternity wear here. Prices range from $1–$75 for apparel, accessories, and shoes. Items are marked down 25 percent after thirty days in the shop and another 25 percent

after sixty days. Kate keeps a detailed list of customers' special requests and calls them when these items arrive. As in other stores of this genre, designer pieces and furs go out as quickly as they come in.

A Chic Conspiracy

7955 W. Third St., Los Angeles. (213) 934-8084.
Hours: Mon.–Fri. 10–5, Sat. 10–5.
Purchases: MC, VISA, cks. Exchanges on gift items. Layaway.
Parking: Street and behind building.

"A mini Rodeo Drive" is how Chic Conspiracy has been described by its customers. At Academy Awards time the store is jammed with women buying gowns. Fifteen notable ladies of society bought their 1981 inaugural ball gowns at this high-fashion resale boutique. "You'd be astounded at some of my resale buyers," says co-owner Roberta Magid, keeping both her customers' and consignees' names confidential. "Even the rich love a bargain. We have limousines parked out front all the time." Designer clothes in sizes 4–16 are featured and 50 percent of the clothing has never been worn. You can shop for complete wardrobes, including shoes, bags, and accessories. "We feel like a public service," laughs Mrs. Magid about the pricing. An Anne Klein jacket selling for $300 at Saks would be $100 here. A Valentino suit which retails for $1400 was selling for $239 the day of our visit and happened to be the most expensive item in the store. Other designers represented include Chloe, Yves St. Laurent, Stavropolous, Adolfo, Maud Frizon, Fendi, and Missoni. New merchandise arrives daily and there's always a sale rack to browse.

D's Potpourri

311 Main St., Seal Beach. (213) 493-1818.
Hours: Tues.–Fri. 11–6, Sat. 11–5.
Purchases: MC, VISA, cks. All sales final. Layaway.
Parking: Street.

This shop has the atmosphere of a small boutique. Throughout the store, clothes are displayed as coordinated outfits—a result of owner Dorothy Landow's long-time interest in fashion. All age groups like to shop here, particularly younger working women. Sizes go from 7–16. Shop the special month-end sales the last three days of each month when 30 percent is taken off the price tags of everything in the store. The merchandise includes all kinds of clothes, as well as furs, jewelry, accessories, and shoes. Prices range from $6–$65.

Dress-Up Shop

521 E. Arrow Highway, Azusa. (213) 331-9071.
Hours: Tues.–Sat. 12–5.
Purchases: Cash or cks. All sales final. Layaway.
Parking: Free lot.

This ten-year-old resale shop stocks a wide range of women's clothes, jewelry, and accessories. You'll occasionally find furs, but the emphasis here is on sportswear and separates by manufacturers such as Leslie Fay, R & K Originals, Graff,

Butte Knits, St. John Knits, KoKo Knits, and Alex Colman. A more mature clientele likes owner Florence Stoehr's emphasis on conservative styles at good values. You'll find more dresses and fewer pantsuits than in the past. Sizes generally run from 5–22 with some large sizes. Call Florence if you're in the market for maternity clothes and she'll notify you when they come in. Prices for most dresses and separates are $25–$35 with a few special things selling for up to $65. The shoe selection features especially low price tags: $2–$6 for good brands.

The Great Name

2315 Wilshire Blvd., Santa Monica. (213) 829-2070.
Hours: Mon.–Sat. 11–6.
Purchases: MC, VISA, cks. All sales final. Layaway.
Parking: Street and free lot. Mailing list.

The five Frost sisters and their consignment boutique are still going strong after five years in the business. They take in new and slightly worn clothing, shoes, and accessories from stars and just plain folks, and resell them on consignment for about one-half the original cost. Designers popular with the women who sell their clothes here include: Galanos, Geoffrey Beene, Pucci, Hanae Mori, Christian Dior, Esteves, Sant'Angelo, Pauline Trigere, Phyllis Sues, Norman Todd, and others. The result is a one-of-a-kind grab bag for the recreational shopper who likes to look as well as buy. The unique feature is the amount of new merchandise the store sells at wholesale prices. The sisters collect overstock and last-season merchandise from Beverly Hills boutiques. The selection of cocktail dresses and evening gowns is consistently strong. Customers have made the shoe department the most popular in the store. Price tags go from $10–$75 for a brand-new pair of Charles Jourdan boots. Sizes go from 5–10 in all widths. One particular consignee brings in her 6½ Maud Frizons and Charles Jourdans and you can imagine they don't last long.

Jean's Star Apparel

15136 Ventura Blvd., Sherman Oaks. (213) 789-3710.
Hours: Mon.–Sat. 10–6.
Purchases: MC, VISA, cks. Exchanges. Layaway.
Parking: Street and rear lot. Mailing list.

Owner Jean Harding began her shop twenty-two years ago with purchases from actresses, hence the store's name. Today her merchandise comes exclusively from wealthy women in Beverly Hills and Bel Air. Some of the very best designers are represented here: Adolfo, Chloe, Yves St. Laurent, Geoffrey Beene, Bill Blass, Oscar de la Renta, Missoni, Jean Muir, Halston, Gucci, Thea Porter, and Zandra Rhodes. Sizes run from 3/4–15/16. Jean cautions that some of the very best designers' things come from slender ladies' closets. If you're a 12 or 14, you might not find quite as many Adolfos in your size. We've listed all these designers names because the store's inventory is shifting gradually to more and more designer merchandise. And we figured you fashion-conscious Glad Raggers like to know where to find some of these labels, especially the European ones. The clothes are in exceptionally fine shape and some are only three or four months old.

Lana & Sybil's Wardrobe

18125 Ventura Blvd., Tarzana. (213) 881-2130.
Hours: Mon.–Sat. 10–5.
Purchases: MC, VISA, cks. All sales final. Layaway.
Parking: Free lot. Mailing list.

Like the proprietors of other really good resale shops around Los Angeles, owner Lana Lampert stocks her cozy store with the clothes of entertainers and wealthy women who have cultivated taste in fine designer labels. The clothes—in excellent condition and well displayed—range widely in style and selection. Cashmere sweaters, pantsuits, jumpsuits, jackets, coats, evening dresses, at-home wear, and furs can all be found at tremendous savings. Check the yellow sale tags for super markdowns. Prices average about 20–50 percent off original retail. Better stores and labels are represented here including Alan Austin, Phyllis Sues, Blassport, Cacharel, Giorgio, Capriotti, Jones New York, and Norman Todd. Since Lana is well connected to the entertainment industry through her producer father and family, she often gets great deals on entire television show wardrobes. Along with belts, scarves, bags, and hats, Lana & Sybil's Wardrobe features a large selection of good costume jewelry and current-style shoes.

Patina

511 S. Glendale Ave., Glendale. (213) 246-7018.
Hours: Tues. and Wed. 11–7, Thurs. and Fri. 11–5, Sat. 10–5.
Purchases: MC, VISA, cks. Exchanges within five days.
  Layaway.
Parking: Free lot. Mailing list.

This cute cottage with its yellow and white shutters, antique furniture, and lace curtains is a refreshing reminder that discount shopping can be fun as well as practical. Appealing clothes tumble out of trunks and armoires; the selection is excellent. The active mother, working woman, and community volunteer will find many items to round out her wardrobe because most of the clothes are brought in by these types of women. New and used items are sold for one-third their original cost. Owner Pat Cheap and her daughter Karen try to keep merchandise current and aren't above refusing items they won't be able to sell to their discriminating customers. Eighty-five percent of the clothes are made of natural fibers: cotton, linen, and wool, with a special emphasis on silk. Unusual pieces, designer labels, and imports from France, Germany and Italy make up a good portion of the inventory. You'll find Cacharel, Jaeger, Valentino, Alan Austin, Missoni, and YSL, as well as Anne Klein, Jag, and lots of Paul Stanley. Occasionally both petite and large sizes are available. A good selection of maternity clothes in better labels (even some European) can always be found here. Brand-new shoes and those with little wear sell for $8–$20 in sizes 5–10. If you're fond of Maud Frizons but don't like to pay full retail, this is the place to pick them up, along with other similar brands.

The Place

8820 S. Sepulveda Blvd., Westchester. (213) 645-1539.
Hours: Mon.–Sat. 10–5:30.
Purchases: MC, VISA, cks. All sales final. Layaway.
Parking: Street and free lot. Mailing list.

Because they have been in business for eighteen years, owners Maureen Clavin and Joyce Brock have helped popularize the entire designer resale boutique concept in Los Angeles. Several hundred celebrities and wealthy socialites regularly clean out their closets for Maureen and Joyce. Consequently, you will find the best designer names from all the chic Beverly Hills boutiques. The sizes are mostly missy in clothes that are in top-notch shape and generally current season. You will find shoes, bags, belts, scarves, and jewelry, too. The saleswomen are talented in helping you put together complete outfits. Most of the clothes are priced at 75 percent off the original retail prices. The store features three rooms, the two in the rear doubling as large, comfortable dressing rooms (men are restricted to the front room). The pantsuit room in the rear also has shoes and the middle room holds slacks, skirts, and jackets. The furs alone are such a buy, they're worth the trip. Lots of great, stylish evening dresses and outfits find their way here, too. Maureen and Joyce have added a special feature to the store: they now carry top California designers' (sorry we can't name names) overruns at wholesale.

Re-Run Plus

372 E. Thousand Oaks Blvd., Thousand Oaks. (805) 495-5553.
Hours: Tues. 12:30–5, Wed.–Fri. 10–5, Sat. 10–2.
Purchases: MC, VISA, cks. All sales final. Layaway.
Parking: Free lot.

Peggy Thompson admits that she got the idea for opening up her store from her twelve grandchildren. She started reselling children's clothes, shoes, and furniture three years ago and has since expanded to include women's apparel and accessories. Good news for you expectant mothers—Peggy carries recycled maternity wear. Size ranges for both women and children are broad: 0–16 for boys, through preteens for girls, and women's small through extra-large. Prices start at 50¢ for infants' undershirts and go up to about $10 for coats and jackets. Peggy gets children's ski boots, sleepwear, toys, games, and baby blankets. As we've discovered elsewhere,

the infants' high chairs, cribs, and car seats don't last long once they come into the store. If you're looking for these items, have Peggy put you on her special "call list." Women's clothing averages about $25 with evening dresses and an occasional fur running higher. There's always plenty of merchandise on sale as a result of the thirty- and sixty-day markdowns.

Second Time Around

3844 E. Foothill Blvd., Pasadena. (213) 449-8658.
Hours: Mon.–Thurs. 10–5, Fri. & Sat. 10–6.
Purchases: MC, cks. All sales final. Layaway.
Parking: Street.

On a warm winter's day when it seemed the temperature in sunny Southern California would never again drop below 80 degrees, we bought three winter coats: two wool (one designed by Paulene Trigere) and one cashmere—all for $30. This kind of bargain is admittedly special, but represents the substantial savings you can enjoy on dresses, separates, shoes, costume jewelry, and furs (from September–February). New and recycled clothes are mixed together. Store owner Gloria buys merchandise from stores that are going out of business, and samples. She carries petite to large sizes and prices are generally one-third of retail and below. For example, an S. Howard Hirsch white crepe dress with an original price tag of $80 was marked down to $30. There's always a half-price rack with dresses under $10.

Second Time Around

3776 Pacific Coast Highway, Torrance. (213) 378-8115.
Hours: Mon.–Fri. 11–5, Sat. 10–5.
Purchases: Cash or cks. All sales final. Layaway.
Parking: Street and rear lot. Mailing list.

More and more labels from designers and better stores find their way to the racks of Second Time Around. Pat Carmer and Harriett Wachrow continually upgrade their inventory as better and better things come in from consignees. Lines common to the shop are Evan Picone, Blyle, Dorce, Anne Klein, Butte Knits, Kimberly, John Meyer, Givenchy, and Breckenridge. They even get quite a few things with the Mr. Blackwell label. Quality continues to be the key policy here. Only gently worn garments are accepted in freshly cleaned condition. The price range is broad—$1.50 for some of the costume jewelry pieces to $175 for the evening ensembles or furs. Sizes go from 5–20. The shoe section continues to be one of the store's strong points with a good selection of nearly new footwear in lines like Ferragamo. All in all, these two ladies run a first-rate store, certainly one you should visit.

Stars & Debs

12424 Ventura Blvd., Studio City. (213) 980-7433.
Hours: Tues.–Fri. 11-4:30, Sat. 10–4.
Purchases: MC, VISA, cks. All sales final. Layaway.
Parking: Street. Mailing list.

Sportswear is the specialty of this first-rate shop begun fourteen years ago by Rose Polinsky and her daughter Michelle. The separates, along with suits and dresses, are purchased from well-to-do socialites and actresses. Career women especially like to shop Stars & Debs. Rose notes that more and more silk pieces, especially blouses and dresses, are sold in the shop. Prices generally run from as low as $3–$70 for the best items in a size range of 4–16. Look for designer labels such as Galanos, Diane Von Furstenberg, Geoffrey Beene, Bill Blass, Alan Austin, Anne Klein, Holly Harp, Yves St. Laurent, and Calvin Klein. The store has an unusually large selection of good shoe values in recent styles for up to $15 for lines like Ferragamo.

That Special Shop

8749 La Tijera Blvd. (near Manchester and Sepulveda), Los Angeles. (213) 670-3441.
Hours: Tues.–Sat. 10–5.
Purchases: MC, VISA, cks. All sales final. Layaway.
Parking: Street and rear lot.

There is a wider range of styles to choose from and a more comprehensive selection *within* each category than at almost any other resale shop we've had the privilege to visit. Like other fine stores in this league, That Special Shop accepts only garments in good condition (some items are brand new, with original price tags) boasting better manufacturer and store labels. An illustration of our point: the large rack of blazers in various colors and cuts we found at the front of the store featured just four labels: Anne Klein, Alan Austin, Calvin Klein, and Evan Picone. All were priced $50–$60. Expect to pay about one-fourth of original retail for clothing in sizes 3–20. Owner Renee Jast advises that the selection in sizes 8 and 10 is especially good. The result of Renee's thirty-five years of retailing experience is a cozy boutique with lots of interesting nooks and crannies to explore. The long and short evening dress sections and shoes (!) hold the most interesting values. We still lust after a $16 pair of Charles Jourdans. Wardrobe departments from several movie and television studios recycle here and a number of apparel buyers bring in brand-new things ahead of season. As for customers, Renee sometimes sends a taxi to the airport to fetch loyal ladies who like to shop at That Special Shop while they're in town on business.

The Tree Top

11542 E. Whittier Blvd., Whittier. (213) 692-1017.
Hours: Tues.–Sat. 10–5:30.
Purchases: MC, VISA, cks. All sales final. Layaway.
Parking: Street and free lot. Mailing list.

Since we first told you about The Tree Top, it's been purchased by a mother-daughter duo, Edith Giardina and Cecelia Nelsen. They have retained the store's informal atmosphere that's so popular with the loyal customers who come to shop and chat. The shop features recent fashions like other resale shops, as well as antique garments such as Japanese kimonos. Customers come in on Tuesdays to put their clothes on sixty-day consignment. During the last two weeks of the consignment, items are marked down and added to the sale rack. The best-selling items come from one particular clothes-conscious consignee who does most of her shopping at I. Magnin. Prices at The Tree Top start as low as $1.50 for blouses and go up to $125 for better things. The store also features jewelry (with an emphasis on the antique), a few pieces of antique furniture, and bric-a-brac.

Two Timer

141 N. Maryland Ave., Glendale. (213) 242-1650.
Hours: Mon.–Sat. 10:30–5.
Purchases: MC, VISA, cks. All sales final. Layaway.
Parking: Street and area lots.

Kitty Kiernan recently moved her shop across the street to more spacious quarters which allowed her to double the inventory and generally give the Two Timer a whole fresh new feeling. Three-fourths of the stock is made up of good-quality used clothing in junior and missy sizes 3–22. The balance of the inventory comes from new goods that Kitty buys specially from manufacturers and sells at 30–70 percent off. The new things are mostly sportswear and sweaters, but the resale merchandise includes every type of clothing, shoes, and accessories. Kitty likes to use the term "affordable quality" when she talks about the store. This is a good way to sum up the values, most of which fall in the $7–$25 range. She also carries blouses and pants for sizes 38–42. On the first of every month, one-third of everything in the store is marked down for that month, so you'll always find a sale in progress.

Whisper

11630 Ventura Blvd., Studio City. (213) 762-3658.
Hours: Mon.–Sat. 11–7.
Purchases: MC, VISA, cks. Exchanges only. Layaway.
Parking: Street and rear lot.

This is the clotheshorse's clothes store. From the elegant, cool grey art deco layout to the neatly arranged and categorized racks of fine resale and vintage garments, it's obvious that owner Claire Roylance herself loves clothes and enjoys operating this store for others who do, too. Claire's husband is also involved in the business, and there are some men's antique garments here as well as women's apparel in sizes

3–14. We could have easily been seduced into browsing all afternoon through the Basiles, Adolfos, Geoffrey Beenes, Halstons, Chloes, Missonis, and Sonia Rykiels, to name a few of the better, designer labels among the resale selection. Most goods in this category sell for $15–$40, the Sonia Rykiel sweaters for only $30–$35. Coats and evening ensembles usually sell for more, although we spotted a classy Halston for a mere $30. Through her connections, Claire can offer a few new goods like Norman Todd blouses at great savings, too. The antique clothes run the gamut from shoes (150 pairs of *new* Andrew Geller alligator pumps in sizes 5½–11 for only $25 a pair), to '40s plastic handbags, suits, '40s jackets, furs, swimsuits . . . we could go on and on. Claire must have a sixth sense for turning up fabulous caches of old gems including lots of old new things—like capri pants and skirts that have never been worn for only $15 and $20. Claire says her favorite era is the '50s, so that must be why that decade is particularly well represented. Other finds include Lilli Ann suits—Claire found a whole warehouse full of them and brand-new mini skirts from the early '60s. As you can well imagine, the local movie and television costumers love Whisper. So will you (but don't say it too loud).

Orange County

Encore
517 N. Harbor Blvd., Fullerton. (714) 871-0852.
Hours: Tues.–Sat. 11–5.
Purchases: MC, VISA, cks. All sales final. Layaway.
Parking: Street and rear lot.

The store's promotional flyer says: "Discover this unique clothing store that has everything from designer apparel and furs to used Levi's for resale from 50¢ to ???" We couldn't have summed it up better. Unique it is. First of all, you'll find all types of current styles from the finer closets in Orange County, Pasadena, and Beverly Hills. What's unusual is that owner Lou Bach's resale clientele also bring in their best antique garments, mostly from the 1940s and '50s. The antique items include furs, suits, beaded sweaters, handbags, hats, and

good jewelry; all are in fine condition at fair prices. There's so much to see, it's a wonder we spent only an hour and a half here. But here's the best and most exciting part: this is where a dozen of the most chi chi Orange County retail boutiques and specialty stores liquidate their end-of-season merchandise (the stuff that doesn't sell after the second or third markdown). Lou displays these goodies on her Carte Blanche rack at the front of the store. Don't let the terms "end-of-the-season" or "third markdown" scare you off. We snapped up a $260 Bagatelle turquoise pigskin jacket for only $90, saw $500 Giorgio Sant'Angelo dresses for $135 and fashions from Harve Benard, Christine Albers, and John Anthony.

Patsy's Clothes Closet

1525 N. Main St., Santa Ana. (714) 542-0189.
Hours: Mon.–Fri. 10–5:30, Sat. 10–4.
Purchases: MC, VISA, cks. All sales final. Layaway.
Parking: Street and rear lot.

This is another one of those shopping experiences you have to see to believe. The bottom thirteen rooms of this converted hospital (circa 1904) comprise a unique resale and sample shop run by Patsy Fowler. It's obvious that she and her salesladies have a ball helping customers find what they want and seeing that they enjoy themselves. The coffee pot is always on and snacks are set out—they serve wine as the day winds down. The front rooms are filled with Breckenridge, Jones New York, Anne Klein, Simple Elegance, Pipe Dreams, and Singer & Spicer samples in sizes 5–10 for half-off retail. You'll find lingerd shoes (Andrew Geller 5 and 5½ samples) in one room, and next door better long and short evening dresses and ensembles. We discovered a whole rack of black dresses for every occasion. The jewelry ranges from $1 for costume pieces to $500 for fine jewelry. The selection of evening shoes and bags is especially good. The back rooms are filled with every garment imaginable, including whole sections of coats, an antique chest full of lingerie, and even leotards and swimwear. You'll find items for any season year round. Blouses and pants are arranged by color and size. Patsy knows how to keep her 3,000 customers and 1,200 active resale accounts happy. She frequently hosts fashion shows in the store and at her home. She recently went on a cruise with seventy other

Orange County area residents and outfitted thirty of the women for the entire trip. While prices for resale items (50 percent of original retail) are higher than most of the other resale stores we've visited, the vast selection makes this a must on your shopping itinerary.

Play It Again

1854 S. Coast Hwy., Laguna Beach. (714) 494-7979.
Hours: Mon. 1–5, Tues.–Sat. 10–5.
Purchases: MC, VISA, cks. All sales final. One-day hold.
Parking: Free lot behind building. Mailing list.

The coffee pot is always on in this quaint, two-story cottage consignment "shoppe" run by owner Elke Standish. The merchandise for sale reflects the owner's classic good taste and we particularly recommend shopping here for suits (none priced over $50 the day of our visit). Prices on all garments, including sportswear, coats and blazers, one- and two-piece dresses, blouses, sweaters, and evening gowns are extremely reasonable. Clothes are from better designers and department stores—Anne Klein, Evan Picone, Charlotte Ford, Givenchy, Oscar de la Renta, and Norman Todd are well represented. Outfits are displayed with accessories to give shoppers fashion inspiration. All garments are cleaned and pressed and in impeccable condition. Sizes range from 3–14 with a good selection of 8s, 10s, and 12s and a few 15s and 16s. Consignees must pick up unsold clothes after two months, so there is always new merchandise to discover. Elke does not accept shoes or lingerie, but in every other area the tailored woman will be satisfied by this classy resale boutique.

Play It Again Fashions

235 N. Euclid, Fullerton. (714) 526-3888.
Hours: Mon.–Fri. 10–6, Sat. 10–5.
Purchases: MC, VISA, cks. All sales final. Layaway.
Parking: Shopping center lot. Mailing list.

We never cease to be amazed at the variety and imagination of discount stores. Play It Again specializes in new and used square dance attire, as well as men's and women's Western apparel and accessories. Owner Bonnie Lee also has slightly irregular Rochelle sweaters (also samples and closeouts) at half price and Ample Togs (large-size) seconds at considerable discount. The size range is 3/4–52! This happily crowded store is a browser's delight. We came upon a Lilli Ann three-piece wool blend suit for $14.50 and a three-piece department store knit for $3. There's a rack of pretty crinolines in rainbow colors for $22 and up, a rack of original square dance dresses and another recycled for $6.50–$30. Large-size blouses are $2.50–$11 and used polyester pants in sizes to 46 are $1.50–$6.50. Costume jewelry, shoes, accessories, and even furs can be found here. There are three preferred-customers sales during the year, as well as weekly specials.

Recycled Rags by Lil' Audrey

2731 E. Coast Hwy., Corona del Mar. (714) 675-5553.
Hours: Mon.–Sat. 10–6, Sun. 12–5.
Purchases: MC, VISA, cks. All sales final.
Parking: Street and rear lot.

Owner Audrey Patterson has been in business ten years. She has attracted over 4300 accounts (including Cher's) with the number of consignees still growing. There are never any special sales, because women snatch up recent, designer-made clothes at one-third to one-half off the original ticket price. This resale shop is distinguished by its more forward-fashion clothes from European designers such as Koos Van den Akker and local talents such as Marlene Stewart for Covers. The classic woman will appreciate Adolfo suits and dresses, and St. John knits (two- and three-piece suits priced at $120–$140 the day of our visit). Audrey also gets men's and women's samples from Levi's. The men's corner featured (new) sample-sized 40 regular men's jackets and safari suits as well as recycled suits and jackets. Women can choose from designers such as Calvin Klein, Anne Klein, Bill Blass,

Galanos, Donald Brooks, and more. You'll find everything from evening gowns and beaded bags to skiwear and tennis skirts. Prices range from 50¢ to $5,000; sizes are 4–14, and clothes are only kept on the floor for thirty days.

Re Runs

205 W. Whittier Blvd., La Habra. (213) 697-8864.
Hours: Tues.–Sat. 10:30–5:30.
Purchases: MC, VISA, cks. Exchanges only. Layaway.
Parking: Street and rear lot.

It's stores like this one that remind us why resale shops continue to be perennial favorites with dedicated bargain hunters. Where else can you shop in a boutique atmosphere for nearly new clothes from all the best lines for one-third the original retail prices? Like other good consignment stores, Re Runs offers a full array of dresses, coats, accessories, sports and activewear in sizes 1–18. Owner Patty Armenta offers an extra service that's made her a favorite among her custom-ers, especially girls from local high schools. She rents beautiful formals, long gowns, and wedding dresses for only $25 (they can also be purchased). We saw a lovely wedding dress for $49 and another beaded, lace ensemble complete with veil for $79. Most things in the store sell for $5–$20; special items, designer labels, and furs go for more. We found an interesting two-piece Calvin Klein outfit for $35. The shoes are especially good values. They're neatly arranged by size and sell for $4–$19 and most have hardly been worn. There are a few racks of girls' clothes for $2–$15. Patty enjoys hosting fashion shows at local country clubs featuring Re Runs clothes modeled by her customers. She keeps up with all the latest fashion magazines and attends trade fashion shows so that she can offer the best and most current fashion assistance to her clientele, many of whom go back ten years to the store's opening.

Second Time Around No. 1

440 E. 17th St., Costa Mesa. (714) 642-8988.
Hours: Mon.–Sat. 11–5.
Purchases: Cks or cash. All sales final. Layaway.
Parking: Street and rear lot.

Recycled clothes on consignment, samples, and closeout inventories coexist comfortably under owner Earlene Abbott's watchful eye. Her shrewd buying makes this an exciting store to shop. We succumbed to a new red angora sweater for $20 that we couldn't touch at retail for less than $60. Better and designer clothes are hung together and garments are grouped by type: e.g., evening gowns hang together on one rack and blouses on another. Shoes range from $4–$20 and you might get lucky and find a hat and bag to match. Prices are very reasonable. Day dresses range from $10–$14, pants average $8, and tennis dresses (some new) are $8–$12 (regularly $30–$40). Clothes are marked down after thirty days and forty-five days, and nothing stays in the store longer than two months. Like most owners of good resale shops, Earlene will call customers when merchandise arrives she thinks they will like.

Second Time Around No. 2

432 32nd., Newport Beach. (714) 675-2864.
Hours: Mon.–Sat. 10–4:30.
Purchases: Cks or cash. All sales final. Layaway.
Parking: Street.

Hazel Little has owned this charming resale boutique for four years, but it has been in business since 1967. (This store has no connection to Second Time Around No. 1 in Costa Mesa.) Their track record proves that shoppers gravitate toward quality and value—both of which are offered here. We were immediately attracted by a stunning mint green and lavender window display coordinated from clothes, shoes, and accessories from the store. Eyeing an Adrienne Vittadini hand-knit sweater for $24, we hurried inside to discover that a shopper could easily outfit herself top-to-toe for $100 or less. On a warm winter day, sweaters were a particularly good buy, but clothes are continually marked down to keep the inventory fresh. We found tempting costume jewelry and lots of belts (new leather belts for $4). The flowered wallpaper, neatly arranged floor space, and regular clientele give this resale shop a homey, comfortable feeling. No wonder women are known to shop here twice-a-year for their complete wardrobes. Sizes range from 3–16 with a particularly good selection of 8s and 10s.

2nds Ltd.

1178 North Coast Hwy., Laguna Beach. (714) 494-0555.
Hours: Mon.–Sat. 11–5, Sun. 12–4.
Purchases: MC, VISA, cks. All sales final. Layaway.
Parking: Street and rear lot.

Customers and consignees of this unique and exciting store are artists and world travelers and the clothes represent their imagination and taste. Rarely have we seen such an interesting mix of old and new, familiar and unique. Clothes are attractively displayed in armoires, chests, and trunks. Old linen sets are folded lovingly and stored in an armoire drawer beneath hanging antique dresses, suits, and jackets (under $50). Drawers of a steamer trunk with echoes of Gypsy Rose Lee hold lingerie, swimsuits, and new and old kid gloves for $5–$8. Costume jewelry, scarves, belts, and shoes are strategically placed around the room. We couldn't resist a pair of new Pancaldi sandals in blush pink for $24. Owner Rose Ortiz buys Levi Strauss samples (size 10) and sells the jeans, pants, skirts, dresses, jackets, and blouses for half of retail. There is also a good selection of tennis dresses averaging $10, and sportswear separates in sizes 4–18. Loungewear, including caftans, robes and peignoir sets, average $20. Rose has more furs than any other resale store. Full-length coats average $300–$600, stoles and capes $100–$150, and hats and collars are under $50.

Antique clothing used to mean anything made before 1950, but with the rediscovery of the Eisenhower decade and now the popularity of the early '60s mod look, definitions are blurring. The price of antique clothing has escalated since *Glad Rags I.* Hawaiian shirts that used to sell for $15–$35 are now $45–$90, but there are still good values to be found. The quality of fabric and workmanship common in the better antique stores listed in this chapter is impossible to duplicate today at comparable prices. Besides being a good source for unique collector's pieces, antique stores are also valuable for classic silhouettes, such as a Chanel suit or fur coat, that remain fashionable over time. Again, each store is unique and may specialize in a particular era or look: you'll find everything from classics to costumes. Many antique stores do alterations and offer expert advice on dry cleaning. Since these clothes are one-of-a-kind, this chapter is dedicated to the budget-conscious clothes connoisseur.

LA County

Aaardvark's Odd Ark

1516 Pacific Ave., Venice. (213) 392-2996.
Hours: Mon.–Sun. 11–6.
7579 Melrose Ave., Los Angeles. (213) 655-6769.
Hours: Mon.–Sat. 10–6, Sun. 11–6.
810 Hermosa Ave., Hermosa Beach. (213) 376-3688.
Hours: Mon.–Sun. 11–6.
3906 W. Sunset Blvd., Los Angeles. (213) 663-2867.
Hours: Mon.–Sat. 10–6, Sun. 12–5.
21435 Sherman Way, Canoga Park. (213) 999-3211.
Hours: Mon.–Sat. 11–7, Sun. 11–5.
Purchases: MC, VISA, cks. Exchanges.
Parking: Street.

When people think of antique clothes, Aaardvark's comes to mind. The store's four convenient locations have been in operation for over a decade and are favorite shopping stops for all kinds of customers. There's a broad mix of merchandise and quality priced accordingly. A few things, which have seen better days, go for low, bargain prices while really rare finds carry higher price tags. In other words, you can spend any amount from $1 to $1,000 here for every single type of clothing for men and women. As you can imagine, the inventory in every store is huge. If you like to browse, you'll love it. If you're pressed for time or hunting for something special, ask one of the knowledgeable, friendly salespeople for help. Besides selling old clothes, owner Joe Stromei likes to dabble in designing and manufacturing clothes from time to time under his own labels. He's recently offered copies of Hawaiian shirts for $10 and satin and velour jackets for $35.

Auntie Mame's House of Fame

1102 S. La Cienega Blvd., Los Angeles. (213) 652-8430.
Hours: Mon.–Sat. 11–5.
Purchases: MC, VISA, cks. All sales final. Layaway.
Parking: Street and rear lot.

Run by owners Estella and Louis Goldstein, this shop features women's clothing from the Victorian era through the 1950s—all in good condition. Stella, who claims to love anything antique, buys from wholesale sources, antique stores, and from individuals. While the store's merchandise includes evening and daytime dresses, jackets, suits, coats, sweaters, blouses, and shirts, the real specialty is the extensive selection of fur coats and jackets of all kinds. The prices range from $100–$1,000 for mouton, lamb, mink, raccoon, squirrel, broadtail, seal, and fox. The rest of the store's merchandise sells for $12–$75 with a few rare items like silk robes and rare Victorian pieces going for more. Besides truly antique items from several decades back, Stella also sells classic dressy sportswear from the past few years. Working women like to save money on their career wardrobes by shopping at Auntie Mame's for these things. Costume rentals of all kinds are a favorite with customers.

The Goldsteins have also opened a men's vintage clothing store called Peabody's next door at 1102½ S. La Cienega. The selection here is quite good and we recommend it to men who like to add a flash from the past to their closets.

Bingo!

5730 Melrose, Los Angeles. (213) 463-6229.
Hours: Wed.–Sat. 12–6.
Purchases: Cks and cash only. Exchanges on gift purchases.
Parking: Free lot behind building.

Bingo! is an off-shoot of one of our favorite *Glad Rags* stores, Repeat Performance. Owner Jean Gould opened her second store to serve a young, new-wave clientele interested in inexpensive, fun clothes from the 1950s and '60s. Women's dresses average $10–$20 for day dresses and $22–$40 for evening gowns. Blouses are $5–$7 and sweaters about $14. Men's clothes are an especially good buy with jackets as low

as $15. Accessorize yourself in go-go boots for $10 and costume jewelry for 25¢–$7. If you're wondering where silver glitter platform shoes go to rest, look here.

Choux

1505 W. Washington Blvd., Venice. (213) 396-0166.
Hours: Tues.–Sat. 12–6, Sun. 12–5. (Sunday hours may vary).
Purchases: MC, VISA, cks. All sales final.
Parking: Street. Mailing list.

Owner Chrystal Smithline specializes in "contemporary-looking" vintage clothing from the 1930s–'50s. "You don't have to look like you're wearing a costume," she says of her classics. You can also find turn-of-the-century through early '60s "mod" apparel. Choux carries a good selection of small sizes (hard to find in antique stores), and we highly recommend the shoes and accessories collection. Shoes, including

cowboy boots for men and women, are priced between $15 and $50. Chrystal says that many of her customers are designers and they help her stay ahead of fashion trends. Thus, you can have the real McCoy while others are wearing knockoffs. Prices are reasonable for quality goods. Check out the bathing suits and trunks from the '40s and '50s priced between $5 and $25. There's always a sale rack out front with $1–$5 bargains.

Cinema Glamour Shop

343 N. La Brea Ave., Los Angeles (213) 933-5289.
Hours: Mon.–Fri. and the first Sat. of each month, 10–4.
Purchases: Cash or cks. All sales final.
Parking: Street.

Tourists and locals have been frequenting this shop since it opened twelve years ago. They flock here to buy clothes brought in by actresses and other women involved in the entertainment industry. All proceeds go to the Motion Picture and Television Fund. The merchandise, which is very carefully selected from donations, features current fashions in all kinds of sportswear, evening ensembles, and furs. Manager Betty Huff says the inventory shows a trend toward more dresses and fewer pants and she notes she's selling more furs than ever before. Prices range from $15–$60 for apparel in sizes 6–12. Shoes average about $10–$15. Men's clothing is also sold here. Suits are priced up to $45. The "better room" holds racks of special treasures, which might include gift items or entire wardrobes.

Junk For Joy

5065 Lankershim Blvd., North Hollywood. (213) 761-5414.
Hours: Tues.–Sat. 12–6, Sun. 1–6.
Purchases: MC, VISA, AE, cks. All sales final. Layaway.
Parking: Street. Mailing list.

If you're alert to the latest fashion looks, love antique clothes, and can mix the two to create a unique style, you've found a shopping paradise in Junk For Joy. Owner Ron Ede also runs a successful vintage clothing wholesale operation and selects the gems from among his vast stock for this retail shop. An example of creating a contemporary silhouette from vintage goods was the entire rack of jodhpurs on display the day of our visit (it was not by accident that jodhpurs were simultaneously hot fashion here and in Europe). Ron prides himself on offering a greater range of merchandise than most other antique clothes stores. He caters to connoisseurs of fine garments from the 1940s–'60s. Wardrobe people from "The Idolmaker," and the latest remake of "Tarzan" along with several television shows outfit their productions here due to the broad selection of both men's and women's clothes, accessories, and shoes.

The Junk Store

11900 Wilshire Blvd., West Los Angeles. (213) 479-7413.
Hours: Mon.–Sat. 12–6, Sun. 12–5:30.
Purchases: MC, VISA, cks. All sales final.
Parking: Street. Mailing list.

"Fine vintage apparel" is Junk Store owner Jerry Brownstein's motto. The classic, tailored looks from the 1930s and '40s remain a steady favorite with the antique clothes lovers who frequent this shop. There's a lot of merchandise displayed here so you might ask for assistance if you're hunting for something in particular. Two full-time restoration seamstresses make sure garments are in tip-top shape before they're hung out for the public. Prices are just a bit more than you might find at other vintage clothes shops, but the quality is correspondingly higher, so you do get more for your money. Most day dresses sell for $30–$80 and jackets for $20–$30. The "u-do-it-2-it" racks hold fixer-uppers and items with minor flaws for $2–$15.

L. A. Woman

881 Alma Real Dr., Pacific Palisades. (213) 459-7116.
Hours: Mon.–Sat. 10–6.
Purchases: MC, VISA, cks. All sales final.
Parking: Street and area lot.

After a stint in Westwood, owner Sally Ball has reopened her shop in Pacific Palisades. She's kept the same cozy Victorian boutique feeling and her many loyal customers feel right at home in the new digs. Every type of fine-quality antique clothing dating from the turn-of-the-century through the 1950s is displayed here. Sally has an especially discerning eye when it comes to selecting merchandise for her shop. She often has very special things from Hollywood's glamour era of the 1920s and '30s. In addition, Sally is talented in putting whole outfits together by combining pieces from different decades to create a unique look. Most clothing sells for $25–$35 with silk garments, evening gowns, furs, kimonos, and other fine pieces going for more. She has also added a rack of new clothes at 10–15 percent off. If you like vintage clothing, L.A. Woman should be added to your list of resources.

La Rue Clothes of Yesterday

5320 Lankershim Blvd., North Hollywood. (213) 762-2072.
Hours: Mon.–Sat. 10:30–5:30.
Purchases: MC, VISA, cks. Exchanges only. Layaway.
Parking: Street and rear lots.

La Rue has three things going for it that distinguish it from most other antique clothes shops: good selection (size and style) in many types of garments (we could have fallen for any one of the superb '40s jackets); the excellent condition of the garments (we found the cleaning tags still on a couple of pieces); and the reasonable prices (15–20 percent below prices in comparable shops). Prices for most sweaters, jackets, day dresses, suits, evening gowns, lingerie, and coats were in the $15–$60 range. In addition to a broad selection of women's and men's clothes from the 1920s to the '50s, there is an unusually large assortment of fine old accessories. Besides the usual lingerie—including slips, nightgowns, robes and kimonos—we found some Merry Widows and crinolines. Perhaps the most special clothes are the evening gowns, dresses, and coats. During our visit, a couple of young women bought 1950s nylon net bouffant prom dresses from the $15–$25 rack of the same at the front of the store. The fur coats come and go quickly. You'll find several wool coats with fur trim and a large glass case protecting the many fine fur collars, stoles, and short jackets.

Lila's

25 N. Fair Oaks, Pasadena. (213) 966-6842.
Hours: Mon.–Sun. 10:30–5.
Purchases: Cash only. Store credit. Thirty-day layaway.
Parking: Street. Mailing list.

The dark, cavernous interior jammed with used men's and women's clothing from the 1920s–'60s makes this store seem forbidding. In fact, it's quite a lot a fun to poke around through this melange of merchandise (including shoes, jewelry, and accessories) if you have the time and inclination to hunt for a diamond in the rough. We found ours—a 1930s wool Catalina swimsuit for $10 that could double this season as a playsuit. Unfortunately, none of the $8 tank suits from a YMCA inventory fit—the syle reminded us of Norma Kamali's current designs. Prices and quality vary considerably, but the dedicated will enjoy the hunt.

Lily et Cie

8121 W. Third St., Los Angeles. (213) 852-0667.
Hours: Thurs., Fri., & Sat. 11–6, Mon. & Wed. 11–7, and by appointment.
Purchases: MC, VISA, All sales final. Layaway.
Parking: Street.

We guess that many of you believe as we do that clothing is an art form, and we want to share a discovery. This is a store unlike any other we've included in *Glad Rags*. It's really a store-within-a-store for the true clothes connoisseur. Lily et Cie is a fashion museum where collector's pieces such as a strapless, bias-cut Vionnet gown made of black hammered satin can not only be admired, but purchased. The tariff for such items as custom-made silk lingerie from the '30s (never worn), and elaborate seventy-five year old Chinese wedding skirts with "forbidden stitch" embroidery start at $125. Not a bargain you say? Well, it costs nothing to look, and proprietor-collector Rita is a knowledgeable tour guide through the history of fashion. The bulk of her antique designer collection is shown by appointment only, but there are many items in stock that make a drop-in visit worthwhile. We were tempted by her excellent selection of costume jewelry at $2.50–$50. The showcase was stocked with sparkling rhinestone and glass pieces, but Rita says the display changes regularly. Rita also stocks current designer pieces and features the handknits of Irene who will create a piece especially for you. Rita's motto is: "I don't care what the clothes are or where they're from as long as they're good." Her enthusiasm is infectious; holding up a jet beaded Erté chemise from the '20s she says, "This is the most beautiful piece I've ever owned!" And it was beautiful.

Melon Patch

1029 E. 4th St., Long Beach. (213) 432-2839.
Hours: Tues.–Sat. 12–6.
Purchases: Cash or cks. Exchanges.
Parking: Street and free lot. Mailing list.

Rather than specializing in a particular era or type of garment, Dorothea Choyce has made the interesting and unusual item her trademark. When she's out hunting for the store's stock, she also keeps an eye out for customers' special requests. She generally carries vintage men's and women's apparel dating from Victorian times through the early '60s. Unlike similar shops that thrive on clothes from the '40s, Dorothea finds that her customers prefer clothes from the '20s and '30s. The Melon Patch has frequent sales—often around a holiday like Valentine's Day or an offbeat occasion like a "black sale" during which the rack of black cocktail dresses are marked down. On the day of our visit, we discovered several top-hat-and-tails combos, Harlowesque silk velvet dresses in fine condition, leather fighter jackets, and even some Japanese WW II leather pilot helmets. Best of all, we found the ruby slippers that grace the back cover of *Glad Rags II* at the Melon Patch. They are about twenty-five years old and were hand-beaded in Hong Kong. We snapped them up for a mere $25.

Memories

8302 W. 3rd St., Los Angeles. (213) 655-4749.
Hours: Mon.–Sat. 12–6.
Purchases: Cash or cks. All sales final. Layaway.
Parking: Street.

Owner Mike Dykeman's impeccable taste and knowledge of fashion history make Memories an outstanding shop for old

and antique clothes. Mike specializes in clothes from the '20s to the '40s. He consistently stocks Hawaiian shirts as well as oriental brocade dresses and jackets. The Western look was available here before the ready-to-wear market picked up on the trend. Prices fluctuate depending on the rarity of the garment. Top price for a Hawaiian shirt is $90. Day dresses range from $30–$45 and evening gowns go up to $150. Slacks start at $20 and go to $35 for pleated wool gabardines. Skirts average $18–$25. During the summer Mike offers a complete array of Victorian whites. Accessories start at two dollars for skinny ties, and for up to $25 you can choose from hats, scarves, pins, gloves, purses, and costume jewelry. Most of the shoes sell for $15–$18.

The Movie Set

3266 Cahuenga Blvd. West, Hollywood (Hollywood Freeway at the Barham offramp). (213) 876-4782.
Hours: Mon.–Sat. 11–6.
Purchases: MC, VISA, cks. Refunds and exchanges. Layaway.
Parking: Free lot and street. Mailing list.

This funky combination antique clothes store and movie costume museum continues to be a favorite among everyone from well-known Hollywood types to just plain dedicated bargain hunters like us. There's a lot to choose from and the prices represent some of the lowest we've found for vintage clothing. The $4.95 and $9.95 racks hold day dresses of all types; cocktail dresses and evening gowns are featured in the $14.95 section. You Hawaiian shirt fans will be glad to know there's always a rack of genuine oldies for only $6.95. Movie Set owners Wanda and Philip Irwin also stock a lot of old furs for up to $75. Besides old garments, there's also a selection of new merchandise (manufacturers' closeouts) at wholesale prices. These are mostly women's things such as blouses, dresses, and jumpsuits. a full-time seamstress handles free alterations on purchases. The popular antique jewelry section has been expanded to twice its former size so customers have even more to chose from.

Norma's LA-LA

8026 W. 3rd St., Los Angeles. (213)651-0423.
Hours: Tues.–Sat. 12–5.
Purchases: MC, VISA, cks. All sales final. Layaway.
Parking: Street. Mailing list.

Owner Norma Hirsch runs a one-woman show here. She does all her own buying and stocks clothing from the '20s through the '70s. She'll help you combine the best from every era into a distinctive look. If you're an antique clothes aficionado you'll ooh and ah over labels from Adrian, Ceil

Chapman, Pauline Trigere, Lilli Ann, and more recent stars, such as Karl Lagerfeld for Chloe and Bob Mackie. Norma stresses *elegant* clothes from days past with oriental kimonos, beaded sweaters, velvet coats, and luxe silk lingerie. Even the men's garments are classy—like the elegant smoking jackets. Prices at Norma's are comparable with other fine vintage shops offering the same kind of first-rate quality. Since new merchandise arrives constantly, Norma is always marking things down for the permanent $5 and $10 racks. There's also a nice selection of $20 coats, dresses, robes, and lingerie. The jewelry assortment is especially good. Norma recently added lovely crystal necklaces in all shades and lengths.

antique-store proprietors. Jeanie's up-swept hair-do would have made the Andrews Sisters jealous and Marv's mutton chops are a dashing complement. Genuine antique, simply old and "new old" clothing and accessories are mixed together. You''ll find new derbys and wool caps, recycled jeans, rayon dresses, furs, bowling shirts, kimonos, sweaters, ivory-handled walking sticks, embroidered jackets, and more. Men's and women's clothing is clean, neatly displayed, and well marked. The silk velvet dresses start about $70, but most other items of varying quality are under $40. There is also a children's rack. "Novelty costume apparel" best describes the mix, so go in the spirit of fun fashion which inspired the store.

Out of the Past
130 Broadway, Santa Monica. (213) 394-5544.
Hours: Tues.–Sun. 12–7.
Purchases: MC, VISA, cks. All sales final. Layaway.
Parking: Street. Mailing list.

Out of the Past is unique for its formal attire—the top hat, white spats, and tails for men and silk velvet gowns for women. Owners Marv and Jeanie certainly dress the part of

Palace Museum
1239 W. Washington Blvd., Venice. (213) 399-9442.
Hours: Mon.–Sat. 11–6, Sun. 12–5.
Purchases: MC, VISA, cks. Exchanges.
Parking: Free lot next door. Mailing list.

Dressed in khaki slacks and a plaid cowboy shirt, owner Roland Tirelli regaled us with colorful stories of riding the rodeo circuit and staging Wild West shows in South America.

Mr. Tirelli opened the first Palace Museum on Ventura Blvd., in Studio City in 1970. He has recently moved into a stunning black-and-white high-tech "environment" that serves as a dramatic background for his vintage and antique clothing. Prices are reasonable and the quality high on a full range of clothes and accessories for men and women. Dresses are the house specialty and day dresses from the '20s–'50s average $20–$40. Gowns are $60–$80, including exquisite velvets and brocades. Blouses are $8–$20 and jackets $25–$35. A special buy the day of our visit was an Ed Mar Original two-piece suit in a black and white op art print for $35. Behind the main room, clothes are stored in bins so there is always more available than meets the eye. January and February are the big sale months.

Paleeze

708 N. Curson Ave., Los Angeles. (213) 653-6359.
Hours: Tues.–Sat. 1–6, or by appointment.
Purchases: MC, VISA, AE, cks. All sales final.
Parking: Street.

This is a shop run by connoisseurs for connoisseurs—to our mind one of the best West-Coast vintage apparel stores.

Owners Karl Holm and Michael Alvidrez have been collecting antique clothes and jewelry for over twenty years. Prices for all types of men's and women's garments are comparable to new things, about $20–$125, but here you'll pick up collector's items. The upstairs salon features the *creme de la creme* of Karl's and Michael's inventory. If you are a true collector or are looking for something quite extraordinary, ask to be shown around. Paleeze stocks an unusual selection of old plastic celluloid jewelry in a rainbow of colors. Display cases are organized by color and there is also some silver jewelry. Prices for the pieces are variable—from $2–$100.

Repeat Performance

7261 Melrose Ave., Los Angeles. (213) 938-0609.
Hours: Mon.–Sat. 11–6.
Purchases: MC, VISA, cks. All sales final.
Parking: Street.

"We take the risk out of buying antique clothes," says owner-buyer Jean Gold. Put yourself in her hands, and you won't be disappointed. Jean handpicks each item that goes into her inviting boutique. A century of clothes (1860–1960) is represented, all in impeccable condition. You can wear anything right off the rack. Prices have increased in the antique clothes business in the last years, and we found somewhat higher price tags here (as we did in other vintage apparel shops we visited). Still, two-piece silk pajama sets, found at nearby stores for $60, are $37 here. The lingerie selection is one of the most elegant we've seen and includes robes for $35 and $50 teddys. Dresses for day run about $38–$35 and Hawaiian shirts are $35–$100. Accessories include shoes, hats, and hand-carved celluloid bracelets. In the spring and summer, Jean sells embroidered lace gowns and antique camisole and slip sets from Victorian times.

Second Time Around

1023 E. 4th St., Long Beach. (213) 437-5787.
Hours: Mon.–Fri. 11–5:30, Sat. 11–4.
Purchases: MC, VISA, no checks. Exchanges.
Parking: Street.

Everyone from fifteen-year-old new wavers to square dancers in their eighties haunts this neat little vintage clothes boutique. Fashion designers and instructors have been known to add to their collections with purchases made here. There's a classic assortment of apparel and accessories for men and women dating from the '20s to the early '60s. Owner Vickie Fell is a real stickler for quality and has resident seamstress Cleo Opera repair many garments to bring them up to snuff. Cleo redesigns '30s and '40s dresses to make them fit slimmer Southern California bodies. She also makes summer playwear from antique pieces and new Hawaiian shirts ($30) from cotton and rayon. Most items sell for $5–$50, including hats, shoes, alligator bags, jewelry, and scarves. In October Vickie rents costumes from her fine and ever-expanding collection for Halloween.

A Store Is Born

727 N. La Brea Ave., Los Angeles. (213) 933-2373.
Hours: Tues.–Sat. 11:30–5:30, and by appointment.
Purchases: Cks and cash only. Exchanges on gift purchases.
  Ten-day hold.
Parking: Street.

To make this store work for you, be sure to ask for owner Terry Warsaw. She's the only one who can go to a rack jammed with evening gowns (or coats, or dressers or . . .) and pull out the exact right size and style to flatter and fit your figure. (Be forewarned, however: it's tough to resist her salesmanship.) Terry loves antique clothes and appreciates their ability to transform the wearer. Wrapping herself in a gold lamé over hand-cut velvet cocoon coat, she became Theda Bara. She'll perform similar magic for her customers and prides herself on rentals for theater productions, photographic sessions and Halloween. The store has a "grandmother's attic" look and feel. Be prepared to rummage through the profusion of suits and suit jackets (mainly from the '40s), lingerie, accessories, shoes, and furs. We saw some designer pieces—an Irene cashmere jacket for $45 and an Adrian suit ($150). Minor alterations and adjustments are done on the premises free. Men's and children's clothing is also available.

Straight Jacket

8046 W. Third St., Los Angeles. (213) 658-8190.
Hours: Mon.–Sat. 11–6.
Purchases: MC, VISA, cks. All sales final. Layaway.
Parking: Street. Mailing list.

It's hard to get used to calling clothing from the '50s and '60s "antique:" Straight Jacket prefers the term "mod clothes for modern people," and we agree that captures more of the fun inherent in this store. One-of-a-kind clothing from both sides of the Atlantic Ocean is featured. Prices range from $3 in their bargain bin to $100 for a Rudi Gernreich topless bathing suit. Clothes for both men and women are reworked when necessary to give an updated, more unique look. A seamstress is on hand for alterations. Shoes, including spike heels and go-go boots average $20, and there is an amusing collection of ear-

Victorian sitting area has just *got* to have noteworthy clothes. One-of-a-kind pieces in fine condition are carefully displayed by owners Jacquelyn and Mariusz Olbrychowski. This couple obviously loves antique clothes and will instruct customers on how to care for their purchases. It's a welcome change of pace to visit a vintage shop that features a real boutique atmosphere. It's easy to shop because garments aren't jammed onto racks. While the majority of the stock is from the '40s (especially jackets) there are pieces from the 1920s through the '60s. The Victorian whites and other garments from that era are real finds (most are stored in the inner sanctum, so be sure to mention that you're looking for Victorian clothes in particular). It's hard to spend more than $35 for sweaters, day dresses, jackets, skirts, and shoes. New French art deco, British sterling, and vintage jewelry sells for $5–$125. Jackie admits to having a real weakness for antique evening dresses and ensembles, and her keen eye and good taste are reflected in the store's extensive assortment. Most sell for $25–$60 with a few rare pieces going up to $250. The really rare dresses are displayed on the walls. The day of our visit we fell in love with a ruby red beaded "flapper" dress from the '20s. Both Jackie and Mariusz cater to their customers in every possible way. Coffee and cookies are always out, and there's champagne on Saturdays. During the busy Halloween season, you can rent your entire costume ensemble including a mask, from a large selection, and have complimentary make-up done by one of the several artists on hand for the occasion.

rings, socks, purses, and other accessories. Owner Genny Body promises an extra discount to anyone who go-go dances in their living window display. The jukebox is well-stocked with vintage rock 'n' roll and local new wave bands. Who can resist?

Time After Time
370½ N. La Cienega Blvd., Los Angeles. (213) 652-2226.
Hours: Mon.–Sat. 11–6.
Purchases: Cash or cks. All sales final.
Parking: Street and side lot. Mailing list.

An antique clothes store that features an oversized pink plastic flamingo hanging out by an old Rock-Ola jukebox in a

Topanga Threads
110 N. Topanga Canyon Blvd., Topanga. (213) 455-1002.
Hours: Wed.–Sun. 12–6.
Purchases: Cash or cks. Exchanges. Layaway.
Parking: Free lot.

This store features a truly eclectic mix, or, as owner J.R. Ball likes to say, "We're sort of a fruit stand for clothes." Plan to spend some time browsing both indoors and out through lots of merchandise. This is the kind of place a recreational shopper can really enjoy. (If you're looking for something in

particular, you can enlist J.R.'s help to save some time.) Good-quality fabrics like cotton, early rayon, and gabardine are available here in different types of garments. Prices generally run anywhere from $2–$75 for adult and some children's items, mostly from the '40s and '50s. J.R. says his clientele from the surrounding Santa Monica Mountains likes to buy its used Levi's and overalls here.

Orange County

Gasoline Alley

4408 E. Chapman Ave., Orange. (714) 639-6550.
Hours: Mon.–Fri. 11–5:30, Sat. 10–6.
Purchases: MC, VISA, cks. All sales final. Layaway.
Parking: Street.

Maybe Gasoline Alley was fated to be: co-owner Donna Saucedo met her husband Bob at a swap meet where they were both buying antiques; ten years later the Saucedos and Gasoline Alley are still going strong. Many theater groups costume their productions from among the 1920s–'50s clothes

and October always brings hordes of shoppers looking for the complete Halloween outfit. We were delighted to discover many items that are difficult to find in quantity at other vintage clothes merchants. There are all kinds of hats on display all over the walls for $5 each. Vintage Navy pea jackets are only $15. We even unearthed some old lederhosen. Cotton gloves sell for $3, leather gloves and shoes for $6, with lizard and alligator fetching up to $15. Like other shops in this genre, Gasoline Alley carries Hawaiian shirts, oriental kimonos, vintage fur collars, muffs, stoles, jackets and coats, silk slips and nightgowns, and men's white dinner jackets. What makes this store unique is the broad selection and the reasonable prices, especially in light of the clothes' superb condition. (No wonder European and Los Angeles vintage clothes dealers buy here at the same prices you and I pay.) Most garments fall into the $6–$20 range, with evening dresses up to $40 and full-length fur coats for $60 and $70. The day and evening dress selection is especially good—we found lots in black. The store also features a whole rack of leather and suede jackets and hundreds of pairs of used, faded jeans for $4–$6.

Children's

The stores in this chapter carry *only* infant through teen apparel from under to outerwear. For a complete list of stores throughout *Glad Rags II* that carry discount apparel for the whole family—including children—see the Type of Merchandise Index. Stores that carry children's footwear are in our Shoes and Accessories chapter.

This new chapter came about as a result of hundreds of requests from mothers who not only want information on how to save money on their *own* clothing, but how to save on their *children's* as well. Once we started to research children's discount stores, we discovered they are fun as well as economical to shop in. The pioneer discount children's clothing merchants have been in business for over twenty years and they report land office business in recent years. The stores listed here are known for quality *and* value. Much of their business is from repeat and referral customers and—especially—grandmothers. We've combined shops carrying new discount clothing, as well as children's resale/consignment stores. The latter category offers remarkable buys on outgrown (but not worn-out) clothing and other necessities.

Discount children's stores specializing in new clothes sometimes carry sample sizes. For girls, these are usually 2, 4, 8, 10, and 10 preteen. For boys, the sizes are 3, 6, 12, and 14. The selection of sizes carried by each store is explained fully.

ℒ𝒜 𝒞𝑜𝑢𝑛𝑡𝑦

Apple Annie's

15194 S. Prairie Ave., Lawndale. (213) 679-4180.
Hours: Wed.–Sat. 11–5:30.
Purchases: Cash or cks. All sales final. Layaway.
Parking: Street.

After Marilyn Salas built up a successful children's resale clothing and furniture business out of her garage, she decided to open up her own store. With such low prices for kids' clothing in sizes 2–8, we can see why Apple Annie's is popular with budget-conscious shoppers from all over the South Bay. Every type of apparel is brand new or in good condition and sells for one-fourth to one-third off original retail prices. Most things go for $1.25–$6. At the end of each month, items are marked down 25–50 percent and, if they're still around after another thirty days, they're priced to move out for only 25¢. With a purchase of $5 or more, customers get three free items. As in other children's resale shops, kids' furniture moves quickly.

Children's Sample Land

22136 Clarendon St., Woodland Hills (behind San Fernando Insurance). (213) 348-0198.
Hours: Thurs. and Fri. 11–3, Sat. 10–2.
Purchases: Cash or cks. Exchanges only.
Parking: Street and rear lot. Mailing list.

Labels have been cut out of the merchandise at Harry Sax's jobbing and discount retail operation, but he assures us these are the same first-quality, current-goods also sold at Penney's, Montgomery Ward's, Sears, and Robinson's. Stock is limited to clothing (no shoes, accessories, or baby furniture) for infants through boys and girls size 14. Overruns and manufacturers cancellations comprise most of Harry's goods with samples filling the balance. Harry says the infants, toddlers, and 4–6x size ranges have the broadest selection, with perhaps a little less to choose from in 7–14. While there are no try-ons, you can exchange garments to get the right fit. The best news of all about Sample Land is the prices—almost everything is under $10.

Davidson's Children's Apparel

8175 E. Wardlow Rd., Long Beach. (213) 430-0706.
Hours: Mon.–Sat. 10–5:30.
Purchases: MC, VISA, cks. Refunds and exchanges. Layaway.
Parking: Free lot. Mailing list.

There were so many mothers busily shopping with their families on the afternoon of our visit, it's a wonder that anyone had a chance to talk to us. No matter—we discovered for ourselves that this cheery shop offers everything from under- to outerwear for newborns through size 14 kids. While the discounts of 10–15 percent may not be overwhelming, the selection of clothing and accessories (including children's umbrellas) is. Better brands are here in first-quality merchandise: Trimfit, HealthTex, Carters, Gloria Vanderbilt, Gunne Sax, Levi's, and Weather Tamer. There's always a sales rack for extra markdowns, as well as Trimfit samples at one-third off retail and 40 percent savings on assorted other samples. There is a selection of girls' preteen clothing.

Everything for Kids

24407 Hawthorne Blvd., (near Pacific Coast Highway), Torrance. (213) 373-4863.
Hours: Tues.–Sat. 10:30–5.
Purchases: Cash or cks. All sales final.
Parking: Free lot and street.

Pat Theberge and Nancy Lepper like to sum up the eclectic nature of their children's apparel and furniture resale store by saying: "There's nothing we haven't had in this store." Mothers

and grandmothers shop here for every type of clothing, shoes, roller skates, baby and youth furniture, toys, and stuffed animals for one-third to one-half of original retail prices. Items are marked down on the first and the fifteenth of every month—there's always plenty on sale. Garments sell in the $1–$10 range, generally in sizes for infants through 14 for boys and preteen for girls. Pat and Nancy mentioned that several women buy for their grandchildren back east. The owners send items all over the world—they even shipped a complete layette ensemble to Paris!

Jack and Jill

10955 W. Pico Blvd., West Los Angeles. (213) 475-4618.
Hours: Mon.–Sat. 9:30–5:30.
Purchases: Cash or cks. Exchanges. Layaway.
Parking: Street.

Bargain hunting may be a new experience to some, but for others getting the most for their money is a way of life. A favor-ite haunt of these shrewd shoppers is Jack and Jill. This children's store is a senior citizen—it just started its sixty-fifth year in business. Young Melissa Couch, who manages the store, represents the third generation of owners. Expect to pay *wholesale* plus ten percent, clearly marked on each ticket, for well-known labels like Billy the Kid, Love Bug, Youngland, Marshall Sinclair, Absorba, Johnston, and Betti Terrell. Sizes run from infants–4, 4–6x, 7–14, and 10 preteen with boys' samples in sizes 3, 6, 12, and 14. Melissa buys samples directly from salesmen and, due to the advance timing in the garment industry, these one-of-a-kind garments end up on the Jack and Jill racks just *before* they appear in other stores. Brittania jeans for girls in size 10 and 10 preteen and boys' slim 12 and 28 waist are featured, as is a broad assortment of boys' shirts by Donmoor and Wonderknit, selling for $3.30–$7.20. Boys Johnston suits are available in infant sizes and other lines are carried in sizes 2–14. Buying is done in Dallas, Chicago, Seattle, and New York. Some of the store's stock is comprised of factory closeouts, especially Imp Originals for boys and a girls' preteen line, Dear Friend. The stock consists of regular school and play clothes and some outerwear. There is sleepwear in girls size 8 and boys size 12, but you won't find underwear or shoes. The large selection of sample christening ensembles (some designers') sells for $9–$53. A smaller part of the store is titled Mr. Jack and Miss Jill and features women's and men's apparel. The women's department is strongest in New York designer lingerie and loungewear. Watch for the new maternity section.

Kids' Mart

Thirty-five locations in Southern California. Consult your
   telephone directory for the store nearest you.
Hours: Mon.–Fri. 10–9, Sat. 10–6, Sun. 12–5.
Purchases: MC, VISA, cks. Exchanges only. Layaway.
Parking: Free lot. Mailing list.

Chains like this one that started from scratch two years ago and have grown so successful that they are opening new stores all the time attest to the expanding discount retail trend. Families especially appreciate the opportunity to save 50–70 percent on children's apparel at Kids' Marts located in convenient shopping centers. The bulk of the merchandise is casual and school separates—you won't find underwear, socks, sleepwear, or very many dresses here. Sizes run from infant–14 and up to 18 for boys' shirts from Kennington, Brittania, Rob Roy, Wonderknit, Luv-It, Trimfit, Carters, Knit-Waves, Tulip Top, and Levi's. Here's an interesting statistic: each and every Kids' Mart sells 1,700 items each week and, naturally, replenishes its stock with the same amount weekly. Selection varies based on the kinds of purchases the chain's buyers make. Watch for quarterly sales—15 percent off everything in the store during spring and back-to-school times, plus big markdowns at the end of the summer and winter.

Kids Snappy Fashions

1240 Beryl St., Redondo Beach. (213) 376-4486.
Hours: Mon.–Sat. 10–6.
Purchases: MC, VISA, cks. Refunds and exchanges. Layaway.
Parking: Free lot. Mailing list.

Customers come from all over Orange County, the Valley, and local communities to save 20–50 percent on a fairly complete mix of children's apparel. Vickie Fell took the store over three years ago and has expanded it to include almost everything for infants through size 14 for girls and up to 16 for boys. The stock ranges from layettes and baby blankets to school and actionwear and jackets for youngsters. You won't find shoes and underwear, although Vickie does carry socks and tights at retail prices. Popular labels are Buster Brown, Youngland, Fawn Togs, Aileen, Baby Grow, and Wrangler. As you can imagine, the back-to-school sale draws 'em out of the woodwork, so get yourself on the mailing list.

Kidstuff

8236 Tampa Ave., Reseda. (213) 993-4420.
Hours: Mon.–Sat. 10–5.
Purchases: MC, VISA, cks. Refunds and exchanges.
Parking: Free lot and street. Mailing list.

If you shop for children (clothing, baby furniture, dolls, toys, games, or books) you'll appreciate the cozy ambience of this consignment shop. (In fact, two families were thoroughly enjoying themselves the afternoon of our visit: the mothers shopped while the little ones amused themselves with the indoor treehouse at the front of the store.) Clothing ranges from infants through size 16 for boys and girls. There's the standard clothing for play and school, as well as pajamas, robes, bibs, bathing suits, socks, hats, and belts. Almost everything falls into the $2–$10 range. Books start at a mere 15¢ and baby blankets fetch $1–$3. Pants and dresses continue to be the most popular sellers. Near the counter, there's an entire rack of Buster Brown, OshKosh, Finger Prints, and Gerber salesmen's samples for $2.50–$13. There are even some lovely

hand-crafted baby items by talented local women. Let owner Kathy Burke know if you're in the market for used baby furniture: the demand is so high that they go out the same day they come in.

Kids'-X-Change/
Los Feliz Dancewear

1943 Hillhurst Ave., Los Angeles. (213) 666-0961.
Hours: Mon.–Sat. 11–5.
Purchases: MC, VISA, cash. All sales final on used clothing; exchanges on new.
Parking: Street and two spaces beside building.

Every inch of space in this tiny store is used. Toys hang from the ceiling and climb up the walls; racks of new and used clothing are jammed together so tightly it's hard to pass between them. Still, it's worth the effort if you're in the market for OshKosh B'Gosh bib overalls, painter's pants, or jumpers. The entire family can walk out dressed alike. Sizes in the Osh-

Kosh line are 0 (six months) to 48 (adult). Kids'-X-Change also carries Buster Brown and Wrangler Kids in sizes 1–16. Owner Frances Miller takes in children's clothing on sixty-day consignment and resells it for about half the original price. Danskin dancewear for toddlers through adult XL is available at $2–$3 below retail. Discounts on new merchandise are generally about 15 percent, but if you come armed with your copy of *Glad Rags*, Frances will give you an additional 10 percent off.

Samplings

10117 W. Washington Blvd., Culver City. (213) 204-1085.
Hours: Mon.–Sat. 9:30–5:30.
Purchases: MC, VISA, cks. Exchanges. Layaway.
Parking: Rear lot and street.

We don't have a children's designer section in *Glad Rags II*, but if we did, Samplings would lead it off. This is one of only two or three stores that offers the very latest fashion looks in children's clothing (some of which comes from divisions of well known New York and French designer houses). Sizes range from infants through boys 14 and girls size preteen 10 (in samples only). There are no basics like underwear or socks. Partner Sylvia Fields used to be a children's apparel buyer for May Co. and enjoys buying unique items for Samplings. With her buying experience and the fact that her husband reps several children's lines, Sylvia stocks the store with samples, manufacturers' promotions and specials, as well as some straight wholesale purchases. There's a lot of merchandise lovingly squeezed in. All three principals, including Dorothy Katz and Dolores Freedman, offer plenty of personal service to their customers. Doting grandparents come from all over and some shoppers stock up during once-a-year buying sprees as part of their annual Southern California vacations. Our best advice is to buy it when you see it. So much merchandise comes in and is sold each week, that you might not find your favorite thing when you look again. Prices are about 20–40 percent below retail and more during the semiannual January and July sales. We can't mention specific labels, but let's see if you can figure out which famous cotton-knit crocodile-emblem shirts are available here in sample sizes for boys and girls. Besides the usual line-up of children's apparel, we saw cute jumpsuits, robes, and nightgowns for girls and special buys on a few pairs of shoes, warm-up suits, and novelty raincoats.

Stork Shop

1868 S. La Cienega Blvd., Los Angeles. (213) 839-2403.
Hours: Mon.–Sat. 10–5:30.
Purchases: Cash or cks. Refunds and exchanges. Layaway.
Parking: Street and rear lot. Mailing list.

Mort and Miriam Silas' business card for the Stork Shop states: "At our prices it pays to have babies." That may be an exaggeration, but it's true that you can save 20–50 percent on all your children's clothing purchases up to size 14 (no shoes, though). The selection includes casual, school, and dressy pieces, underwear, coats, jackets, rabbit-fur jackets, and pajamas. The infants' apparel (including layette), furnishings, and furniture selection is about as complete as you can get. Wise shoppers have made this thirty-two-year-old establishment a one-stop shopping center for babies' needs. The Stork Shop functions like a self-service warehouse, but the employees are happy to help locate a size or whatever you need. There are no try-ons, but the full refund and exchange policy ensures customer satisfaction. Ninety percent of the stock consists of closeouts and the rest is samples of all types. Occasionally, Mort buys the entire stock of a children's store that has gone out of business and customers get even greater savings as a result. We are not able to list brand names, but rest assured they include all the better, well-known labels found in major retail and department stores.

Sugar 'N Spice

10836½ Washington Blvd., Culver City. (213) 838-5343.
Hours: Mon.–Sat. 9:30–5:30.
Purchases: Cash or cks. All sales final. Layaway.
Parking: Street.

Nancy Sweeney and Debbie Berger decided to open their children's consignment shop when they realized one day that no one knows more about children's clothes than two mothers who have a total of seven children. (We met them when we spoke to a Mothers of Twins Club.) Better brands of "gently used" clothing, infant sizes through 14, for boys and girls are neatly displayed in this small and cheerful shop. A fair amount of the goods, especially for infants, are brand new with the original tags still attached. Nancy and Debbie also sell used baby furniture, car seats, baby buggies, strollers, as well as toys and games in their well-organized store. The front of the store features a gift section with new hand-crafted bibs, quilts, craft aprons, bags and hair ribbons, and a unique "baby safe" holder for $9.50 (available at Bloomingdales for $22.50). One last thing—these two capable mothers have become, as you can imagine, children's clothes laundering experts and here's their hot tip for *Glad Rags* readers: dishwasher soap removes stains from most types of fabrics.

Orange County

California Kids
801 Lakeview Ave., Suite A, Placentia. (714) 779-1170.
Hours: Mon.–Fri. 10–6, Sat. 10–5, Sun. 12–5.

Just For Kids
18927 Colima Rd., Rowland Heights. (213) 912-6612.
Hours: Mon.–Sat. 10–6, Sun. 11–5.
Purchases: MC, VISA, cks. Refunds and exchanges. Layaway.
Parking: Free lot and street.

Among all the discount children's stores we visited, these two offer especially low prices. We were impressed by the wide range of sizes (infants through girls' preteen and boys' student) and the depth of merchandise selection within each size range. Pregnant women and new mothers can meet every baby need, including infant clothing, shoes, and furnishings such as sheets, quilts, bassinet fittings, and diaper bags. At the opposite end of the spectrum, you'll find boys' student sizes (small through extra large in shirts and sweaters and 25–30 waist in pants) and girls' preteen (8–14 teen). Prices are 20 to 70 percent below retail, depending on the good buys cousins Nancy Davis and Penny Morales can get. You'll not only find all types of casual and school clothes, but also belts, hats, purses, backpacks, even bibs, overalls, and nylon and down jackets for skiing or just plain keeping warm. Nancy and Penny stock plenty of the highly popular Southern California labels: O.P., Off Shore, Lightning Bolt, Bottom Line, HealthTex, and Buster Brown. An example of the low prices we mentioned earlier—$30 Bottom Line pants sell here for only $14. Dresses in sizes 7–14 go for $5–$20 and preteen sizes for $5–$25. The stores also feature sections of name-brand men's and women's casual sportswear and actionwear for $1–$25. One final comment about the pleasing shopping atmosphere: the decor and layout of the store and its merchandise are plush but not too fancy or intimidating—ideal for family shopping.

The Clothes Gallery
2930 Brea Blvd., Fullerton. (714) 990-1751.
Hours: Mon.–Thurs. 10–6, Fri. 10–8, Sat. 10–5, Sun. 1–5.
Purchases: MC, VISA, cks. Refunds and exchanges. Layaway.
Parking: Free lot. Mailing list.

The merchandise at this shop for mothers and daughters is bought at straight wholesale like a regular retail store, but Bruce and Peggy Seldeen take a lower mark-up to attract a loyal following of satisfied customers. Two other big pluses are the store's service and selection. There were six saleswomen helping customers the afternoon of our visit. Mothers can drop little children off in the store's playroom so they can shop in peace. While the discounts of 8 to 12 percent may not be as great as you're used to in other stores, the broad selection of better labels in girls sizes 7–14 and preteen 6–14, as well as ladies' junior contemporary sizes 0–15 and missy 4–16 is noteworthy. The girls and preteens section meets every apparel need from underwear, sleepwear, and hosiery to sporty and dressy looks—even swimsuits and lightweight jackets. Girls labels represented are Gunne Sax, Kim, and Les Girls, and, in preteen, Day One, Dijon, Sting Bee, Jodeen, and KnitWaves. Bruce told us that some petite-proportioned women buy preteen clothing in the more junior-styled lines. The women's section concentrates on casual and career coordinates with some lingerie and swimwear from such lines as Sue Brett, Jody Tootique, Gunne Sax, and Esprit de Corp.

Jennifer's Pride 'n Joy
2552 E. Chapman Ave., Orange. (714) 639-0634.
Hours: Mon.–Sat. 10–5:30.
Purchases: MC, VISA, cks. Exchanges only. Layaway.
Parking: Free lot. Mailing list.

While the savings of 10–15 percent are less than those of some other discount stores, the broad array of first-quality, current merchandise makes a stop at Jennifer's well worth

your while. This is actually a small department store chock full of children's apparel for infants through size 14. Don't let all the frilly dresses hanging from everywhere fool you—there's an equally good selection of boys' clothing, as well. Prices range from $2 for underwear to an occasional $50 dress. Labels include Martha's Miniatures, HealthTex, Aileen Girl, Youngland, Nannette, OshKosh, Donmoor, Doe Spun, and Peter Piper. Like other children's stores, Jennifer's carries the usual jeans, pants, shorts, dresses, blouses, shirts, and jackets. Jennifer's considers itself a full-service store: it also carries christening ensembles, stuffed animals, and baby toys, lots of cute baby shoes, as well as pajamas, slips, nightgowns, socks, tights, belts, jumpsuits. They'll even special order any type of baby furniture.

Kids For Less

821 N. Tustin Ave., Orange. (714) 633-4131.
122 E. Yorba Linda Blvd., Placentia. (714) 996-9480.
753 E. Whittier Blvd., La Habra Heights. (213) 697-0850.
5414 Walnut Ave., Irvine. (714) 559-8131.
3652 S. Bristol St., Santa Ana. (714) 979-8111.
Hours: Mon.–Fri. 10–9, Sat. 10–6, Sun. 11–5.
Purchases: MC, VISA, cks. Refunds and exchanges. Layaway.
Parking: Street and free lot. Mailing list.

This is a real no-nonsense store—and so are the prices. You'll save 40–70 percent on most children's apparel needs (with the exception of underwear) for infants to toddler size 4, 4–6x, and 7–14 for boys and girls. The store itself is set up in a self-serve way: every type of garment is displayed clearly by size and style. There's even an O.P. brand section in the Orange store. Jeans, pants, tops, and shirts count for much of the volume here in lines such as Billy the Kid, Lightning Bolt, Wrangler, Levi, Kennington, Off Shore, and Tulip Top. The selection also includes Nannette and Polly Flinders dresses for girls with prices in the $5–$20 range for sizes 7–14. You'll also find a big selection of seasonal merchandise, such as coats and jackets, swimsuits, leotards, playsets, and rompers. Owner Gary Mann stocks from many sources and even buys in Miami several times a year. All merchandise is first quality and current. About 5 percent of the stock is samples. Prices start at $1 or $2 for infants sizes up to $13–$16 for shirts and tops and $19 for designer jeans for older children. There's a clearance section in every store with the sale price reflected on the ticket, which also shows the discount and regular retail prices. Make sure you get on the mailing list for the twice-yearly sales (in January and at the end of the summer) and watch for the frequent sidewalk sales.

Margaret's Kiddie Korner

17912 Magnolia St., Fountain Valley. (714) 963-0522.
25422 Narbonne Ave., Lomita. (213) 325-3210.
Hours: Mon.–Sat. 10–5:30.
Purchases: MC, VISA, cks. Refunds and exchanges. Layaway.
Parking: Free lot and street.

Here's one of those unique stores best described as a treasure trove: it's filled to overflowing with everything you could possibly want or need for kids in one-of-a-kind samples and manufacturers' promotional goods. Though Margaret requested that we keep mum about the specific labels, we can tell you that you'll discover favorite, well-known brands as a result of Margaret's eighteen years in the business and her long-standing relationships with suppliers. As a matter of fact, the Kiddie Korner is the exclusive outlet for a number of lines. Savings of one-third and more can be realized on apparel for infants through size 14 with a few girls preteens. In addition to clothing, the store has a nice assortment of toys, stuffed animals, school supplies, and baby quilts. This is one of the few discount stores that carries christening clothes. Margaret's customers include lots of grandmothers and second-generation Kiddie Korner shoppers who have grown up and now have children of their own. One final bit of shopping advice: come early during the Christmas season. One of the experienced saleswomen told us that it's so busy during this heavy gift-buying time that the store is jammed morning to night.

The Team Deal

221 W. Katella Ave., Suite C, Orange. (714) 771-5690.
158 Roy Mar Rd., Oceanside. (714) 439-0700.
Hours: Mon.–Sat. 9:30–5.
Purchases: MC, VISA, cks. Exchanges only.
Parking: Street and free lot. Mailing list.

This just might be the answer to every mother's shopping needs—the outlet for Lightning Bolt, Off Shore, O.P. (Ocean Pacific), and Hang Ten. Most of the stock is first quality: the few irregulars are clearly marked. Boys and girls sizes 4–14 are available in shorts, shirts, T-shirts, jeans, pants, and rompers for $7–$13.50 (50–70 percent below retail). Happily, Mom can shop for herself while she's picking up a few things for the kids. All kinds of casual separates, dresses, and actionwear are displayed in sizes 3–13 from O.P., Off Shore, and Beach Town. Prices?—$5 for T-shirts to $29 for ski jackets and vests by Sea and Ski. There's a big selection of men's apparel from these same manufacturers, too, in sizes 28–36 for pants and small–extra large in shirts. The Team Deal's big deal is its annual January sale and you'll always find several sale racks throughout the store.

Alphabetical Index

Geographical Index

LA County

Orange County

Type of Merchandise Index

Silk Goods

Sweaters

Swimwear and Coverups

Type of Store Index

Children's Index

Men's Clothing Index